.NET Security Programming

A Note from Gearhead Press

Gearhead Press is dedicated to publishing technical books for experienced Information Technology professionals—network engineers, developers, system administrators, and others—who need to update their skills, learn how to use technology more effectively, or simply want a quality reference to the latest technology. Gearhead Press emerged from my experience with professional trainers of engineers and developers: people who truly understand first-hand the needs of working professionals. Gearhead Press authors are the crème de la crème of industry trainers, working at the companies that define the technology revolution. For this reason, Gearhead Press authors are regularly in the trenches with the developers and engineers that have changed the world through innovative products. Drawing from this experience in IT training, our books deliver superior technical content with a unique perspective that is based on real-world experience.

Now, as an imprint of John Wiley & Sons, Inc., Gearhead Press will continue to bring you, the reader, the level of quality that Wiley has delivered consistently for nearly 200 years.

Thank you.

Donis Marshall
Founder, Gearhead Press
Consulting Editor, Wiley Computer Publishing

Gearhead Press Books in Print

(For complete information about current and upcoming titles, go to www.wiley.com /compbooks/)

Books in the Gearhead Press *Point to Point* Series

Migrating to Microsoft Exchange 2000 by Stan Reimer, ISBN: 0-471-06116-6

Installing and Configuring Web Servers Using Apache by Melanie Hoag, ISBN: 0-471-07155-2

VoiceXML: 10 Projects to Voice Enable Your Website by Mark Miller, ISBN: 0-471-20737-3

Books in the Gearhead Press *In the Trenches* Series

Windows 2000 Automated Deployment by Ted Malone and Rolly Perraux, ISBN: 0-471-06114-X

Robust Linux: Assuring High Availability by Iain Campbell, ISBN: 0-471-07040-8

Programming Directory Services for Windows 2000 by Donis Marshall, ISBN: 0-471-15216-1

Programming ADO.NET by Richard Hundhausen and Steven Borg, ISBN: 0-471-20187-1

Designing .NET Web Services Using ADO.NET and XML by Richard Hundhausen and Steven Borg, ISBN: 0-471-20186-3

Making Win32 Applications Mobile: Porting to Windows CE by Nancy Nicolaisen, ISBN: 0-471-21618-6

Mastering SQL Server 2002 Security by Mike Young and Curtis Young, ISBN: 0-471-21970-3

Microsoft.NET Security Programming by Donis Marshall, ISBN: 0-471-22285-2

.NET Security Programming

Donis Marshall

Wiley Publishing, Inc.

Publisher: Joe Wikert
Editor: Ben Ryan
Developmental Editor: Kathryn Malm
Managing Editor: Pamela Hanley
New Media Editor: Brain Snapp
Text Design & Composition: Wiley Composition Services

This book is printed on acid-free paper. ∞

Copyright © 2003 by Donis Marshall. All rights reserved.

Published by Wiley Publishing, Inc., Indianapolis, Indiana

Published simultaneously in Canada

No part of this publication may be reproduced, stored in a retrieval system, or transmitted in any form or by any means, electronic, mechanical, photocopying, recording, scanning, or otherwise, except as permitted under Section 107 or 108 of the 1976 United States Copyright Act, without either the prior written permission of the Publisher, or authorization through payment of the appropriate per-copy fee to the Copyright Clearance Center, Inc., 222 Rosewood Drive, Danvers, MA 01923, (978) 750-8400, fax (978) 646-8700. Requests to the Publisher for permission should be addressed to the Legal Department, Wiley Publishing, Inc., 10475 Crosspoint Blvd., Indianapolis, IN 46256, (317) 572-3447, fax (317) 572-4447, E-mail: permcoordinator@wiley.com.

Limit of Liability/Disclaimer of Warranty: While the publisher and author have used their best efforts in preparing this book, they make no representations or warranties with respect to the accuracy or completeness of the contents of this book and specifically disclaim any implied warranties of merchantability or fitness for a particular purpose. No warranty may be created or extended by sales representatives or written sales materials. The advice and strategies contained herein may not be suitable for your situation. You should consult with a professional where appropriate. Neither the publisher nor author shall be liable for any loss of profit or any other commercial damages, including but not limited to special, incidental, consequential, or other damages.

For general information on our other products and services please contact our Customer Care Department within the United States at (800) 762-2974, outside the United States at (317) 572-3993 or fax (317) 572-4002.

Wiley, the Wiley Publishing logo and related trade dress are trademarks or registered trademarks of Wiley Publishing, Inc. in the United States and other countries, and may not be used without written permission. Gearhead Press, In the Trenches and Point to Point are trademarks of Gearhead Group Corporation. All other trademarks are the property of their respective owners. Wiley Publishing, Inc. is not associated with any product or vendor in this book.

Wiley also publishes its books in a variety of electronic formats. Some content that appears in print may not be available in electronic books.

Library of Congress Cataloging-in-Publication Data:
ISBN: 0-471-22285-2

Printed in the United States of America

10 9 8 7 6 5 4 3 2 1

CONTENTS

Acknowledgments   **xiii**

Introduction   **xv**

Chapter 1   **.NET Architecture**   **1**

  .NET Is Web Enabled   3

  .NET Components   3

  .NET Framework Architecture   5

  Managed Languages and Common Language Specification   6

  Common Type System   7

  .NET Framework Class Library   8

  ASP.NET   11

  XML Web Services   13

  Windows Forms and Console Applications   15

  ADO.NET   16

  .NET Remoting   18

  Common Language Runtime   19

  Just-in-Time Compilation   19

  Garbage Collector   20

  Basic C# Application   22

  What's Next   24

Chapter 2   **.NET Security Core Concepts**   **25**

  Common Language Runtime   27

    Metadata Verification   28

    Code Verification   29

  Application Domain   32

  Strongly Named and Shared Assemblies   36

    Hashing of a Shared Assembly   39

    Delayed Signing   39

Download Cache 41

Instrumentation and Auditing 45

Obfuscators 51

Win32 Security 52

Integrating Win32 Security in .NET 54

What's Next 56

Chapter 3   Runtime Security Policy **57**

Overview of the Runtime Security Policy 59
Evidence 59
Permission and Permission Sets 59
Code Groups 60
Policy Levels 60
Runtime Security Policy 61

Runtime Security Policy Tools 62

Evidence 63

Permissions and Permission Sets 67

Code Groups 72
Zones 73
Code Group Hierarchy 74

Policy Levels 76
Policy Level Modifiers 78

Refining the Runtime Security Policy 79

Security Neutral Code 79

Fully Trusted versus Partially Trusted Assemblies 81

Refining the Runtime Security Policy 82

Runtime Security Policy in Practice 83
Security Policy for WriteToFile 84
Security Policy for WriteToFile3 88
Resolving Assembly Permissions 88

What's Next? 90

Chapter 4   Code Access Security **91**

Overview of Code Access Security 94

Declarative Security 96

Imperative Security 100

Stack Walk 101

Demand and Link Demand 104

Inheritance Demand 107

Assert 112

Deny 116

PermitOnly 117

	ReverseAssert, ReverseDeny, RevertPermitOnly, and RevertAll	118
	Unmanaged Code	120
	Performance Optimizations	122
	What's Next	123
Chapter 5	**Role-Based Security**	**125**
	Policy Defaults	129
	Identity	132
	Generic Identity	132
	GenericIdentity Constructors	133
	Windows Identity	133
	WindowsIdentity Constructor	134
	Principal	135
	Principal Permission	136
	Imperative	137
	Declarative	138
	CallContext	138
	Propagating Principals	141
	CallContext and Remoting	143
	Impersonation	146
	What's Next	149
Chapter 6	**ASP.NET Security**	**151**
	ASP.NET Pipeline	153
	IIS Security	154
	Basic Authentication	156
	Digest Authentication	156
	Integrated Windows Authentication	156
	Anonymous Access	156
	Delegation	157
	Configuration Files	158
	ASPNET User	161
	ASP.NET Impersonation	163
	Authentication	165
	Windows Authentication	165
	Forms Authentication	165
	Credentials in web.config File	167
	Cookie Security	168
	A Sample Forms Authentication Application	169
	Passport Authentication	171
	"None" Authentication	172

	URL Authorization	172
	File Authorization	173
	Tags Configuration File	175
	What's Next	177
Chapter 7	**Cryptography**	**179**
	Key Terms of Cryptography	182
	CryptoAPI	187
	Getting Started with CryptoAPI	188
	Random Number Generation	189
	Encryption	190
	Decryption	194
	Hashing	196
	Verifying the Hash	200
	Digital Signatures	203
	Confirming a Digital Signature	206
	.NET and Cryptography	208
	CryptoStream	210
	Configuring .NET Cryptography	211
	Cryptographic Parameters	213
	Encryption with .NET	214
	Decryption with .NET	217
	Hashing with .NET	219
	Verifying a Hash in .NET	221
	Digital Signatures in .NET	223
	Confirming a Digital Signature in .NET	225
	What's Next	227
Chapter 8	**Customizing .NET Security**	**229**
	Custom Evidence	230
	Creating Custom Evidence	231
	Custom Evidence Scenario	231
	Custom Evidence Sample Code	232
	Adding Evidence to an Assembly	232
	Custom Membership Condition	235
	Creating a Custom Membership Condition	235
	Custom Evidence Scenario	236
	Custom Membership Condition Sample Code	236
	Using a Custom Membership Condition	239
	Custom Code Groups	242
	Creating a Custom Code Group	242
	Custom Code Group Scenario	244
	Custom Code Group Sample Code	244
	Using a Custom Code Group	246

Custom Permissions 248
    Creating a Custom Permission 249
    Custom Permission Scenario 251
    Custom Permission Sample Code 251
    Using a Custom Permission 255
What's Next 259

Chapter 9   **System.Security Namespace**   **261**
Classes in the System.Security Namespace 261
    CodeAccessPermission 261
    NamedPermissionSet 263
    PermissionSet 266
    SecurityElement 268
      Sample Code 269
    SecurityException 270
      Sample Code 271
    SecurityManager 272
      Sample Code 274
    SuppressUnmanagedCodeSecurityAttribute 274
    VerificationException 274
    XmlSyntaxException 275
What's Next 276

Chapter 10   **System.Security.Permissions Namespace**   **277**
Classes of System.Security.Permissions 277
    CodeAccessSecurityAttribute 278
    EnvironmentPermission 278
      Sample Code 279
    EnvironmentPermissionAttribute 280
    FileDialogPermission 280
    FileDialogPermissionAttribute 281
    FileIOPermission 281
    FileIOPermissionAttribute 282
      Sample Code 282
    IsolatedStorageFilePermission 283
    IsolatedStorageFilePermissionAttribute 284
    PermissionSetAttribute 284
      Sample Code 285
    PrincipalPermission 285
    PrincipalPermissionAttribute 286
    PublisherIdentityPermission 287
      Sample Code 287
    PublisherIdentityPermissionAttribute 288
    ReflectionPermission 289
      Sample Code 289
    RegistryPermission 291
    RegistryPermissionAttribute 292
    ResourcePermissionBase 292

ResourcePermissionBaseEntry 293
SecurityAttribute 294
SecurityPermission 295
    Sample Code 295
SecurityPermissionAttribute 296
SiteIdentityPermission 296
SiteIdentityPermissionAttribute 297
StrongNameIdentityPermission 297
StrongNameIdentityPermissionAttribute 297
UIPermission 298
UIPermissionAttribute 298
UrlIdentityPermission 299
UrlPermissionAttribute 299
ZoneIdentityPermission 299

Index 301

ACKNOWLEDGMENTS

More than any previous book that I have written, this effort is collaborative. With the assistance of key individuals, and the patience of many more, this book was made possible. Joe Wikert, Ben Ryan, and Kathryn Malm of Wiley Publishing, Inc. encouraged when necessary and pushed when required. Jerry Olsen helped whip the book into production shape and more. Scott Stabbert and Michael Dunner, both at Microsoft, are ascribed special appreciation. Their infallible support, technical prowess, and responsiveness made this book a reality.

No person is taller than his or her family and friends. I am very tall. My family and friends have lifted me during a challenging year. There are too many to individually mention. To everyone, thanks.

.NET is an amazing technology. This book conveys my enthusiasm for an excellent product. .NET marks the beginning of a new technology revolution. Over the next few years a new generation of products will begin to appear. .NET will be the impetus for this and the widening of the universe of computing. It brings down the artificial boundaries in computing and ushers in a world where computing devices are ubiquitous. This book is my contribution to the new technology revolution.

S cott Stabbert, a Microsoft engineer, first introduced me to .NET security programming. Scott described .NET security as a complete departure from native Win32 security. Shortly into the conversation, he used the words *"really* different." After hearing the intricacies of .NET security from Scott, I realized that this phrase was inadequate. .NET did not use security attributes, security descriptors, Discretionary Access Control List, System Access Control List, access control entries, NTLM, and other remnants of traditional Win32 security. The old security model had been completely abandoned. I was stunned. After investing considerable intellectual capital in Win32 security APIs, I felt like someone that had lost his or her best friend.

.NET security is a new approach to persistent security problems that have plagued the computing industry. Scott's unfettered enthusiasm for .NET security peeked my interest. I researched .NET security independently and was equally impressed. Shortly thereafter, I began teaching .NET security programming at Microsoft and other companies. Writing a book about .NET security seemed the natural extension of my interest in this subject.

The basic premise of .NET security is that code, not the user, is the proper focus of a security strategy. This simple but radical shift addresses longstanding security problems, such as shared security context and luring attacks. Everyone has received a potentially suspicious email—email from a vaguely recognizable name with an ambiguous header. Worse, the email has had an attachment. However, the attachment ploy has received such widespread publicity that no rational person would open an attachment from a potentially unknown source. However, sometimes simply opening an email is enough to spur an attack. Therefore, you sit there pondering whether to open this suspicious email. Assigning a separate security context to embedded code would resolve this problem. Lowly code, such as an attachment, would be granted limited permissions and prevented from launching a security attack. Now, you can open that email, even the attachment, with little concern for the consequences other than being spammed.

How are assemblies assigned a security context? In Win32 operating systems, the most common authentication scheme is Challenge/Response authentication. The challenge is essentially the password of a known user. The trust authority calculates the password locally, which is compared to the challenge. If identical, the user is authenticated and assigned an access token, which determines that user's security context. The response is the access token sent to the requesting machine. .NET adopts a similar model for code. The Common Language Runtime (CLR) challenges an assembly for evidence instead of a password. The CLR is the trust authority. Based on evidence submitted on behalf of the assembly, a trust level is assessed and appropriate permissions are granted. For example, code running in the download cache is partially trusted and conferred limited rights.

Despite apocalyptic warnings against this practice, virtually everyone still logs on with administrator privileges on the local machine. Those guilty of this practice, raise your hand.

Everyone, put your hand down. Programs running on the local computer will inherit your security context. This is the "shared security" context problem. Should every program on your computer be trusted with administrator rights? The answer is a resounding "no." .NET accesses code separate of the user context and assigns a trust level and security context based on the merits of the application rather than the user. The security context of the user is still enforced by the operating system. However, .NET adds another layer of security dedicated to code. For this reason, .NET security offers the best of two worlds.

Managed Language

The roster of managed languages includes C#, Visual Basic .Net, Jsharp .Net, Jscript .Net, and is expanding daily. In the near future, there will be Perl .NET, Fortran .NET, Ada .Net, and probably COBOL .Net (aghast!).

C# is the managed language of choice for this book. This decision is immaterial. If you are a Visual Basic or Java programmer, keep reading. .NET security classes reside in the Framework Class Library (FCL), which is almost identical in all .NET languages.

Look at the following C# and Visual Basic .NET version of the same security program. Here is the C# version of the program.

```
// C# Security Code
using System;
using System.Security;
using System.Security.Permissions;
class Starter
{
    public static void Main()
    {
```

```
        FuncA();
        StreamWriter s=new StreamWriter(@"c:\test.txt", true);
        s.WriteLine("Test");
        s.Close();
    }
    void FuncA()
    {
        FileIOPermission p =
            new FileIOPermission(FileIOPermissionAccess.Read,
                @"C:\test.txt");
        p.PermitOnly();
    }
}
```

This is the Visual Basic .Net version of the program.

```
' VB Security Code
imports System
imports System.Security
imports System.Security.Permissions
imports System.IO
public class Starter
    public shared sub Main()
        FuncA()
        dim s as new StreamWriter("c:\test.txt", true)
        s.WriteLine("VB Test")
        s.Close()
    end sub
    public shared sub FuncA()
        dim p as new _
FileIOPermission(FileIOPermissionAccess.Read, _
                "C:\test.txt")
        p.PermitOnly()
    end sub
end class
```

These programs are almost identical. The biggest differences are that C# is case sensitive and requires semicolons at the end of every statement. Bill Gates, the chairman and chief software architect of Microsoft, called choosing a managed language a lifestyle choice. C# fits my lifestyle best.

Visual Basic .NET sample code for this book is posted at its Web site at www.wiley.com/compbooks.

Security issues worthy of special attention in this book are highlighted in a security alert. Here is an example:

SECURITY ALERT

Security alerts, similar to this one, highlight especially dangerous behavior, little-known facts, clarifications, and general but important facts.

Other highlighted material is marked as notes. Here is an example:

NOTE
■■■■ **Notes similar to this one emphasize other significant or tangential points.**

Chapter Overview

The objective of *.NET Security Programming* is to provide a broad understanding of security programming for professional developers. Code access security, role-based security, cryptography, and .NET security customization are some of the topics discussed. Individual topics, such as cryptography and ASP.NET Security, could be easily expanded beyond a single chapter. For these topics, the objective is to provide a basic understanding that the reader can build on.

As with any new technology, .NET introduces a blizzard of new terms, concepts, and syntax. Fortunately, whenever assistance was needed, Michael Dunner was available. He is also an engineer at Microsoft. The syntax of .NET security is not that difficult. Understanding the new concepts and terms are probably more challenging. For that reason, special emphasis is placed on explaining the precepts of .NET security.

The following sections provide an overview of the chapters in this book.

.NET Architecture

A basic understanding of the .NET Framework is beneficial when learning .NET Security programming. This chapter explores .NET architecture, managed languages, and Common Language Runtime (CLR). Common terms and concepts of .NET are also explained. A tour of Web Forms, ASP.NET, XML Web Services, ADO.NET, and .NET remoting is provided. The CLR is the engine of .NET. Services of the CLR, such as Just-in-Time Compilation and Garbage Collection, are documented. The chapter closes with an explanation of a basic C# application.

.NET Security Core Concepts

Building a secure perimeter around an application is the goal of this book. This chapter discusses some of the smaller bricks of that perimeter beginning with verification. Manifest and code verification confirm the correctness of an assembly. Next, application domains are reviewed. Application domains are lightweight processes and afforded the same protection as separate processes. Strongly named and shared assemblies are more secure than private assemblies. The merits of strongly named assemblies are literally hashed over. Code downloaded from the Internet and an intranet execute in the download cache and are granted limited permissions. Many more bricks of this perimeter are also discussed in the chapter.

Runtime Security Policy

The Runtime Security Policy is a roadmap for .NET security. It maps assemblies to security permissions. The CLR uses this roadmap to determine the trust level of an assembly and ordains an assembly with the correct permissions at load time. An assembly will never have more permissions then those granted at load time. This chapter explains the components of the Runtime Security Policy: code groups, permission sets, permissions, and evidence. Microsoft Framework Configuration and Caspol tools are provided in .NET as the means to administer the Runtime Security Policy. Both tools are demonstrated in this chapter.

Code Access Security

Code access security enforces the Runtime Security Policy. The principal command is Demand, which performs a stack walk to confirm that callers have required permissions. Demand a permission associated with a sensitive resource to protect access to that resource. Code access security also allows developers to comment on and refine Runtime Security Policy. Developers can name optional permissions, designate a minimal set of permissions, and deny unneeded permissions. This chapter provides instruction on code access security.

Role-Based Security

.NET has not completely forgotten about the user. Role-based security offers both generic and Windows users. Generic identities and principals are non-Windows users. Conversely, Windows identities and principals are Window users who have been authenticated, probably with NTLM. Windows principals are wrappers for access tokens. Roles are groups, but not necessarily Windows groups. This chapter shows how to assign a thread of execution a security context, how to impersonate a Windows user, and how to manage roles in an enterprise application.

ASP.NET Security

ASP.NET and Web forms are integral to the mission of .NET, which is software that is highly available, accessible from any platform, and deployable to devices large and small. As wireless becomes the dominant standard, ASP.NET will emerge as the preeminent desktop. Since the modalities are disparate, securing a Web application is significantly different than securing a client-side application. Web applications operate in a public forum and are exposed to a myriad of security attacks. This chapter elucidates unique security requirements of ASP.NET applications, including forms authentication, URL authorization, role-based security, and more.

Cryptography

Cryptography is about keeping secrets and confirming identity. The anatomy of cryptography must be understood before delving into implementation details. This chapter begins with the disclosure of important cryptographic concepts and terms. Critiques of encryption, decryption, hashing, and digital signatures are provided. As a precursor to discussing cryptography in .NET, the Crypto APIs are discussed with plenty of sample code. The chapter concludes with a detailed exploration of cryptography in .NET, notably the CryptoStream class.

Customizing .NET Security

Microsoft made .NET extensible. New attacks are constantly being plotted, and algorithms to guard against these attacks are being created. In the field of security, nothing is static. In addition, each application is unique, with unique requirements. Microsoft could not predict every permutation of security requirements. The solution was to make .NET security extensible. This chapter deals with customizing objects found in the Runtime Security Policy. Permissions, permission sets, code groups, and evidence are easily customized in .NET.

System.Security Namespace

The System.Security namespace encompasses most of the .NET security infrastructure. Knowledge of this namespace is the first step in a basic understanding of security in .NET. This chapter explains classes of this namespace and provides sample code.

System.Security.Permissions Namespace

System.Security.Permissions contains many of the classes used by the Runtime Security Policy and code access security. This chapter explains those classes and complements the Runtime Security Policy, Code Access Security, and Customizing .NET Security chapters.

Enjoy the book.

.NET Architecture

.NET security is not an island of technology, but a slice of a larger entity called the .NET Framework. Basic understanding of the .NET Framework is required before attempting .NET security programming. This chapter presents the basic concepts of the .NET Framework architecture and programming. This is an overview and is not intended to replace the independent study required for a mastery of this subject. (For a comprehensive discussion on the .NET Framework from a developer's perspective, I recommend *.NET Framework Essentials* by Thun L. Thai and Hoang Q. Lam, O'Reilly & Associates, February 2002.)

Microsoft .NET is not just a different spin on the Win32 operating model. Furthermore, despite reports to the contrary, it is not Java in wolf's clothing. You will never understand or adequately explain .NET simply by comparing it to existing products. .NET is new. As such, .NET introduces a fresh operating modality and perspective on computing software and devices.

Are there similarities to Java? Are there similarities to Win32? Yes, but there are many more differences. Successfully programming in .NET requires embracing this new technology as new and fully understanding the many things that make .NET unique. When object-oriented languages were introduced, developers faced a similar challenge and, unfortunately, mindset. Many programmers quickly learned the syntax and ported their C application to C++ or SmallTalk. However, without the requisite understanding of object-oriented programming, these new applications were procedural programs draped in the syntax of an object-oriented language. Some developers invested the time to learn object-oriented programming—not just the syntax, but the philosophy and intent. Their resulting applications were true object-oriented programs that provided all the benefits envisioned for the new programming modality. Similarly, understanding the philosophy and architecture of .NET is essential for creating applications that offer new solutions. Some industry analysts assert that Microsoft has gambled the company on .NET. I would not agree. .NET does represent a massive investment. However, Microsoft is a diversified and multibillion dollar company with many products and a sizable market share in many segments of the software industry. In addition, Microsoft is no longer simply a software company, having expanded into many markets outside their traditional stronghold.

But recognizing that Microsoft is not teetering on a precipice named .NET does not diminish the importance of .NET. .NET does represent a new philosophy in product development. From .NET will emerge an entirely new family of products that will drive Microsoft sales into the stratosphere over the next 5 to 10 years. If the .NET initiative fails, or more likely is adopted slowly, Microsoft will recover and continue, although maybe with a little less luster. Importantly, .NET allows Microsoft to escape the Windows conundrum. Although Windows has been enormously successful, it is still a box. .NET helps Microsoft emerge from that box and develop applications for a universal audience. This new opportunity will fuel growth not just for Microsoft, but for software developers everywhere.

I attended the formal launch of Microsoft .NET at the Professional Developers Conference in Orlando, Florida several years ago. William Gates III (aka Bill) was the keynote speaker. Part of his speech included an entertaining video. The video portrayed .NET as a new standard that will allow software to run anywhere, at anytime, on any platform, and on devices large and small.

Anywhere. This has reported many times, but it is worth repeating: "Microsoft was late to realize the importance and then embrace the Internet." Recently, Microsoft has been making up for that late start. .NET marks the next major step in that journey. The Internet is not an adjunct of .NET, but is interwoven seamlessly into the product. The Internet was planned, integrated, and implemented into .NET—including the embracing of open standards such as XML and HTTP. Essentially, any platform that offers a browser that understands XML or HTML is a potential .NET client.

Anytime. The Internet is open 7 days per week and 24 hours per day. The Internet never closes. Since .NET leverages the Internet, .NET applications such as a Web service are fully accessible at anytime.

Any platform. .NET is a multilanguage and multiplatform operating environment. Compare this to Java, which is single-language and multiplatform. .NET offers C#, Visual Basic .NET, and many more .NET-compliant languages. Programming in .NET does not require learning an entirely new language. To program to the Java Virtual Machine (JVM) requires learning the Java language. For many, this is a substantial drawback. The common language runtime is the common runtime of all .NET languages. In addition, Microsoft publishes the Common Language Infrastructure (CLI) document, which is a set of guidelines for creating a .NET common language runtime for any platform, such as Linux. To view one such initiative, visit www.go-mono.com. In the future, developers can create .NET applications in Windows and run them in Linux, Unix, Macintosh, or any platform that offers a common language runtime.

Devices large and small. NET marks Microsoft's first extensive support of open standards, even if it is rather tepid. Microsoft adopts HTTP, SMTP, SOAP, XML, and many more standards. This means that any device that supports these standards can actively participate in a .NET conversation. This will liberate personal digital assistants (PDAs), hand-held, and embedded devices. These devices lack the girth to run powerful applications, such as full-blown Microsoft Office. Using open standards, these devices can tap the power of a back-end server and run virtually any program. The embedded chip in your refrigerator could access Microsoft Word remotely, compose a grocery list, and print it to a networked printer. Refrigerators with word-processing capabilities—way cool!

.NET Is Web Enabled

Microsoft .NET is Web empowered. Developers can use ASP.NET, XML Web services, and ADO.NET to easily create feature-rich Web applications. This represents the front, middle, and bottom tier of an *n*-tiered enterprise application. Despite this, do not believe the rhetoric stating that Microsoft has abandoned client-side applications—some applications will never be well suited for server-side operations. Windows Forms, a new forms generation engine, and other additions in the .NET Framework make development of traditional Windows applications more intuitive, while adding additional features.

.NET Components

.NET introduces a new component model that is largely implicit. The messiness of COM (Component Object Model) is removed. In .NET, developers use standard language syntax to create, publish, and export components. There is nothing else to learn. .NET addresses many of the shortfalls of COM, including susceptibility to DLL Hell, language incompatibilities, reference counting, and more.

Coding COM at the API level is exacting. Interfaces such as IUnknown, IDispatch, IConnectionPoint, and system functions such as CoGetClassObject and CoFreeUnusedLibraries represent a massive learning curve. MFC (Microsoft Foundation Classes), ATL (Active Template Library), and Visual Basic provided some relief, but offered different solutions for creating COM objects for different languages.

How do you create a component in .NET? In the server application, you define a public class, using the syntax of the preferred .NET language. In the client, you import a reference to the component application and then create an instance of the component class. That is it. You can then use the component. The arcane syntax of COM is gone.

The developer controls the lifetime of a COM object. AddRef and Release live in infamy. They are methods of the IUnknown interface and control the persistence of the COM object. If implemented incorrectly, a COM object could be released prematurely or, conversely, never be released and be the source of memory leaks. The .NET memory manager, appropriately named the Garbage Collector, is responsible for managing component lifetimes for the application—no more AddRef and Release.

COM was largely a Windows standard, and building bridges to components in other platforms was difficult. COM was still a worthwhile endeavor and did indeed advance the concept of component development. However, now the torch has been handed to .NET. Using open standards, .NET components are potentially accessible to everyone at anytime.

Component versioning was a considerable problem with COM and contributed to DLL Hell. Another contributor was COM's reliance on the Windows Registry. Let us assume that two versions of the same in-process server (COM DLL) are installed on the same computer, and the newer version is installed first. The older version will override the Registry settings of the newer component, and clients will be redirected to the incorrect version. Clients using newer services will immediately break. .NET does not rely on the Registry for component registration, which diminishes the possibility of DLL Hell.

I have been teaching .NET to developers for some time and usually start class with a question for my students: Can someone describe the benefits of .NET for end users? Students quickly mention the common language runtime, ASP.NET, XML integration, Garbage Collection, and so on. They are all great things, but they benefit programmers rather than end users. Why would clients give a whit about .NET? The benefit of .NET to users is the new generation of software that .NET introduces: software that runs anywhere, at anytime, on any platform, and from devices large and small.

.NET Framework Architecture

.NET is tiered, modular, and hierarchal. Each tier of the .NET Framework is a layer of abstraction. .NET languages are the top tier and the most abstracted level. The common language runtime is the bottom tier, the least abstracted, and closest to the native environment. This is important since the common language runtime works closely with the operating environment to manage .NET applications. The .NET Framework is partitioned into modules, each with its own distinct responsibility. Finally, since higher tiers request services only from the lower tiers, .NET is hierarchal. The architectural layout of the .NET Framework is illustrated in Figure 1.1.

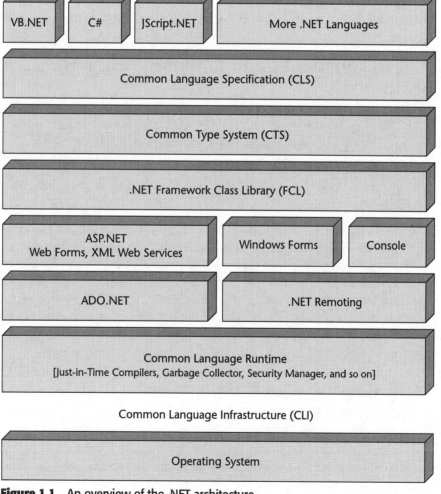

Figure 1.1 An overview of the .NET architecture.

The .NET Framework is a managed environment. The common language runtime monitors the execution of .NET applications and provides essential services. It manages memory, handles exceptions, ensures that applications are well-behaved, and much more.

Language interoperability is one goal of .NET. .NET languages share a common runtime (the common language runtime, a common class library), the Framework Class Library (FCL), a common component model, and common types. In .NET, the programming language is a lifestyle choice. Except for subtle differences, C#, VB.NET, or JScript.NET offer a similar experience.

.NET abstracts lower-level services, while retaining most of their flexibility. This is important to C-based programmers, who shudder at the limitations presented in Visual Basic 6 and earlier.

Let us examine each tier of the .NET Framework as it relates to a managed environment, language interoperability, and abstraction of lower-level services.

Managed Languages and Common Language Specification

.NET supports managed and unmanaged programming languages. Applications created from managed languages, such as C# and VB.NET, execute under the management of a common runtime, called the common language runtime.

There are several differences between a compiled managed application and an unmanaged program.

- Managed applications compile to Microsoft Intermediate Language (MSIL) and metadata. MSIL is a low-level language that all managed languages compile to instead of native binary. Using just-in-time compilation, at code execution, MSIL is converted into binary optimized both to the environment and the hardware. Since all managed languages ultimately become MSIL, there is a high degree of language interoperability in .NET.

- Metadata is data that describes data. In a managed application, also called an assembly, metadata formally defines the types employed by the program.

- Wave a fond goodbye to the Registry. Managed applications are sweeping away the Registry, Interface Definition Language (IDL) files, and type libraries with a single concept called metadata. Metadata and the related manifest describe the overall assembly and the specific types of an assembly.

■ Managed applications have limited exposure to the unmanaged environment. This might be frustrating to many programmers, particularly experienced C gurus. However, .NET has considerable flexibility. For those determined to use unmanaged code, there are interoperability services.

NOTE

In .NET, a managed application is called an assembly. An *assembly* adheres to the traditional Portable Executable (PE) format but contains additional headers and sections specific to .NET. MSIL and metadata are the most important new additions to the .NET PE. When the .NET Framework is installed, a new program loader recognizes and interprets the .NET PE format. In future Windows operating systems, the first being .NET Server, the .NET loader is automatically provided.

What is a managed language? If someone wants to create Forth.NET, are there established guidelines? Common Language Specification (CLS) is a set of specifications or guidelines defining a .NET language. Shared specifications promote language interoperability. For example, CLS defines the common types of managed languages, which is a subset of the Common Type System (CTS). This removes the issue of marshaling, a major impediment when working between two languages.

Common Type System

The Common Type System (CTS) is a catalog of .NET types—System.Int32, System.Decimal, System.Boolean, and so on. Developers are not required to use these types directly. These types are the underlying objects of the specific data types provided in each managed language. The following is the code for declaring an integer in C# and Visual Basic .NET. Either syntax maps to a System.Int32 object.

```
// C# integer
int nVar=0;
' VB.NET
dim nVar as integer=0
```

Preferably, you should use the syntax of the language and not the underlying object type, leaving .NET the flexibility to select the most appropriate type and size for the operating environment.

The common type system is a pyramid with System.Object at the apex. .NET types are separated into value and reference types. Value types, which are mainly primitive types, inherit from System.ValueType and then System.Object. Reference types—anything not a value type—are derived from System.Object, either directly or indirectly. Value types are short-term objects and are allocated on the stack. Reference types are essentially pointers and allocated on the managed heap. The lifetime of reference types is controlled by the Garbage Collector.

NOTE There are many more differences between a value type and reference types, which is a subject beyond the context of this book.

Value types can be converted to reference types, and vice versa, through processes called boxing and unboxing, respectively. Boxing is helpful when a developer needs to change the memory model of an object.

The contributions of CTS extend well beyond the definitions of common data types. CTS helps with type safeness, enhances language interoperability, aids in segregating application domains, and more. Type verification occurs during just-in-time compilation, ensures that MSIL safely accesses memory, and confirms that there is no attempt to access memory that is not formerly defined in metadata. If so, the code is treated as a rogue application. CTS provides a shared type substratum for .NET, enhancing language interoperability. Finally, .NET introduces lightweight processes called application domains. Application domains are processes within a process. Application domains are more scalable and less expensive then traditional Win32 processes. .NET must police application domains and guarantee that they are good neighbors. Code verification, type safeness, and CTS play a role in guaranteeing that application domains are safe.

.NET Framework Class Library

The .NET Framework Class Library (FCL) is a set of managed classes that provide access to system services. File input/output, sockets, database access, remoting, and XML are just some of the services available in the FCL. Importantly, all the .NET languages rely on the same managed classes for the same services. This is one of the reasons that, once you have learned any .NET language, you have learned 40 percent of every other managed language. The same classes, methods, parameters, and types are used for system services regardless of the language. This is one of the most important contributions of FCL.

Look at the following code that writes to and then reads from a file. Here is the C# version of the program.

```
// C# Program
static public void Main()
{
    StreamWriter sw=new StreamWriter("date.txt", true);
    DateTime dt=DateTime.Now;
    string datestring=dt.ToShortDateString()+" "+
        dt.ToShortTimeString();
    sw.WriteLine(datestring);
    sw.Close();
    StreamReader sr=new StreamReader("date.txt");
    string filetext=sr.ReadToEnd();
    sr.Close();
    Console.WriteLine(filetext);
}
```

Next is the VB.NET version of the program.

```
' VB.NET
shared public sub Main()
    dim sw as StreamWriter=new StreamWriter("date.txt", true)
    dim dt as DateTime=DateTime.Now
    dim datestring as string=dt.ToShortDateString()+" " _
        +dt.ToShortTimeString()
    sw.WriteLine(datestring)
    sw.Close()
    dim sr as StreamReader=new StreamReader("date.txt")
    dim filetext as string=sr.ReadToEnd()
    sr.Close()
    Console.WriteLine(filetext)
end sub
```

Both versions of the program are nearly identical. The primary difference is that C# uses semicolons at the end of statements, while VB.NET does not. The syntax and use of StreamReader, StreamWriter, and the Console class are identical: same methods, identical parameters, and consistent results.

FCL includes some 600 managed classes. A flat hierarchy consisting of hundreds of classes would be difficult to navigate. Microsoft partitioned the managed classes of FCL into separate namespaces based on functionality. For example, classes pertaining to local input/output can be found in the namespace System.IO. To further refine the hierarchy, FCL namespaces are often nested; the tiers of namespaces are delimited with dots. System.Runtime.InteropServices, System.Security.Permissions, and System.Windows.Forms are examples of nested namespaces. The root namespace is System, which provides classes for console input/output, management of application domains, delegates, garbage collection, and more.

Prefixing calls with the namespace can get quite cumbersome. You can avoid needless typing with the *using* statement, and the namespace is implicit. If two namespaces contain identically named classes, an ambiguity may arise from the *using* statement. Workarounds for class name ambiguity are provided by defining unique names with the *using* directive. Here is a simple program written without the *using* statement.

```
public class Starter
{
    static void Main()
    {
        System.Windows.Forms.MessageBox.Show("Hello, world!");
        System.Console.WriteLine("Hello, world");
    }
}
```

This the same program with the *using* statement. Which is simpler? Undeniably, the next program is simpler and more readable.

```
using System;
using System.Windows.Forms;
public class Starter
{
    static void Main()
    {
        MessageBox.Show("Hello, world!");
        Console.WriteLine("Hello, world");
    }
}
```

It is hard to avoid the FCL and write a meaningful .NET application. Developers should fight the tendency or inclination to jump to unmanaged code for services provided in .NET. It may appear simpler because you have used that unmanaged API a hundred times. However, your program then becomes less portable, and security issues may arise later. When in Rome, do as the Romans do. When in .NET, use managed code.

ASP.NET

ASP.NET is used to create dynamic Web applications and is the successor to ASP. While IIS 5 and 6 support side-by-side execution of ASP and ASP.NET, ASP.NET is not merely an upgrade of ASP, as evidenced by the lack of upward compatibility. The view state, configuration files, validation controls, and a total reconstruction of the ASP architecture is the short list of numerous changes. The theme of these changes is scalability, extensibility, and improving the programmer experience.

Microsoft emphasizes scalability in ASP.NET. Free threads boost responsiveness and prevent internal bottlenecks. ASP.NET uses ADO.NET, server-side controls, and other techniques to promote a highly distributed and scalable model. Also, ASP.NET hosts Web applications in application domains within the worker process (aspnet_wp.exe) to heighten performance and lower overhead. Finally, ASP.NET uses compiled pages instead of interpreted pages to improve performance.

Speaking of scripting languages, many developers did not learn ASP because of the necessity of learning yet another language. In addition, some C-based programmers have an aversion to scripting languages on principle, such as VBScript. ASP.NET is coded in the managed language of choice: C#, VB.NET, SmallTalk .NET, or whatever. The complication of learning a new language solely for Web development has been removed. There is an additional, probably unintentional, but positive side effect. Converting a client-side application written in a managed language to a Web-based program is considerably easier since the language now remains the same. This removes the final excuse for not moving all your applications to the Web.

NOTE Of course, this excludes device driver developers. You can continue to happily code to your platform.

Web Forms (see Figure 1.2), is the forms generator for Web applications in ASP.NET and replaces Visual Interdev. Web Forms closely resembles Windows Forms or the Visual Basic 6 forms engine, one more consideration that helps developers move between client and Web programming. A variety of server- and client-side controls are supported. Web Forms controls are server-side controls and typically more complex than HTML controls. The calendar control typifies a Web Form control that maps to multiple tags. HTML controls by default are client-side controls and map to a single tag. Web controls are instances of managed classes that write HTML tags. Developers create custom controls by having them inherit from the Control class and coding the Control.Render method to output desired tags.

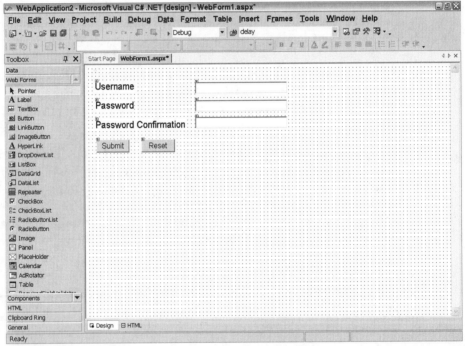

Figure 1.2 This Web form submits a username and password. This form is built from Web Forms controls.

Developers can view and edit the generated HTML by switching to the HTML pane, shown in Figure 1.3. Actually, developers can opt out of the Web forms and build controls directly into the HTML pane or even Notepad.

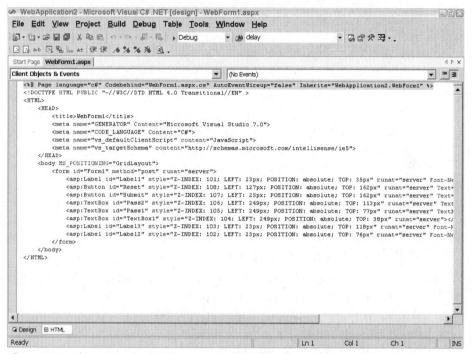

Figure 1.3 The HTML view of the username and password form.

XML Web Services

Web services are the basis of the programmable Web and distributed applications that transcend hardware and operating environments. Web services are not unique to Microsoft. Microsoft, IBM, Sun, and other vendors are promoting Web services as integral components of their recent initiatives. Web services promote remote function calls over the Internet. The promotion and hype surrounding Web services has been deafening.

A Web service exposes functionality to the entire world—any device at any time. Not coincidentally, this is the very definition of .NET and explains the importance of a Web server to .NET. Anyone with Web-enabled software, such as a browser, that understands HTML and HTTP can access a Web service. Any device, large or small, that is Web enabled can access a Web service. This revolutionizes embedded devices, bringing an array of services to these devices that were not previously practical. The Internet never closes, which means that Web services are available 24/7. The explosion of computers and PDAs that are continuously wired to the Internet creates a burgeoning audience for Web services.

XML Web services are part of ASP.NET and leverage open standards, such as HTTP and XML, to publish public functions to the Internet. In addition, creating Web services in .NET is remarkably easy. Web pages publish presentation data with limited functionality over the Internet. Open standards, namely HTML and HTTP, are the backbone of Web pages and deliver them to almost anyone with a browser. Web services expose functionality over the Internet using open standards—the combination of HTTP, XML, SOAP, and the Web Service Description Language (WSDL), which are the underpinning of this exciting technology. SOAP is the preferred protocol for XML Web services.

Visual Studio .NET removes the challenge of creating a Web service. Developers can create Web services with limited or no knowledge of SOAP, XML, or WSDL. The first step is to create an ASP.NET Web service project. The new project is a starter kit for a Web service application. A Web service class, sample Web method, web.config file, global.asx file, and the remaining plumbing of a Web service are provided. See Figure 1.4. The developer is left with only one task—writing the functions to be exposed as Web methods.

Consuming a Web service is equally easy. Start by creating a proxy from the WSDL of the Web service. Create the proxy in Visual Studio .NET by adding a Web reference or externally using the WSDL.exe tool. After creating the proxy, compile it into the Web service client or into a separate assembly, and then bind it to the client. In the client code, create an instance of the proxy and call the Web service methods as local functions. The proxy connects to the Web service, uses SOAP to invoke a remote method, and then return any values. The parameters, return value, and other Web service data are transported in XML envelopes.

```
{
    /// <summary>
    /// Summary description for Service1.
    /// </summary>
    public class Service1 : System.Web.Services.WebService
    {
        public Service1()
        {
            //CODEGEN: This call is required by the ASP.NET Web Services Designer
            InitializeComponent();
        }

        Component Designer generated code

        // WEB SERVICE EXAMPLE
        // The HelloWorld() example service returns the string Hello World
        // To build, uncomment the following lines then save and build the project
        // To test this web service, press F5

//      [WebMethod]
//      public string HelloWorld()
//      {
//          return "Hello World";
//      }
    }
}
```

Figure 1.4   The Web service class and method are generated for the ASP.NET Web service project.

Windows Forms and Console Applications

Windows Forms is the form generator for client-side applications and is similar to the forms engine of Visual Basic 6. Visual Basic programmers using VB.NET will be familiar with the look and feel of Windows Forms, but this similarity is largely cosmetic and there are substantial differences in the implementation. Windows Forms is new to Visual C++ programmers, who previously had to code every aspect of a program's graphical user interface. This excludes the dialog editor of Visual C++, which is a limited forms engine.

Microsoft Foundation Classes removed some of the drudgery, but it was far from a visual tool. C-based developers can now focus more on the application and less on the mechanics of creating edit boxes, coding buttons, managing a status bar, and attaching a menu to a window. Windows Forms is primarily a code generator, generating managed classes for forms, buttons, text boxes, menus, and other graphical user interface elements.

NOTE

C++ developers do not have access to Windows Forms as a forms generator. They are restricted to coding the graphical user interface from managed classes found in the Windows.Forms namespace. There is no visual assistance. C-based programmers must use C# for full access to Windows Forms visual tools.

Console applications have been available to C-based, but not to Visual Basic, programmers. In .NET, console applications are available to all managed languages. Console applications are useful for logging, instrumentation, and other text-based activities.

ADO.NET

ADO.NET is an exceptional and a worthy successor to ADO. ADO.NET accentuates disconnected data manipulation, is highly scalable, integrates open standards, and is perfected for Web application development. ADO.NET offers managed providers for Microsoft SQL and OLE DB databases and is a set of managed classes in the System.Data namespace. The System.Data.SqlClient namespace contains classes related to Microsoft SQL, while System.Data.OleDb encompasses classes pertaining to OLE DB providers.

The differences between ADO.NET and ADO are significant. In ADO, everything revolves around record sets. ADO.NET does not support record sets, which underscores that there are fundamental differences between ADO.NET and ADO. ADO.NET is an entirely different model. Record sets, client-side cursors, and server-side cursors are not supported in ADO.NET. Instead, these constructs are replaced by data readers on the server side and data sets for client-side disconnected management of data. Data readers are server side, and support read-only and forward-only access of the database. Data sets are client side, bidirectional, and modifiable.

ADO.NET is more scalable then its predecessor and embraces the disconnected model. Data sets are more flexible then records sets, supporting the client-side transfer of multiple tables and relations. The ability to transfer multiple tables of a database as a unit was not easily supported in ADO. With more relevant data on the client side, the application can remain disconnected longer, which improves scalability and enhances customer satisfaction.

XML is ubiquitous in the .NET Framework—no more so than in ADO.NET, where you bump into XML everywhere. Data sets particularly rely heavily on XML as the standard for transmitting data from the server to the client. In data sets, building relations between tables from different databases is trivial, since regardless of the origin, everything is ultimately XML. There is no concept of an SQL or OleDb dataset. When the data reaches the data set, it is fully homogenized. This provides ADO.NET with unprecedented flexibility. Data sets are initialized using data adapters.

Data adapters play a critical role in ADO.NET and are the bridge between the data source and the client-side data set. The data adapter is the connection between the data source and the disconnected database. First, a data adapter fills the data set with content from the data source. Second, using command builder objects, data adapters update the data source with changes incurred in the data set. Data adapters are the glue that makes the disconnected model work.

An ADO.NET data set is an ensemble of collections, beginning with the tables collection. Iterate the tables collection to find the individual tables stored in the data set. Each table has a rows collection and a data column collection. The rows collection contains the records of the table, while the data column collection is the schema of the table. Each row has a collection of values, normally called fields. Iterate the fields to extract the individual values of each record. Therefore, browsing a database is series of iterations, which is made easier with the *foreach* statement.

The following code creates a data set from the authors table and then iterates each record, outputting the author names from within a *foreach* loop.

```
using System;
using System.Data;
using System.Data.SqlClient;
public class Starter
{
    public static void Main()
    {
        string conntext= "Initial Catalog=pubs;"
            +"Data Source=localhost;"
            +"Integrated Security=SSPI;";
        SqlConnection conn= new SqlConnection(conntext);
        SqlCommand command=new SqlCommand("SELECT au_lname,
            au_fname FROM authors", conn);
        SqlDataAdapter da= new SqlDataAdapter(command);
        DataSet ds=new DataSet();
        da.Fill(ds);
        DataTable dt=ds.Tables[0];
        foreach(DataRow row in dt.Rows)
        {
            Console.WriteLine(row["au_lname"]+
                ", "+row["au_fname"]);
        }
        conn.Close();
    }
}
```

Figure 1.5 This is the data toolbox from a Web application project in Visual Studio .NET.

The Data toolbar of Visual Studio .NET shown in Figure 1.5 provides a full complement of controls for rapid application development using ADO.NET. ADO.NET code can be complicated and long. The data tools generate the code for you and can be a welcome time saver.

.NET Remoting

.NET Remoting is a second option for remoting objects in the .NET Framework. The first mentioned was XML Web services. .NET Remoting is similar to Web services conceptually. However, with .NET Remoting the developer chooses the transmission protocol, data protocol, data port, and other aspects of the remoting architecture necessary to open a channel for client-server communication. In essence, a developer is setting the specifications of the remoting infrastructure. In this way, .NET Remoting offers unlimited possibilities. Like Web services, .NET Remoting can leverage open standards, such as XML, HTTP, and SMTP. .NET Remoting is fully extensible. Custom or and proprietary standards can also be plugged in.

The namespace for .NET Remoting is System.Runtime.Remoting. Remoted objects can be copied or used as a reference (marshal-by-reference). If copied, the object is duplicated in the address area of the client and is then accessible as a local object. Alternately, remoted objects can be accessed by reference via a proxy that connects to the object on the server machine. The indirection of a proxy affects performance. However, not all remoted objects are good candidates for copying. Some are either too large, have software dependencies on the server side, or require the server machine.

For server-side or referenced objects, .NET controls the activation of remoted objects as either Singleton or SingleCall objects. Singleton objects are created once, then shared among multiple clients. With SingleCall objects, each client receives a unique instance of the remoted object. RemotingConfiguration.RegisterWellKnownServiceType is the method that establishes the activation mode.

Like MSRPC (Microsoft RPC), the server application must be running for clients to connect. There is no Service Control Manager (SCM), as exists in COM, to bootstrap .NET Remoting server applications.

Example of .NET Remoting can be found in Chapter 5, "Role-Based Security."

Common Language Runtime

The common language runtime is the engine of .NET and the common runtime of all managed languages. In addition, as the final layer resting atop of the operating environment, the CLR provides the first level of abstraction. Since assemblies run within the context of the common language runtime, they are independent of the underlying operating environment and hardware. Assemblies or managed code are portable to any environment offering a .NET-compliant common language runtime, as defined by the Common Language Infrastructure (CLI).

Managed code is managed by the common language runtime. common language runtime manages security, code verification, type verification, exception handling, garbage collection, a common runtime, and other important elements of program execution. When an assembly is executed, mscoree.dll is loaded into the memory of the running process, and the imported entry point _CorExeMain is called. Mscoree contains the common language runtime, which then manages the executing application.

Of the many services offered by the common language runtime, we will focus on the two most important: code execution and memory management.

Just-in-Time Compilation

Assemblies contain MSIL, which is converted into native binary and executed at runtime, using a process aptly named Just-in-Time compilation, or jitting. An assembly is subjected to two compilations. First, managed code is compiled to create the actual assembly. Managed compilers, such as csc and vbc, compile C# and VB.NET source code into an assembly that contains MSIL and metadata. Second, the assembly is compiled at load time, converting the MSIL into native binary that is optimized for the current platform and hardware. When an assembly is jitted, an in-memory cache of the binary is created and executed. Just-in-Time compilers are called Jitters. There is a Jitter for each supported hardware architecture.

Converting an entire program to native binary may be inefficient and compromise the performance of the application. The Jitter converts to binary only methods that are called; there's no need to convert methods that are never used to native code. Only the parts of the program used during the current execution are loaded into memory, which conserves resources. When the assembly is loaded, the class loader stubs the methods of each class. At this time, the stubs point to a Jitter routine that converts MSIL to native binary. Upon invocation of a stubbed method, the conversion routine is called that compiles MSIL into native binary, which is then cached in memory. The stub is then updated to point to the in-memory location of the native binary and the code is executed. Future calls to the same function skip the conversion routine and execute the native binary directly.

If you chart the runtime performance of a jitted assembly, you will see a series of small peaks and valleys. Based on usage patterns, the type of application, and the size of the application, this may not be the most efficient model for executing the assembly.

Consider a large application in which the user touches 80 percent of the functionality and where performance is a concern. A few peaks and valleys may not be noticeable, but a few hundred might be problematic. In this scenario, a different model will work better. In the alternate model, you compile and cache the native binary of the entire assembly. Running the assembly from the cache should improve performance. Instead of a blizzard of peaks and valleys, the new chart would show an acute spike at the beginning and then flat line for the remainder of the program. To adopt the later model, use the Ngen tool to generate the cached native image of the .NET assembly.

Garbage Collector

In .NET, the Garbage Collector manages the memory associated with new objects. Ceding memory management to the runtime is not a radical concept for Visual Basic programmers. However, this is indeed a radical concept for C-based programmers accustomed to managing their own memory. Despite the messiness, C-based programmers relish pointers. This approach will also be foreign to low-level COM programmers, who are accustomed to the IUnknown interface and to calling the AddRef and Release methods to manage the lifetime of components. However, I believe there will be few COM pro-grammers marching to protest the lost of AddRef and Release—these methods have never been a developer favorite. The Garbage Collector will hopefully eviscerate inadvertent memory leaks or problems caused by prematurely releasing an object. Memory management, regardless of the application, typi-cal follows known patterns. There is absolutely no reason for every developer to implement a private memory management model. The Garbage Collector implements a common memory model that is applied to all managed code. The public interface of the Garbage Collector is the System.GC managed class.

Garbage collection manages the heap using a concept called generations, which is based on certain tenets:

- Small objects are generally short lived and frequently accessed.
- Larger objects are longer lived.
- Grouping like-sized objects together decreases heap fragmentation.
- Segmenting the heap offers efficiencies, such as defragmenting only a por-tion of the heap.

The managed heap is divided into generations. As new objects are created, they are placed in Generation 0. Eventually, memory reserved for Generation 0 will be exhausted. The generation is then compacted. If these steps do not free enough memory to satisfy the pending allocation request, the current gen-eration is aged to Generation 1 and a new Generation 0 is started. Existing objects are now in Generation 1, and the pending object is allocated in the new Generation 0. The next time memory is depleted, these steps are repeated, now for Generation 0 and 1. If insufficient memory is recovered, the existing gener-ations are aged and Generation 0 is reinitialized.

There are a maximum of three generations: Generation 0, 1, and 2. Sufficiently, large objects (larger than 20,000 bytes) are automatically copied to the large object heap, which is Generation 2. This model keeps short-lived objects group together in younger generations. Large objects are group in older generations. In addition, the smaller objects, which require more frequent aligning, can be compacted without having to recompact the entire heap.

In C#, a developer allocates memory for an object with the *new* statement. The Garbage Collector creates the object on the managed heap. However, there is no *free* or *delete* command to deterministically remove the object from memory. Cleanup of .NET objects is nondeterministic. When there are no outstanding references to the object, the Garbage Collector eventually removes the object from the managed heap. At that time, if the object has a destructor, the destruc-tor is called and the object is afforded the opportunity to release unmanaged resources. This includes closing files, releasing tokens, and deconstructing socket connections.

Starting at the initialization, objects with destructors are weighted with non-trivial additional overhead. The management of objects with destructors at times seems counterintuitive and destined to draw the wrath of many developers. This is a perfect example of what happens when a good idea goes afoul. When an object with a destructor is instantiated, not only is the object allocated on the managed heap, but also a reference to the object is placed in the finalization queue. When there are no outstanding references to the object, the Garbage Collector does not immediately remove the object, as it would an object without a destructor. It spends the garbage collection cycle moving the object from the finalization queue to the freachable queue. The freachable queue contains references to objects pending finalization. There is a dedicated thread that services the freachable queue. This thread eventually wakes up and calls the destructors of objects found in the freachable queue. On the next cycle of garbage collection, these objects are finally deleted. Destructors should be omitted from all .NET objects unless required. Alternately, consider using an IDisposable.Dispose method, which can be called deterministically, without the overhead of a destructor.

This is a cursory explanation of garbage collection. For more details, consult MSDN, including two articles from Jeffrey Richter, "Garbage Collection: Automatic Memory Management in the Microsoft .NET Framework, Parts I and II."

Basic C# Application

C# is used throughout this book. Visual Basic .NET examples can be downloaded from the companion Web site for the book. Depending on the application, I switch between using NotePad and Visual Studio .NET as the development platform.

Chapter 1 of every programming book must have a Hello World application. This chapter offers the Hello World application twice.

```csharp
using System;
using System.Windows.Forms;
public class Starter
{
    static void Main()
    {
        try
        {
            Console.WriteLine("Please enter your name : ");
            string name=Console.ReadLine();
            MessageBox.Show("Hello "+name);
            Console.WriteLine("Hello, {0}", name);
            Console.WriteLine("Please enter your age : ");
            string sAge=Console.ReadLine();
```

```
            XAge age=new XAge();
            age.IsYoung(int.Parse(sAge));
        }
        catch(Exception e)
        {
            MessageBox.Show(e.Message);
        }
    }
}
public class XAge
{
    public void IsYoung(int _Age)
    {
        nAge=_Age;
        if(nAge<40)
            Console.WriteLine("You are very young!!");
        else
            Console.WriteLine("Well, you are young also.");
    }
    public XAge()
    {
        // Do nothing constructor
    }
    ~XAge()
    {
        // Do nothing destructor (costly)
    }
    private int nAge=0;
}
```

This is a short, but representative C# program. Helpful notes on the hello program and general comments on C# follow.

- The using statements name the namespaces required in the program. System.Windows.Forms is required for the MessageBox.Show method.

- All methods must be contained in a class, including the entry point of Main. C# does not support global functions.

- The entry of a C# executable is Main. It must be a static method and there is only one entry point per program.

- The try block is guarded code, protecting against an exception. If an exception is raised, execution is transferred to the catch block and the error is displayed. System.Exception is the base exception and traps all exceptions.

- Finally, XAge is a public class that contains instance methods, such as a constructor, destructor, and IsYoung. There is also a single private data member called nAge. In Main, an instance of XAge is created and used. When the Main method ends, there is no outstanding references to the instance and it becomes a candidate for garbage collection.

- The program is compiled from the Visual Studio .Net command line using the csc compiler. As the result, hellorevised.exe, a console application is created through the following command: *csc hellorevised.cs*. Use the target option to compile to a library or Windows application. The reference option is used to bind to assemblies that contain external references required by the target through the following command: *csc /t:library /r:another.dll mylib.dll*.

With the example presented in this section, you should be able to understand most of the code presented in this book.

What's Next

This chapter offers the core concepts of the .NET Framework, while the next chapter covers the fundamental concepts of Win32 security. Win32 security is not replaced by .NET security. This is the first, but not the last, time this is mentioned in the book. Win32 and .NET security are partners, each providing a secured perimeter protecting securable resources.

The first gate usually entered is Win32 security. If Win32 security denies access to a securable resource or task, this will often preempt .NET security. Therefore, the importance of Win32 security is not diminished in .NET.

Win32 security consists of multiple systems working together to protect securable resources. Win32 security is end to end and starts at logon, when the user is authenticated and an access token is assigned. Later, processes inherit the access token and run in the security context of the related user. When processes attempt to access a secured resource on behalf of the user, authorization occurs and is coordinated by the security subsystem. The next chapter explains authentication, authorization, and impersonation in the Win32 environment.

The nuts and bolts of the security APIs and structures can be mind numbing and challenging even to an experienced Windows programmer. A discussion of security descriptors, security attributes, DACL, and ACEs, can be painful, but is nothing that a good explanation and some thorough examples will not rectify.

Finally, Windows XP Professional ships with an assortment of new security features and updates. The next chapter reviews what is new in Windows XP for security.

CHAPTER 2

.NET Security Core Concepts

.NET takes an active, not a passive, role in security. The common language runtime adopts a proactive approach to protecting applications from security attacks. This is the very definition of managed code. The common language runtime manages the execution of a managed application, which includes monitoring of potential security foibles.

This chapter reviews some of the little things that .NET, mainly the common language runtime, does on behalf of a managed application to create a secure environment. In security, little things matter considerably. There are a variety of tools in the .NET security toolbox that protect .NET applications and users. Broad topics, such as code access security and cryptography have individual chapters dedicated to them in this book. However, each of the eclectic topics discussed in this chapter is narrow, but significant, in securing the .NET operating environment.

The more important responsibilities of the common language runtime are to nab rogue applications, prevent viruses and buffer overruns, and more. The common language runtime uses various techniques to ensnare ill-behaved applications, including manifest and code verification.

This protection does not extend to unmanaged applications. Unmanaged applications, such as COM objects, exist outside the sphere of .NET and subsequently the control of the common language runtime. For managed applications, .NET security is not the magic bullet. Traditional security practices must also be followed to erect an effective security perimeter around managed applications. For example, something as simple as using an effective logon password, which is then kept secret, is still the greatest deterrent. Logging on as someone *not* in the administrator group is also important. If the security perimeter of an application is pierced, there is no reason to automatically bestow the extraordinary powers of an administrator on someone. However, the security perimeter .NET builds around an application is formidable and consists of many components.

Verification is one component. Verification is an important tool in the common language runtime security toolbox that detects ill-behaved or ill-formed code. Verification is separated into manifest and code verification. Manifest verification confirms the existence of a properly constructed manifest before an application is loaded and executed. Code verification inspects the Microsoft Intermediate Language (MSIL) of a .NET assembly to determine if it is well formed. This includes confirming that the MSIL consists of only valid instructions. MSIL verification includes type verification, which flags an assembly that attempts to access data that is not formally defined. Since code and metadata cohabit in the same assembly, the check is easy to perform. The common language runtime validates parameters and references to information found in the metadata. Verification makes applications behave. One benefit of verification is that isolation of processes is no longer mandatory.

Application domains are lightweight processes or "processes within a process." In .NET, processes do not face forced isolation in a 4-GB virtual address sandbox. Processes can share a single application. The common language runtime prevents cross-pollution and essentially keeps each application safely within its application domain borders. Verification techniques reveal to the common language runtime any application that inadvertently or purposely attempt to access a foreign application domain. The common language runtime will terminate such an application. This is one more example of the common language runtime acting as the .NET security police, making managed applications behave.

As with application domains, the common language runtime is especially vigilant and protective of shared assemblies. A shared assembly, which is also a strongly named assembly, is reusable code, and the potential for abuse is enormous. To prevent exploitation, shared assemblies use cryptographic algorithms to detect identity attacks. Shared assemblies are signed and hashed to protect against identity and other attacks. Shared assemblies are typically placed in the Global Assembly Cache (GAC).

The download cache is another cache used by .NET. Web or mobile code is downloaded into this cache and receives special attention. Mobile code is often the source of security attacks. The true origin of mobile code is more difficult to establish and easy to spoof, and therefore is an ideal medium in which to launch a security challenge. For this reason, code running in the download cache is granted limited permissions in .NET. For example, Internet applications are unable to write to the local drive and limited to isolated storage for data storage.

The content of an assembly is one of the most sensitive resources in .NET. Code access security, role-based security, and other security specifics are written directly into the assembly. The metadata and MSIL of the assembly can be read as a road map, offering a snapshot of an application's security strategy. Cracking this information is trivial using ildasm and similar tools. Not only are security details potentially exposed, but the intellectual capital and maybe trade secrets of the software vendor are compromised.

Obfuscators (discussed in a later section of this chapter) are possible solutions. An obfuscator encrypts a static assembly, which is then decrypted at load time. This prevents prying eyes from viewing the sensitive details of an assembly.

The common language runtime guards an application against all sorts of malfeasance. However, this does not exempt users and developers from acting responsibly. Effective security is a partnership between you and the operating environment. Even if a municipality employs a sizable police contingent, residents of a locale are not absolved of responsible practices. Neighborhood watches, citizen patrols, and simply locking the front door of one's home are basic security precautions that anyone should take. If the front door is left unlocked, it is difficult to blame the police when one is vandalized. Developers should not leave the front door open either—protect your password. In addition, watching for suspicious activities is also prudent. Logging and various notification schemes are available in .NET to audit suspicious activity or access to sensitive resources.

The namespaces System.Security and System.Web.Security abstract Win32 security services, but not completely. For example, the Framework Class Library (FCL) offers little support for access tokens. In addition, support for Discretionary Access Control Lists (DACL) and System Access Control Lists (SACL) is minimal. Developers wanting to use security features not offered in the FCL must call the unmanaged API directly using .NET Interoperability.

Common Language Runtime

The common language runtime tosses a security net over .NET. The net catches rogue or unstable applications before they have an opportunity to wreak havoc. The common language runtime is proactive and collects evidence about an assembly at load time. This evidence is used to group assemblies and grant appropriate permissions—more about this in Chapter 4, "Code Access Security."

In this chapter, the focus is on verification. *Metadata* and *code verification* are the two important types of verification.

Metadata Verification

Metadata is data about data, and describes the content of the assembly. Types (classes), member methods, fields, and other data points in the assembly are recorded in the metadata. Metadata is a hierarchy of cross-referenced tables. For example, there is a table of types, containing a record for each class previously defined in the source code . Each record in the type table contains references to a method table. In the method table, each record represents a member function. Each row of the method table contains references to the parameter table, and so on. Metadata tables also use one of four heaps for dynamic data, such as names. Figure 2.1 is high-level illustration of metadata tables.

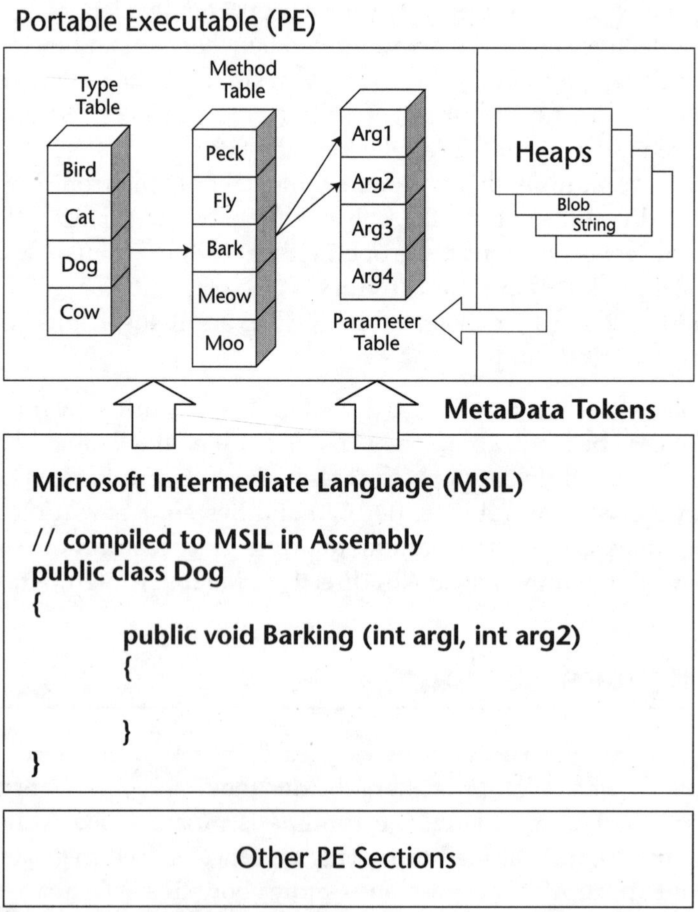

Figure 2.1 A high-level depiction of a portable executable with an expanded view of metadata.

Code Verification

Metadata verification occurs when an assembly is loaded as a private assembly into the Global Assembly Cache (GAC) or download cache. The primary goal of metadata verification is to confirm that there is a stable workplace for the common language runtime to operate in. Metadata verification performs *error*, *warning*, and *CLS* validation. Error validation checks for manifestations in the manifest that would be harmful to the common language runtime. Warning validation seeks areas of the manifest that could be improved, but would not necessarily deter the common language runtime from operating correctly. CLS validation confirms that the metadata adheres to the Common Language Specification guidelines and is interoperable. These are some of the tests performed during metadata verification:

- Checking metadata tables for valid reference to other tables
- Identifying duplicate rows in metadata tables
- Verifying references to the string, blob, understring, or GUID heap
- Confirming relative virtual addresses (RVA), which are offsets from the base addresses of the applications in a metadata table

Source compilers, such as csc or vbc, create assemblies that contain both MSIL and metadata. When assemblies are loaded, a just-in-time compiler incrementally converts MSIL code into optimized native binary. This is an opportunity for the common language runtime to verify the validity of the MSIL code, and type verification is performed at this point. Confirming that MSIL code has valid opcodes is an example of code verification. Identifying buffer overflow attacks is another part of type verification. A VerificationException is thrown when code verification fails.

Verification is a sensitive task, and disabling verification could open security holes. The SkipPermission flag of the SecurityPermission object protects verification as a sensitive resource. This permission is automatically granted to local applications, which are fully trusted. Unless the default runtime security policy is altered, code verification is not performed on locally executing applications.

During code verification, the levels of safeness applied to the MSIL are:

Invalid MSIL.   Invalid MSIL is not convertible into a valid native instruction. A MSIL instruction with an invalid opcode is an example of Invalid MSIL.

Type-safe MSIL.   Type-safe MSIL code restricts access to types that have been previously defined in the metadata and the types of the public interface. For example, MSIL code that manipulates private members of a type is considered unsafe.

Valid MSIL. Valid MSIL is well formed and translatable into native code.

Verifiable MSIL. Verifiable MSIL code passes a strident algorithm designed to uncover flawed MSIL code. Even some valid MSIL code will not pass this conservative test. However, all verifiable MSIL code is also valid.

No verification scheme is perfect. Some safe code will fail the verification test. Non-Microsoft compilers for .NET may generate safe, but unverifiable, MSIL code. Conversely, on rare occasions, unsafe code may be incorrectly categorized as safe. Unmanaged code exists outside the umbrella of common language runtime verification. The common language runtime cannot and does not comment on the safeness of native applications. Actually, the common language runtime views unmanaged code as hazardous.

These are some of the tests performed during code verification:

- Valid instruction jumps
- Object initialization
- Valid stack manipulation
- Unsafe use of pointers
- Attempts to access private members

This is an abbreviated list of tests performed during type verification:

- Appropriate casts
- Use of types as defined in metadata
- Buffer overflow

PEVerify is a helpful tool that confirms MSIL code as verifiable. This is particularly useful for anyone emitting MSIL code, such as a .NET macro language. The md option requests metadata verification, while the il option initiates code verification. If no options are provided, both tests are administered by default. Unless explicitly requested, code verification is conducted only if metadata verification is completed successfully.

The following MISL code is verifiable:

```
.assembly Mammal{}
.class Dog{
    .method private static void Bark(string) il managed
    {
        ldarg.0
        call void [mscorlib]System.Console::WriteLine(string)
        ret
    }
    .method public static void Main() il managed
```

```
      {
            .entrypoint
            ldstr "Barking dog"
            call void Dog::Bark(string)
            ret
      }
}
```

The program successfully compiles into an assembly, using the ilasm tool. When executed, it displays "Barking Dog" in a console window. Next, the IL code is modified, and the Bark method is modified to have an int32 parameter. However, a string is still pushed on the stack prior to the Dog.Bark call. This is obviously bad code, which PEVerify will detect. Here is the modified program:

```
.assembly Mammal{}
.class Dog{
    .method private static void Bark(int32) il managed
    {
        ldarg.0
        call void [mscorlib]System.Console::WriteLine(string)
        ret
    }
    .method public static void Main() il managed
    {
        .entrypoint
        ldstr "Barking dog"
        call void Dog::Bark(string)
        ret
    }
}
```

The program is once again compiled using ilasm. Figure 2.2 is the error message displayed when verification is performed on the resulting assembly using PEVerify.

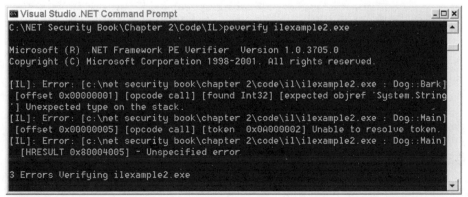

Figure 2.2 When verification was performed on a poorly formed assembly, errors are reported by PEVerify.

Application Domain

A famous quote from Alphonse Karr is, "The more things change, the more they remain the same." Application domains allowed processes to share memory. This is something old that is now new. In 16-bit Windows, processes shared memory through a global heap. For example, 16-bit applications shared the Windows clipboard through the global heap. Unfortunately, 16-bit applications often acted like misbehaving children sharing a common sandbox. An inferior application could throw sand and worse on other applications and the operating system. This allowed a single application to ruin the party for all the other children.

In Win32 operating systems, particularly in Windows NT, Windows 2000, and Windows XP, a better code of conduct is enforced on all applications. These operating systems isolate applications in a 4-GB virtual address area, which other applications are prevented from directly accessing. In essence, each process now plays in a private sandbox. The enforced isolation makes the entire environment more stable. However, replicating the 4-GB address area for each process makes this model more expensive and not as scalable. An application domain is a lightweight process. .NET applications start with one application domain, but others can be added easily. Similarly to 16-bit Windows, because of application domains, processes can once again share memory.

An application domain is often termed a lightweight process or "process within a process." Instead of running in a dedicated process, an assembly launched as an application domain shares an assembly with other processes executing in sibling application domains. An application domain is not simply an application running on a single thread. Actually, an application domain can consist of several threads.

The best example of an application domain in the .NET Framework is the worker process (aspnet_wp.exe) of ASP.NET. Instead of spawning a separate process for each Web application, ASP.NET launches a single process called the worker process. As new ASP.NET Web applications are requested, they are housed within application domains created in the worker process. This is much more scalable then creating a separate application for each Web application. Figure 2.3 shows the relationship between ASP.NET, Web applications, and the worker process.

NOTE IIS 6 adopts a different model than IIS 5. IIS 6/ASP.NET does not offer an aspnet_wp.exe worker process.

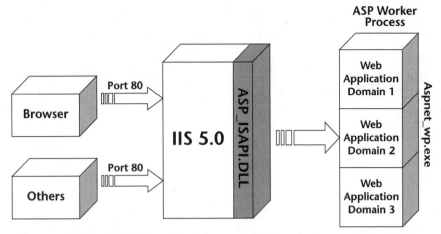

Figure 2.3 ASP.NET Web applications run within a single process, each in a separate application domain.

The common language runtime verifies that code in an application domain behaves. The common language runtime detects any attempt by an application to veer into another application domain. The key is verification: manifest, code, and type verification. Programs executing in an application domain are expressly prohibited from directly accessing memory and other resources of another application domain. Such behavior is detected by the common language runtime, and the offending application is terminated. Within a process, the common language runtime isolates application domains as if they were in separate processes. To that extent, application domains cannot communicate directly and must use .NET Remoting or similar technology to send messages. Therefore, the isolation between processes and application domains are logically equivalent.

For additional protection, the Runtime Security Policy evaluates each application domain separately. This allows developers and administrators to apply appropriate security permissions based on the merits of the application domain rather than the overall container process.

An application domain is an instance of the System.AppDomain class. A default application domain is erected when a .NET application assembly is executed. The assembly will run within this application domain. This is considered the parent domain, and the application can create additional application domains as children. Parent domains, such as the host, are responsible for submitting evidence to the common language runtime on any new child domains. With this evidence, the common language runtime grants the child domain the correct permissions. Based on the parent domains' trust of the child assembly, more or less permission can be granted, as determined by the evidence.

Here is sample code that creates multiple application domains within a single process. There are two assemblies. The first assembly is the Hello assembly, which will be loaded into two application domains. The second assembly is the Driver assembly, which is the main application and creates two application domains therein. The Hello assembly executes in the child application domains of the Driver application.

```
// Hello (AppDomain)
using System;
using System.Threading;
using System.IO;
public class Hello
{
    public static void Main()
    {
        string
            name=AppDomain.CurrentDomain.FriendlyName;
        StreamWriter sw=new
            StreamWriter(@"c:\"+name+".txt");
        sw.WriteLine("Hello, world");
        sw.Close();
        while(true)
            Thread.Sleep(5000);
    }
}
```

The preceding Hello assembly is simple and outputs "Hello, world" to a text file. Using the friendly name, the text file will have the same name as the assembly.

```
// Driver
public class Hello
{
    static public Evidence e;
    public static void Main()
    {
        Zone z=new Zone(SecurityZone.Intranet);
        object [] hostevidence={z};
        e=new Evidence( hostevidence, null);
        Thread t1=new Thread(new
            ThreadStart(StartDomain));
        t1.IsBackground=true;
        t1.Name="AD1";
        t1.Start();
        Thread.Sleep(1000);
        Thread t2=new Thread(new
            ThreadStart(StartDomain));
```

```
        t2.IsBackground=true;
        t2.Name="AD2";
        t2.Start();
        Console.WriteLine("Press <Ctrl-C> to exit");
        Console.ReadLine();
    }
    public static void StartDomain()
    {
        AppDomain appHello =
            AppDomain.CreateDomain(
            Thread.CurrentThread.Name);
        appHello.ExecuteAssembly("Hello.exe");
        appHello.ExecuteAssembly("Hello.exe", e);

    }
}
```

In Driver, the parent domain, there are two functions, Main and StartDomain. The Main method creates evidence for the child assemblies and starts threads that create the child domains. Evidence is a combination of host and assembly evidence. Main creates only host evidence, which is the Intranet zone. Two instances of StartDomain are spawned as a background thread. In StartDomain, an application domain is created. The thread name is used as the name of the spawned application domain. The ExecuteAssembly method loads and executes Hello.Exe in the new domain.

There are two versions of the ExecuteAssembly command in the StartDomain method—the second is commented out. When ExecuteAssembly is called without evidence, Hello runs successfully, and the files AD1.txt and AD2.txt correctly contain the text, "Hello, world."

The second version of ExecuteAssembly in our sample code submits the name of the assembly with evidence. As the creator (host) of the child domain, Driver can submit evidence to the common language runtime about the Hello assembly. Evidence is submitted that Hello.exe belongs to the Intranet zone. Applications in the Intranet zone are not fully trusted and are not granted File I/O permission. Uncomment the second ExecuteAssembly, and comment the first. When the Hello executes, the following error is reported by the common language runtime:

```
Unhandled Exception: System.Security.SecurityException: Request for the
permission of type System.Security.Permissions.FileIOPermission,
mscorlib, Version=1.0.3300.0, Culture=neutral,
PublicKeyToken=b77a5c561934e089 failed.
```

This example demonstrates the effectiveness of submitting evidence when creating an application domain.

SECURITY ALERT

▬▬▬▬▬ **Do not be lulled into a false sense of security. Verifications performed by the common language runtime do not provide absolute protection for application domains. Attacks can be made on the unmanaged resources of the processes. Such attacks can exhaust existing resources and render the entire application, including any application domains, inoperable.**

Strongly Named and Shared Assemblies

.NET addresses many of the issues related to unsafe versioning of DLLs, commonly know as DLL Hell. Win32 and COM libraries (known as in-process servers) are plagued with versioning problems related to the Registry, shared DLLs, and no enforcement of a common versioning strategy. This makes the deployment of DLLs unnecessarily perilous.

Unmanaged or native DLLs are shareable by default. At load time, unmanaged DLLs become essentially alternate paging files backing the loaded DLL. When a second application runs and requests the same library, the paging file of the DLL is shared and the DLL is not reloaded. Lazy evaluation prevents the different applications from sharing private data through the DLL. When private data is modified, that page is copied into the regular paging file, and the application is redirected to the pagefile.sys for that page. This model is efficient and scalable. However, this model is fertile territory for versioning problems. In addition, there is no implicit protection from security attacks. Binding is based solely on the path and name of the DLL. Spoofing, or launching a Trojan Horse attack in this model, is trivial and almost invited.

In .NET, assemblies are private by default. Versioning is not an issue when each application receives a private copy of the requested DLL. At build time, the private assembly is copied into the directory of the dependent assembly. Like native libraries, private assemblies are bound using only the simple name. For this reason, private assemblies are susceptible to many of the same attacks as an unmanaged DLL. In addition, the economies of a shared assembly, which is a strongly named assembly, are not available. However, shared assemblies avoid most of the problems associated with DLL Hell and are infinitely more secure.

Naturally, a strongly named assembly requires a strong name. A strong name consists of the following ingredients. The elements of the strong name and the strong name itself are written into the manifest of the strongly named assembly.

- Cryptographic public key of a public-private key pair
- Four-part version number
- Simple name
- Culture

If using Visual Studio .NET, the AssemblyInfo.cs file is present in most types of .NET projects and contains varied assembly attributes, including attributes required to create a strong name. The AssemblyCulture, AssemblyVersion, and AssemblyKeyFile attributes assign a culture, version, and public key to the assembly, respectively. The simple name is not found in the AssemblyInfo file, but extracted from the name of the assembly. For example, the simple name for the Hello.dll assembly is "Hello."

Here is an abbreviated AssemblyInfo.cs file with entries for a strongly named assembly:

```
using System.Reflection;
using System.Runtime.CompilerServices;
[assembly: AssemblyTitle("")]
[assembly: AssemblyDescription("")]
[assembly: AssemblyConfiguration("")]
[assembly: AssemblyCompany("")]
[assembly: AssemblyProduct("")]
[assembly: AssemblyCopyright("")]
[assembly: AssemblyTrademark("")]
[assembly: AssemblyCulture("en-US")]
[assembly: AssemblyVersion("2.0.0.0")]
[assembly: AssemblyDelaySign(false)]
[assembly: AssemblyKeyFile("mykey.snk")]
[assembly: AssemblyKeyName("")]
```

The public key is read from the file stipulated in the AssemblyKeyFile attribute. Sn is the command line tool used to create the key file that contains a key pair. The next statement creates a key pair that is saved in the mykey.snk file.

```
sn-k mykey.snk
```

Strongly named assemblies can be shared, while private assemblies cannot be shared. The Global Assembly Cache (GAC) is the repository for shared assemblies. Only strongly named assemblies can be installed in the GAC.

Rules enforced by the GAC eliminate DLL Hell. Open the subdirectory \%system%\assembly to view the GAC, which starts the shfusion.dll (Assembly Cache Viewer) shell extension. Figure 2.4 is a snapshot of the GAC.

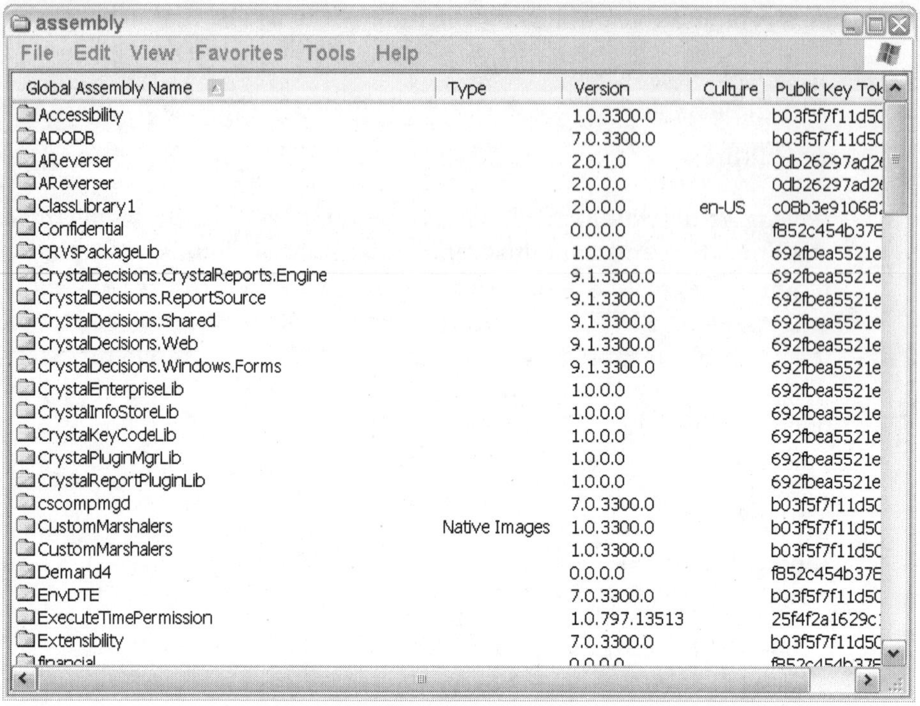

Figure 2.4 A view of the GAC.

A unique directory is created in the GAC for each version of the shared assembly. The unique directory name is \%system%\assembly\gac*simple name**mangled name*. The directory name containing the assembly is mangled and combines parts of the strong name. Mangled directories containing different versions of a Hello assembly are shown in Figure 2.5.

There are three different methods that can be used to install a strongly name assembly easily in the GAC:

- Install it into the GAC using the gacutil command line tool and the –i option. The following statement installs an assembly in the GAC.

```
gacutil-i hello.dll
```

- Install it into the GAC using Windows Explorer. Copy the assembly from its current location into the Assembly Cache Viewer presented in \%system%\assembly.

- Install it into the GAC using the Microsoft .NET Framework Configuration Tool, which is located in Administrative Tools of the Control Panel.

The common language runtime offers strongly named and shared assemblies addition security, mostly derived from the public-private key pair.

```
Visual Studio .NET Command Prompt                                    _ □ ×
 Directory of C:\WINDOWS2\assembly\GAC\hello

07/10/2002  10:18 AM    <DIR>          .
07/10/2002  10:18 AM    <DIR>          ..
07/10/2002  04:31 AM    <DIR>          2.3.1.2__a275f120156983b0
07/10/2002  10:18 AM    <DIR>          3.0.0.0_en-AU_a275f120156983b0
07/10/2002  10:07 AM    <DIR>          3.0.0.0__a275f120156983b0
                0 File(s)              0 bytes
                5 Dir(s)   5,183,184,896 bytes free
```

Figure 2.5   The GAC of this machine has three versions of the Hello assembly installed.

Hashing of a Shared Assembly

Hashing algorithms are used to confirm the integrity and identity of a strongly named assembly. First, individual hashes are created of each file in the assembly and inserted into the manifest. A particular hashing algorithm can be chosen with the AssemblyAlgIDAttribute attribute or the assembly generation tool (al.exe). Second, a hash of the entire assembly is formulated and signed with the private key of the vendor.

The SHA-1 algorithm is used and cannot be changed. The hash of the assembly is written not into the manifest, but into a reserved area of the assembly. When the assembly is loaded, each hash is regenerated and compared to the hashes in the manifest. In addition, the signature of the assembly hash is also recreated and compared. If either comparison fails, the assembly is not loaded.

Hashing of strongly named assemblies prevents an assortment of attacks and is another reason for using strongly named assemblies.

Delayed Signing

A private key should be just that—private. Software companies guard the private key. While the public key is freely distributed, the private key is kept at a secured location or stored in a secured electronic device.

Circumventing the security of a shared assembly is simpler with the private key. With the private key, an interloper has both sides of the hashing algorithm puzzle and can break the protection afforded a shared assembly. For these reasons, most companies limit access to the private key—even employees have limited access. Vendors delay exposing the private key until the latest possible moment in the development process, usually using it only when building the released product. This means that the key is not available during beta builds of the product. The absence of the private key makes beta testing a strongly named assembly difficult. Delayed signing is the answer.

Delayed signing substitutes an empty placeholder for the private key. This allows the beta development and testing of a product without the private key. The placeholder is replaced with the actual private key when the released product is built and distributed. Since the beta product does not have an actually private key, it does not have the same level of protection as an assembly that is properly signed.

SECURITY ALERT
■■■■ **Never distribute a released product that contains delayed signing. It is no more secure than a private assembly. Delayed signing should be used in debug versions of assemblies only.**

These are steps for delayed signing of an assembly:

1. Using the sn tool with the -p option, extract the public key from the key pair of a key file. This command creates another key file containing only the public key. The following statement extracts the public key from mykey.snk and embeds the key in mypublic.snk. There are other strategies for isolating a public key of a key pair.

   ```
   sn -p mykey.snk mypublic.snk
   ```

2. Follow the normal steps for creating a strongly named assembly, except use the public key file. Add the additional step of setting the Assembly-DelaySignAttribute attribute to true. Alternately, build modules using the language compiler and create the assembly with the al tool. The /key and /delay option will delay the signing of the assembly. This statement creates a delayed signed assembly:

   ```
   al hello.netmodule /t:lib /out:hello.dll /delaysign+
   /keyfile:myPublic.snk
   ```

3. Since the assembly does not have a private key, attempts to hash and sign the assembly will fail. The -Vr option of the sn tool disables assembly hashing and signing. The delayed signed assembly is ready for deployment.

   ```
   sn -Vr classlibrary1.dll
   ```

4. At the end of the development cycle, run sn to properly sign the assembly. The–r option reads a key file containing the public-private key to correctly hash and sign the assembly.

   ```
   sn -R classlibrary1.dll mykey.snk
   ```

5. Deploy the secured assembly.

Shared assemblies are installed in the GAC. Conversely, Internet-downloaded assemblies are installed in the download cache and have their own security concerns.

Download Cache

Applications running in the download cache are downloaded into the memory of the client from the Web server. Thus, applications in the download cache run locally. In addition, smart clients also execute in the application store of the download cache. Zones in IIS categorize the assembly as belonging to the Intranet or Internet zone. A downloaded assembly originates from a Web or virtual directory on the source Web server. Applications running in the download cache represent foreign applications and should be granted few permissions.

To list or clear the contents of the download cache, use the gacutil utility. The -ldl option lists the assemblies in the download cache, and the cdl option clears the cache.

You download an assembly in the download cache by using one of the following three methods:

- The <object> tag of an ASP.NET page
- The Assembly.LoadFrom method
- Browse to the URL of the assembly

Writer is a Windows application and resides in a virtual IIS directory. It creates a text file called Foo.txt and then writes, "this is foo" into the file. The application is loaded from Internet Explorer with the following URL: http://local-host\foo\writer.exe. After the program is launched, the contents of the download cache are displayed. See Figure 2.6.

Execute the Writer program and click the "Click to Write" button to create and write to Foo.txt. Figure 2.7 displays the resulting error message.

Figure 2.6 Writer is presently the only item in the download cache.

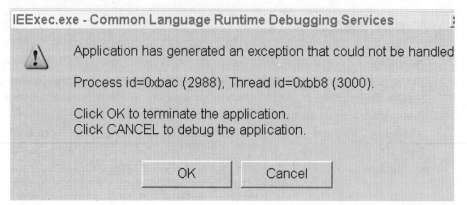

Figure 2.7 Error message generated when running Writer as a partially trusted assembly.

What is the problem? Writer is considered an Internet application and granted restrictive permissions as a partially trusted assembly. Instead of granting enhanced permissions to all assemblies in the Internet zone, Writer alone can be elevated to a fully trusted assembly. Obviously, you must be confident of the intent of an assembly before boosting its permissions. This is further discussed in Chapter 3, "Runtime Security Policy," and Chapter 4, "Code Access Security." Until then, the .NET Framework Configuration Wizard is a quick and simple way to increase the trust of an assembly.

The .NET Framework Configuration Wizard, as shown in Figure 2.8, is found in the Control Panel in the Administrative Tools group.

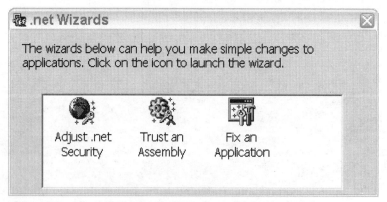

Figure 2.8 The .NET Framework Configuration Wizard tool.

After launching the wizard, here are the steps to promote Writer to a fully trusted assembly.

1. Click Trust an Assembly icon in the Main window of the wizard.

2. On the second page, select Make Change to this Computer or Make Changes for the Current User Only to affect this assembly in the context of a specific user. See Figure 2.9.

3. On the third page, enter the path of the target assembly. This can be a local file path or a URL. See Figure 2.10.

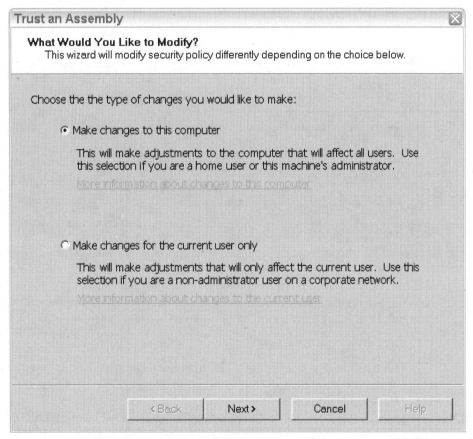

Figure 2.9 From this page, set the security change to affect a machine or a specific user.

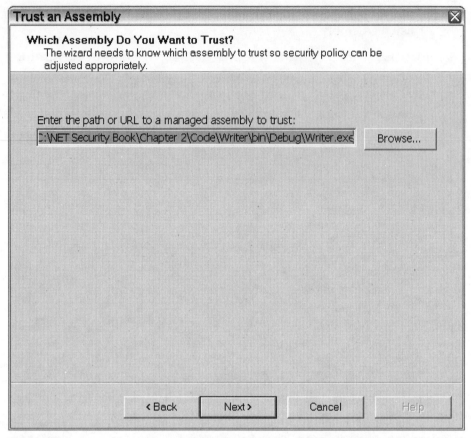

Figure 2.10   From this page, enter the path of the assembly that is affected by this security adjustment.

4. On the fourth page, choose the desired trust level for the assembly. To have the File I/O permission, Full Trust is chosen for the Writer assembly. See Figure 2.11.

5. The final page is a summary. Confirm the details and click Finish, or choose the Back button to correct earlier details.

After running the wizard, Writer.exe executes without causing an exception.

Choices in the .NET Framework Configuration Wizard are limited. They work but are not very granular. The Runtime Security Policy offers a more exact approach. A specific permission, such as the File I/O Permission, can be granted using the Runtime Security Policy. Hopefully, this is more than a subtle nudge to read the upcoming chapters on Runtime Security Policy and Code Access Security.

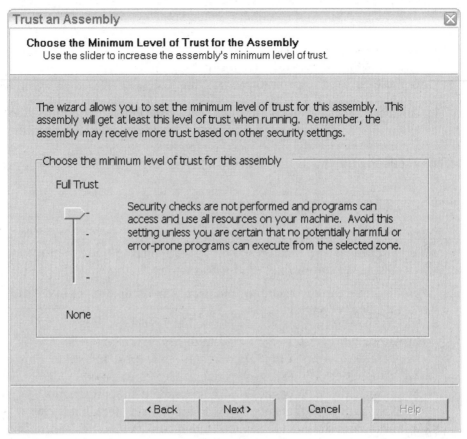

Figure 2.11 The .NET Framework Configuration Wizard supports changing the trust level of an assembly.

Instrumentation and Auditing

Auditing is an important component of security and not directly provided in .NET. However, auditing can be effected with instrumentation. Win32 applications can enable auditing within the security infrastructure.

Auditing is attached to a securable resource and described in a System Access Control List (SACL). The SACL is part of the security descriptor and security attributes assigned to a Win32 securable object. The SACL is an array of access control entries (ACE) that describe who is audited and under what conditions.

Unfortunately, similar functionality is not provided in the Framework Class Library (FCL). Through interoperability services, the Win32 APIs can be called directly to implement an auditing strategy. Calling Win32 security APIs directly is the last topic of this chapter. Some sensitive resources within .NET are not accessible to unmanaged code using Win32 APIs. The Execute permission is one such example. It is hard to attach a SACL to an object that does not exist outside of managed code. In these circumstances, the only option is building an audit log within .NET, using managed code and instrumentation.

Instrumentation in .NET logs messages to a variety of targets, such as the event log or a log file. Instrumentation targets are called listeners. Instrumentation can be enabled or disabled remotely, using switches and without altering the underlying code. Other benefits of instrumentation in .NET are:

- The cost of auditing is only incurred when warranted and auditing is undertaken.
- Keeping a separate audit-enabled and release assembly is not necessary.
- Auditing is switched on and off without interfering with or having to shut down the audited production server.
- Auditing can occur largely undetected, making it easier to detect improper behavior.

Instrumentation classes are found in the System.Diagnostics namespace. Listeners, switches, and other classes required for instrumentation are found in this namespace. The Diagnostics namespace contains other classes helpful in diagnosing the state of the .NET environment (thus the name System.Diagnostics), such as the Process, ProcessThread, and StackFrame classes. Quality information is the basis of any effective security plan, and System.Diagnostics contains a wealth of information.

These are the steps for instrumenting an application:

1. Select the resources to audit.
2. Select the events to be audited. Step 1 and 2 are the "who" and "when."
3. Decide on the information and messages to be recorded.
4. Create listeners or targets of instrumentation.
5. Create a Boolean or trace switch.
6. With the Trace command and switches, output information to the listeners.
7. Create an application configuration file for remote enabling and disabling of auditing.

Instrumentation is predicated on listeners, switches, and outputting with a Trace or Debug command.

Instrumentation commands output to listeners. Valid listeners are the output window, event log, and log file. DefaultTraceListener, EventLogTraceListener, and TextWriterTraceListener are the managed classes for each listener, and TraceListener is the common base class. The default listener is the output window. Multiple listeners can be selected and accessed from a listeners array. Trace.Listeners.Add adds a listener to the listeners array, while Trace.Listeners.Clear erases the listeners array. Add and Clear are both static methods. By default, a DefaultTraceListener object is the only element of the listeners array.

Switches enable or disable instrumentation. Switches can be altered programmatically or through a configuration file. There are two types of switches: Boolean and trace. The state of a Boolean switch is either true or false. True enables instrumentation. False disables instrumentation. A Boolean switch is an instance of the BooleanSwitch class. The BooleanSwitch.Enabled property gets or sets the state of a Boolean switch.

A trace switch is more granular than a Boolean switch and offers severity levels instead of a simple on or off switch. In order of importance, the severity levels are Off, Error, Warning, Info, and Verbose. Off is the least severe, while Verbose is reserved for the worst conditions. TraceLevel is an enumeration of the severity levels. Verbosity should increase as the severity increases, and error messages are cumulative. An Error condition should write only error messages. However, a Verbose error condition will output Error, Warning, Info, and Verbose messages—the accumulation of verbose and less severe messages. A trace switch is an instance of the TraceSwitch class. TraceError, TraceWarning, TraceInfo, and TraceVerbose are read-only properties of the TraceSwitch class and return the state of an individual severity level.

The constructor of the TraceSwitch and TraceBoolean class are identical. The first argument of the constructor is the name of the switch, while the second is a description. The name identifies a particular switch in a configuration file. Description is a general description or the long name of the switch.

```
[C#]
public TraceSwitch(string displayName, string description);
public BooleanSwitch(string displayName, string description);
```

Both the Trace and Debug class write to listeners contained in the listeners array. To instrument only the debug version of an assembly, output information to the listeners using the Debug class. The Debug class is automatically stripped from the release version of an assembly. When you are writing about either a debug or release version of an assembly, Trace is the appropriate class. Other than this single anomaly, both Trace and Debug are essentially identical and have the same methods. The Trace or Debug compiler constants must be set or Trace and Debug commands are ignored.

The Write, WriteLine, WriteIf, and WriteLineIf methods of the Debug and Trace class write to listeners. Write and WriteLine are not conditional and do not accept switches. WriteIf and WriteLineIf accept a switch, and the state of the switch determines the level, if any, of instrumentation. These two methods are more suitable for auditing. They support varying levels of auditing and remote management of auditing. For this reason, the focus in this chapter is on the later two methods. This is one prototype of the WriteIf and WriteLineIf methods:

```
public static void WriteIf(bool, string);
public static void WriteLineIf(bool, string);
```

The first parameter of WriteIf and WriteLineIf is the switch. If true, the second parameter, which is a string, is written to any listeners. Otherwise, the write is suppressed. Both methods are overloaded in a variety of ways.

As mentioned previously in this chapter, the state of a BooleanSwitch or TraceSwitch can be set programmatically. BooleanSwitch has the Enabled property and TraceSwitch exposes a Boolean property for each severity level, such as TraceLevel.Error. These properties are used as the first parameter of a WriteIf method.

In addition, switches can be added to an application configuration file. An application configuration file has the same name as the affected assembly, except for the addition of the .config extension, and they reside in the same directory. Writer.exe.config is the application configuration file for a Writer.exe assembly. Within the configuration file, set trace switches between the <switches> paired tags, which are between the <system.diagnostics> tags. The <add> single-tag element adds a single trace switch. The bounding tags of an application configuration file are the <configuration> tag, as in the following example.

```
<configuration>
    <system.diagnostics>
        <switches>
        <add name=switchname value=value />
        </switches>
    </system.diagnostics>
</configuration>
```

NOTE When using a configuration file, use integral values for trace switches. Substitute 0, 1, 2, 3, and 4, for Off, Error, Warning, Info, and Verbose trace levels, respectively. Boolean switches are 0 and 1.

Writer2.exe is a sample application that leverages instrumentation for auditing. Writer2 outputs data to a file, runs locally, and is thereby fully trusted. The write functionality is relegated to a library, which Writer2 loads into the download cache. Reflection is used for late binding and then invoke the Tester method of the library. The Tester method writes to a file on the local hard drive. Residing in the download cache, the library assembly is not granted the File I/O permissions, and a security exception is thrown on the write. An audit trail of this event is written into the event log. Administrators viewing the log would be notified of a potential failed attack. This is a fragment of the code from the application.

```
EventLogTraceListener listener = new EventLogTraceListener("Writer");
string writerlibURL=@"http://localhost\foolib\writerlib.dll";
BooleanSwitch auditing=new BooleanSwitch("auditing", "auditing trail");
private void button1_Click(object sender, System.EventArgs e)
{
    try
    {
        Assembly a=Assembly.LoadFrom(writerlibURL);
        Type t=a.GetType("WriterLib.Writer", true);
        MethodInfo Tester = t.GetMethod("Tester");
        object writerlib=Activator.CreateInstance(t);
        GenericPrincipal principal=
            new GenericPrincipal(new
            GenericIdentity("WriterLib"), null);
        IPrincipal oprincipal=Thread.CurrentPrincipal;
        Thread.CurrentPrincipal=principal;
        Tester.Invoke(writerlib, null);
        Thread.CurrentPrincipal=oprincipal;

        // remainder of program
        listener.Close();
    }
    catch(Exception error)
    {
        if(error.InnerException is SecurityException)
        {
            if(Thread.CurrentPrincipal.Identity.Name
                =="WriterLib")
            {
                MessageBox.Show(error.InnerException.Message);
                Trace.WriteLineIf(auditing.Enabled,
                    "Source is \n"+writerlibURL+
                    ".\n"+error.InnerException.Message);
            }
        }
    }
}
private void Form1_Load(object sender, System.EventArgs e)
{
    Trace.Listeners.Clear();
    Trace.Listeners.Add(listener);
}
```

This is the application configuration file used with Writer2.Exe.

```
<configuration>
    <system.diagnostics>
        <switches>
        <add name="auditing" value="1" />
        </switches>
    </system.diagnostics>
</configuration>
```

Let us review the code. Above the button click handler, an EventLogListener, BooleanSwitch, and string are declared as data members of the form. The EventLogListener is initialized to the "Writer" section of the application log. In the constructor, the BooleanSwitch is named "auditing." Finally, the string is assigned the URL of the library, which contains code to write to a file. Because of the HTTP protocol, the library is downloaded into the download cache and executes with few permissions.

The button click handler starts a try block. Next, Assembly.LoadFrom loads the assembly into the download cache. WriterLib exposes a Writer class and a single method called Tester. Tester attempts to write to a file on the local drive. Reflection is used to late bind to the Writer.Tester method. The downloaded assembly runs on the thread of the host application. Before invoking the Tester method, WriterLib is impersonated. If an exception is raised, this helps to identify the proper context. A generic principal is created, with WriterLib as the identity. Impersonation begins when the current principal is replaced with this new principal. Next, the Tester method is invoked through reflection. After the call, the security principal is reset and impersonation stopped. If an exception occurs, execution is transferred to the catch statement. In the catch block, we check Exception.InnerException to confirm that the exception was raised elsewhere (that is, in the WriterLib assembly). If this happens, the identity of the thread is checked. If the identity is Writerlib, we know that the exception occurred while in the role of WriterLib. If so, auditing details are written to the event log. Writing only occurs in this example when the switch is enabled in the application configuration file. This the entry for the switch in the configuration file:

```
<add name="auditing" value="1" />.
```

The entry declares a Boolean switch named auditing, which matches the switch declared in the program. The switch is set to true, and auditing is enabled.

Run the application and click the "Write" button. An exception is raised. Open the event log to confirm the audit trail. Figure 2.12 is the property sheet of the audit entry in the event log.

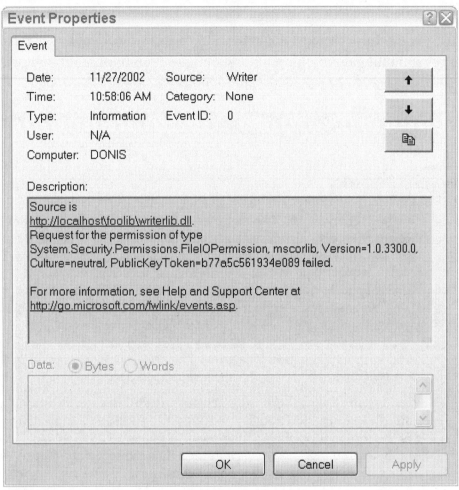

Figure 2.12   Audit information is written to the Event Log.

Obfuscators

Obscuring the content of an assembly, metadata, and MSIL not only protects intellectual investment, but also is an important security strategy. Most of your security settings and commands are written directly into the assembly. Attackers can examine an assembly using ildasm or a similar tool to obtain a blueprint to your security strategy. Plotting a security attack then becomes much easier.

Obfuscators use various algorithms to encode assemblies and block access to sensitive data and code within the assembly. The assembly is automatically decoded when loaded into memory. .NET then executes the plain assembly.

Several vendors sell obfuscators. This is a short list of those vendors:

- Dotfuscator from PreEmptive Solutions (www.preemptive.com)
- Demeanor for .NET from WiseOwl (www.wiseowl.com)
- .NET IL-Obfuscator from 9Rays (www.9rays.net)

Obfuscators' prices range from several hundred to several thousands of dollars.

Win32 Security

The .NET Framework Class Library is not a wrapper for Win32 security. Discretionary access control, system access control, and privileges, the pillars of Win32 security, are largely ignored in the Framework Class Library. The FCL focuses primarily on Win32 security related to securing enterprise or Web-based applications. Cryptography, certificate management, and Message Queue are some of the enterprise services offered by the FCL. The FCL is more than a thin wrapper of the Crypto or MSMQ APIs and extend each technology with important new functionality. In addition, the FCL offers new security tools, such as Code-Based Security, Role-Based Security, and the Runtime Security Policy.

Win32 security is not disabled and is fully enforced, even for managed applications. A file accessed from a managed application is still protected by a security descriptor regardless of the security policy of .NET. Win32 security is simply one more perimeter of protection for a managed application—another lock on the door helping to keep intruders away.

Actually, Win32 security takes precedence over .NET security. For example, when Win32 denies access to a file, .NET security cannot subjugate that decision. Therefore, Win32 security is one of many important tools in the arsenal of a managed application. Unfortunately, interfacing with Win32 security is a tad more difficult.

What is traditional Win32 security? Win32 security evolves around the security context of the user. At logon, users must present their public identity and some secret data. This is typically accomplished at a logon screen, but there are many other options. NT Lan Manager (NTLM) or Kerberos is used for authentication. Once the user is authenticated, an access token is built and assigned to the user. Users are granted individual rights and restrictions. This includes the rights of whatever groups that the user is a member of.

The access token is the security badge of the authenticated user and is presented when the user attempts to access a securable resource. A process is a surrogate for a user. A user launches a process to perform a specific task on behalf of that user. Thus, a process inherits the access token and security context of the user. If the user is an administrator, the process runs with the authority of an administrator. Access tokens contain a security identifier (SID) and relative identifier (RID) that uniquely identify the user and group membership. Based on the SID and RIDs, various machine privileges are granted to the user. Privileges include the following, among others:

- Creating a paging file
- Increasing the process priority of an application
- Loading and unloading device drivers
- Accessing the audit log
- Performing a complete backup and restore

Privileges grant rights to the entire machine and should be considered macrorights. Permissions grant access to a specific resource and are microrights. Whoever creates the first handle to a securable resource controls that resource and has discretion to set the security of that object—thus the term discretionary access control, at the discretion of the owner. Basically, if you own an object, you set the rules. Security is described in a security attributes structure, which is a parameter of the method used to create the securable kernel resource. The security attributes structure references a security descriptor. The security descriptor structure is a container for discretionary and auditing permissions.

Following is the signature of two APIs used to create kernel resources. Object security is defined in the SecurityAttributes parameter.

```
HANDLE CreateMutex( LPSECURITY_ATTRIBUTES lpMutexAttributes,
    BOOL bInitialOwner, LPCTSTR lpName)

HANDLE CreateFileMapping( HANDLE hFile, LPSECURITY_ATTRIBUTES
    lpAttributes, DWORD flProtect, DWORD dwMaximumSizeHigh,
    DWORD dwMaximumSizeLow, LPCTSTR lpName)
```

A security descriptor contains a Discretionary Access Control List (DACL) and a System Access Control List (SACL). Each is an array of access control entries (ACEs). Each ACE contains a SID or RID and a permission. The SID or RID identifies a user or group that the ACE will control. In a DACL, ACEs grant or deny permission to a kernel object. With a SACL, each ACE applies to auditing.

There are a variety of ACE types. For further detail, I recommend consulting the Microsoft Knowledge Base. When the security resource is opened, the ACEs of the securable resource are read and compared to the SID or RIDs of the user. If a match is found in DACL, the ACE is evaluated and access is granted or denied. In the SACL, the ACE is evaluated for auditing. This is how Win32 security secures securable resources.

Win32 security APIs are unmanaged code. Use the interoperability classes to access these security APIs from a managed application. The interoperability classes are provided in .NET to build bridges between managed and unmanaged code.

Integrating Win32 Security in .NET

Access Win32 security APIs using interoperability classes. Use the DllImport statement to build a bridge between managed code and unmanaged functions published in a native DLL. The interoperability classes and services are found in the System.Runtime.InteropServices namespace. Also, assemblies must be granted the unmanaged code permission to call an unmanaged function. Fully trusted assemblies, such as an application running on the local machine, are automatically granted this permission.

The DllImportAttribute class describes an unmanaged call. Unmanaged calls are implemented as a static method of a class. To limit how much code must be granted the unmanaged code permission, if possible place all unmanaged calls in a single class. Here is a basic version of DllImportAttribute:

```
[DllImport("unmanaged library name")]
    public static extern returntype FunctionName(parameters)
```

The following code reads the security descriptor of a file, obtains the SID of the owner, and converts the SID to a string, which is displayed using a Message-Box. Three unmanaged security APIs are required to accomplish these tasks: GetFileSecurity, GetSecurityDescriptor, and ConvertSidtoStringSid.

Converting an unmanaged signature to a managed signature is the biggest challenge facing a developer. First, the managed signature must be found in the Knowledge Base. Second, the return type and parameter of the unmanaged call must be matched to managed types. Following is the sample code from the application and typical of any assembly calling Win32 security APIs from managed code:

```
public class API
{
    [DllImport("Advapi32")] public extern static bool
        GetFileSecurity(string lpFileName, int
        SecurityInformation, IntPtr pSecurityDescriptor,
        int nLength, out int lpnLengthNeeded);
    [DllImport("Advapi32")] public extern static bool
        GetSecurityDescriptorOwner(IntPtr
        pSecurityDescriptor, out IntPtr pOwner,
        out bool lpbOwnerDefaulted);
    [DllImport("Advapi32")] public extern static bool
        ConvertSidToStringSid(IntPtr Sid, out string
        StringSID);
}
private const int OWNER_SECURITY_INFORMATION=1;
private void button1_Click(object sender, System.EventArgs e)
{
    int needed;
    bool resp=API.GetFileSecurity(@"c:\cat.txt",
        OWNER_SECURITY_INFORMATION, IntPtr.Zero,
        0, out needed);
    IntPtr pSecurityDescriptor=Marshal.AllocHGlobal(needed);
    resp=API.GetFileSecurity(@"c:\cat.txt", 1,
        pSecurityDescriptor, needed, out needed);
    IntPtr pOwner;
    bool lpbOwnerDefaulted;
    resp=API.GetSecurityDescriptorOwner(pSecurityDescriptor,
        out pOwner, out lpbOwnerDefaulted);
    string StringSID;
    API.ConvertSidToStringSid(pOwner, out StringSID);
    MessageBox.Show(StringSID);
}
```

In the preceding code, API is a managed class and contains references to unmanaged calls. DllImport creates a connection to the GetFileSecurity, GetSecurityDescriptorOwner, and ConvertSidToStringSid

In the button click event GetFileSecurity is called twice. First, GetFileSecurity is called to obtain the size of the security descriptor. Using the resulting size information, memory for the security descriptor is allocated with the Marshal.AllocHGlobal method. GetFileSecurity is called again to obtain the security descriptor attached to the cat.txt file. GetSecurityDescriptorOwner reads the SID of the owner from the security descriptor. ConvertSidToStringSid converts the SID into a string, which is displayed with the MessageBox.Show method.

SECURITY ALERT

Unmanaged code permissions can potentially open a backdoor and security hole into a managed application. Use this type of permission selectively in a managed application.

What's Next

The Runtime Security Policy, code access security, and role-based security are the most important new concepts implemented in .NET Security and are applicable to most any managed applications.

The Runtime Security Policy organizes assemblies into code groups. Membership in a group is based on evidence. Assemblies are granted permissions from the groups of which they are members. Additionally, the Runtime Security Policy is organized into policy levels. Policy levels represent realms of security, and an assembly receives the permission at the intersections of the policy level. Administrators and developers configure the Runtime Security Policy to reflect their security policy. The default Runtime Security Policy is conservative and implicitly creates a safe environment for deploying managed applications.

The Runtime Security Policy can be viewed as a set of security laws, while code access security is the police, enforcing those laws on managed code. The Runtime Security Policy defines the superset of permission granted to an assembly at load time. The list of permissions granted to an assembly at load time by the Runtime Security Policy cannot be expanded; but can be restricted. Code access security checks code against the Runtime Security Policy by demanding required permissions. Code executing without the necessary permissions is incarcerated and thrown into the local .NET security jail.

The Runtime Security Policy is discussed in the next chapter.

CHAPTER 3

Runtime Security Policy

A ssemblies are security principals in .NET and are granted permissions for securable resources or operations. This is the essence of the Runtime Security Policy. Traditionally, users are the primary security principals in Windows. The Runtime Security Policy adds an additional layer of security, wherein assemblies have their identity challenged and are assigned permissions. An assembly, the basic unit of security in .NET, is assigned permissions at run time. Changes in the manner that software is acquired have necessitated an extra layer of security dedicated to protecting users from malicious software.

A decade ago, most software applications were purchased at local computer stores or from a mail order company. This approach, referred to as sneaker distribution, requires shipping software from a vendor to a distribution center, and then ultimately to the client. Sneaker distribution is costly and time-consuming, but provides inherent security safeguards. High costs associated with this type of distribution prevent most malcontents from distributing malicious software in this manner. The identity of the distributor is easily traced back to the origin when using conventional transportation—this is not ideal for someone intent on disseminating malicious software. With sneaker distribution, subterfuge while in transit is unlikely. Hijacking a United Parcel Service (UPS) truck to nefariously exchange benevolent software with malicious software is a high-risk venture, even for the most brazen hacker. Finally, because of the potential liability, established retailers are unlikely to distribute unknown software from an unverifiable source. If a crate of unknown software arrived at their depot, it is highly improbable that a retailer would resell that software to unsuspecting consumers. For these reasons, until recently, acquiring software has been a relatively innocuous experience. Sneaker distribution offered both preventative and punitive security, which was not entirely dependent on the end user. Therefore, administrators faced fewer security holes inadvertently opened by careless users. In this environment, where code is basically trusted, security based on user identity is usually adequate.

Fast forward to today, where sneaker distribution is simply one of many methods used to acquire software. The percentage of software downloaded from the Web or licensed software that runs remotely has increased dramatically. This simple but revolutionary shift in software distribution benefits individuals and small software companies. The original distribution model favored software behemoths, such as Microsoft, Corel, IBM, Apple, and Adobe. The proliferation of boutique software firms is the direct result of the new paradigm. However, Microsoft, IBM, and other leading technology companies are moving quickly to capitalize on this new model as well, which includes embracing Web services and open standards. The new distribution model removes or lessens many of the implicit security safeguards of sneaker distribution. What is the distribution cost of software sold online? Erecting a Web site to distribute software is possible at a fraction of the cost of conventional distribution. When one purchases software online, is the identity of the source easily traced? Disguising one's identity is part and parcel of the activities of someone intent on distributing rogue applications via the Web. Are Internet transmissions implicitly safe? Interception of a Web transmission is possible, is done every day, and compromises security regularly. Finally, users can download programs from anywhere at anytime. This is a security concern because users are no longer isolated islands, but part of a larger enterprise. The security hole that a user inadvertently opens on one machine can potentially destabilize the entire enterprise. Within an enterprise, security is only as robust as the worst user. For these reasons and more, user identity alone is no longer sufficient for security purposes. Applications now pose a measurable security risk, which demands that their identity also be challenged and operations monitored. Mobile code epitomizes the new challenges.

The emergence of mobile code, such as email attachments, in recent months has placed the spotlight on deficiencies of Win32 security model. The explosion of Web services and embedded devices will further hasten the proliferation of mobile software. An important tenet of Microsoft .NET is delivering software components that run on devices large and small, anytime, and anywhere. Open standards help .NET deliver mobile software to a wide variety of devices. With this open architecture, comes considerable security challenges including determining the origin and safeness of code.

Overview of the Runtime Security Policy

In .NET, assemblies are accorded varying levels of trust, based on their identity or origin. Fully trusted assemblies have unfettered access to securable resources and operations, while partially trusted assemblies are accorded fewer rights. For example, programs installed locally on a computer are fully trusted. Conversely, assemblies downloaded from an Internet site are partially trusted and cannot write to the local hard drive, cannot access the Registry, and execute with other limitations. Therefore, an e-mail attachment cannot erase the hard drive as a malicious act. This describes the default policy of the runtime security policy. The elements of runtime security policy are evidence, permissions, permission sets, code groups, and policy levels.

Evidence

Evidence is an object that encapsulates the identity or origin of an assembly. It answers one of two questions: who or where. Evidence, such as a strong name or Authenticode, identifies who the assembly is. URL address or application directory are examples of evidence of the origin of an assembly. Identity evidence is stored in the metadata of the assembly and extracted by the common language runtime, while the host that launches an assembly submits evidence of origination for that code. With Web applications, ASP.NET is the host and submits the requested evidence. Based on the evidence, assemblies are categorized and granted permissions.

Permission and Permission Sets

Permissions are also objects and grant access to a securable resource or operations. .NET offers a wide variety of standard permissions, from the File Input/Output permission that grants access to a specific file to the Printing permission that enables printing. For convenience, permissions are grouped into permission sets that reflect a certain level of trust.

Permission sets, not individual permissions, are assigned to assemblies at run time. Permission sets consist of one or more permissions. Standard permission sets are called named permission sets. FullTrust, Internet, and Nothing are examples of named permission sets. Each code group has a single permission set, which establishes the rights of assemblies that are members of that code group.

Code Groups

Code groups classify assemblies based on trust. Assemblies inherit the permissions of every code group where the membership criteria are met. There are three parts to a code group: membership condition, permission set, and attributes. Membership condition is the criterion that assemblies must meet to join a group, as determined by evidence (input). The permission set represents the permissions assigned to member assemblies of a code group (output). Figure 3.1 shows the relationship between membership condition, evidence, and permission sets. Attributes, such as LevelFinal, alter the default behavior of the Runtime Security Policy. Code groups are organized in levels, mirroring the administrative responsibilities of an enterprise.

Policy Levels

Policy levels represent administrative realms of responsibility. There are four policy levels: Enterprise, Machine, User, and Application domain. Enterprise administrators configure the Enterprise level, domain and local administrators configure the Machine level, users manage the User level, and hosts are responsible for specific Application Domain levels. This partitioning of responsibility allows the enterprise manager to set enterprise-wide policy, while a local administrator sets policy that affects a single machine.

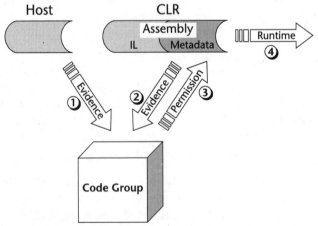

Figure 3.1 Relationship between evidence, code group, and permissions.

Runtime Security Policy

The components that have been described, when assembled, form the Runtime Security Policy. Understanding the Runtime Security Policy begins with understanding Win32 security. Let's explain Win32 security first. At logon, users are challenged and required to provide evidence of identity—typically, a username and password. The WinLogon process submits the evidence to an authority, which authenticates the credentials. If authentication is successful, an access token (security badge) is granted to the authenticated user. At the completion of the logon process, the shell is started and inherits the access token. Processes and threads inherit a copy of the access token and execute in the security context of the user. This describes the default. The default security context can be overridden in the Win32 environment. Users also accumulate the privileges and rights of groups that they are members of. Securable resources designate an array of permissions, called access control entries (ACE), that define permissions for specific users. An abbreviated list of securable resources includes semaphores, files (NTFS), Registry keys, and pipes. A process requests specific permissions when opening a securable resource. This is compared to the granted rights, and the request is either allowed or denied.

Similarities between Win32 security and the Runtime Security Policy are undeniable. Substitute assemblies for users, permissions for ACEs, and code groups for groups to transform the algorithm from Win32 security into the Runtime Security Policy. At load time, assemblies are challenged for evidence. An assembly may offer multiple pieces of evidence. Evidence is evaluated by the Runtime Security Policy to determine what code groups an assembly belongs to. The assembly accumulates the permissions of all code groups of which it is a member. When a securable resource is opened or operation performed, the assembly requests specific permissions. The request is compared to permissions granted to the assembly, and the request is either allowed or denied. Figure 3.2 depicts the Runtime Security Policy.

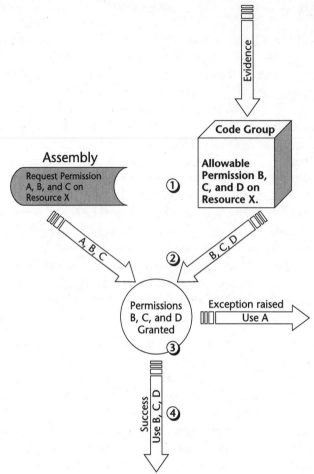

Figure 3.2 Runtime Security Policy.

Runtime Security Policy Tools

The .NET Framework includes tools for viewing and configuring the Runtime Security Policy. The Mscorcg (Microsoft Core Configuration) and Caspol (Code Access Security Policy) tools are distributed with the framework. Mscorcfg and Caspol are both found in the %system%/Microsoft.Net/Framework/*version number* directory. Mscorcfg is a Microsoft Management Console (MMC) document and provides a graphical interface for viewing and configuring the Runtime Security Policy (see Figure 3.3). Caspol is an equivalent command-line tool (see Figure 3.4). Mscorcfg is preferred for ease of use, while Caspol offers flexibility and additional functionality.

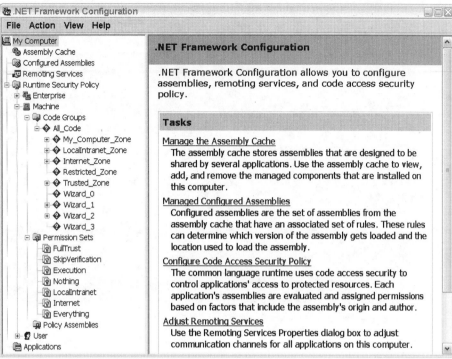

Figure 3.3 An Mscorcfg MMC document.

NOTE

Consult Microsoft's Knowledge Base for detailed instructions on using Mscorcfg and Caspol.

Evidence

Evidence is proof of code identity or origin—what and where—used to organize assemblies into code groups and set appropriate permissions therein. Evidence is obtained from two sources. First, evidence of identity is found in metadata of the related assembly, is extracted using reflection, and is submitted by the common language runtime to the Security Manager. Second, a host, such as ASP.NET, submits evidence confirming the origin of an assembly. The only qualification for evidence is being a managed component, or anything derived from System.Object.

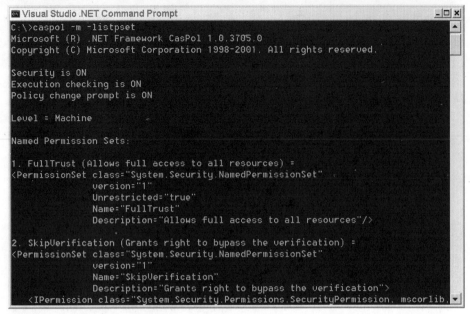

Figure 3.4   A Caspol command.

NOTE

The Security Manager is part of the common language runtime and is responsible for resolving permissions for an assembly. Based on the evidence submitted, the Security Manager maps an assembly to one or more code groups. Use the System.Security.SecurityManager managed class to interface with the Security Manager.

Code groups use evidence to set membership conditions. Assemblies can have multiple piece of evidence and thereby be members of several code groups. Evidence of an assembly can be enumerated using the Assembly.Evidence read-only property. The following program, in the ListEvidence method, enumerates evidence of the calling assembly. The evidence is then listed to a console window.

```
// AE.dll library
using System;
using System.Collections;
using System.Reflection;
using System.Security.Policy;
[assembly: AssemblyKeyFile("foo.key")]
[assembly: AssemblyVersion("1.0.0.0")]
namespace Donis
{
```

```
public class AssemblyEvidence
{
    public static void ListEvidence()
    {
        Assembly a=Assembly.GetCallingAssembly();
        Evidence e=a.Evidence;
        foreach(System.Object o in e)
            Console.WriteLine("Evidence : "+ o.ToString());
    }
}
}
```

The Foo application calls AssemblyEvidence.ListEvidence to enumerate its evidence.

```
// Foo.exe application
using System;
using System.Reflection;
using Donis;
[assembly: AssemblyKeyFile("foo.key")]
[assembly: AssemblyVersion("2.0.0.0")]
namespace FooNamespace
{
    public class Foo: AssemblyEvidence
    {
        public static void Main()
        {
            AssemblyEvidence.ListEvidence();
        }
    }
}
```

.NET provides a standard assortment of evidence—listed in Table 3.1.

Table 3.1   Evidence for Code Access Security

NAME	DESCRIPTION
Hash	Hash of assembly
Publisher Certificate	Authenticode
Strong Name	Combination of public key, name, and version number
Site	Source Web site
URL	Source url (http:, ftp:, file:, and so on)
Zone	Internet zones (derived from Internet Explorer)
Application Directory	Installation directory

In Mscorcfg, the list of available evidence can be viewed while editing or creating a new code groups. Within the code group properties, evidence is presented on the Membership property sheet. Unfortunately, the listing of available evidence cannot be obtained independently of a code group. You cannot simply list evidence. The Caspol tool also does not offer commands to list evidence.

Evidence can be listed programmatically. Using a SecurityManager object, the following program enumerates code groups based on specific evidence, the MyComputer zone evidence. Standard evidence is defined in the System.Security.Policy namespace.

```
using System;
using System.Security;
using System.Security.Policy;
using System.Collections;
namespace EnumerateEvidence
{
    class EnumerateEvidence
    {
        public static void Main()
        {
            Zone z=new Zone(SecurityZone.MyComputer);
            Evidence e=new Evidence();
            e.AddAssembly(z);
            IEnumerator enumerator=
                SecurityManager.ResolvePolicyGroups(e);
            while(enumerator.MoveNext())
            {
                Object o=enumerator.Current;
                Console.WriteLine(((CodeGroup)o).Name);
            }
        }
    }
}
```

Permissions and Permission Sets

The basic unit of the Runtime Security Policy is the permission, which is a right to access a securable resource or task. Securable resources are a diverse array of objects, each with a unique set of rights and properties. Figures 3.5 and 3.6 show the attributes of FileIOPermisson and SocketPermission objects, respectively, and highlight the differences between permissions. Refer to the documentation of each permission object for an explanation of specific rights and usages.

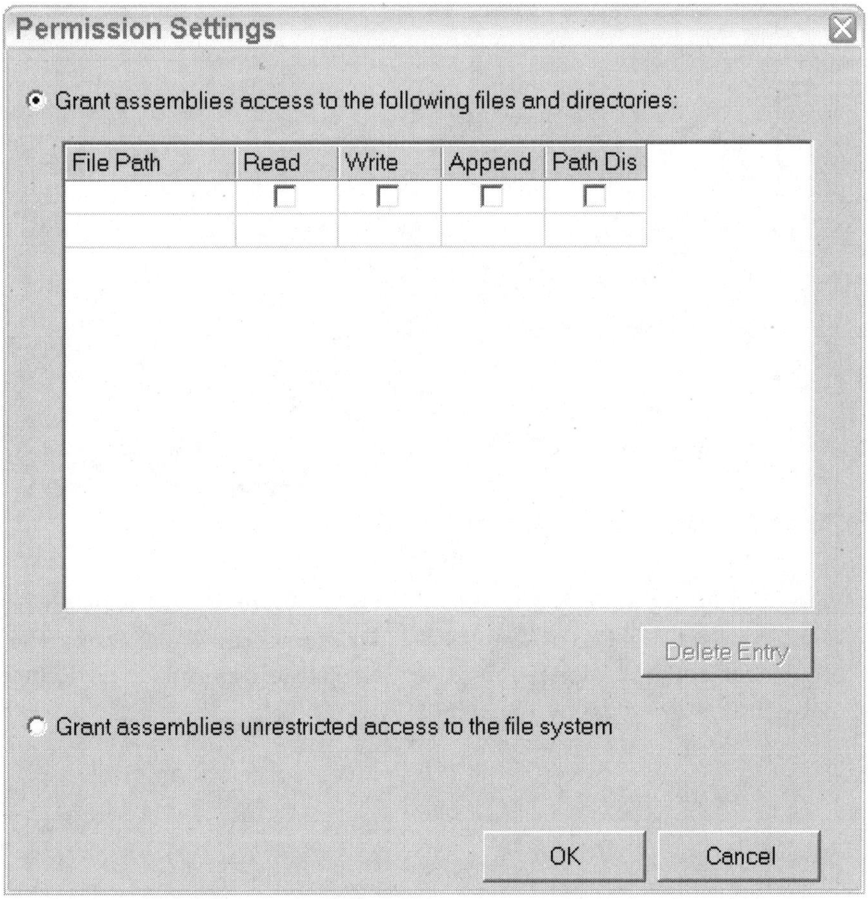

Figure 3.5 FileIOPermission attributes.

Figure 3.6 Socket access permission.

Permissions are managed objects derived directly or indirectly from the System.Security.CodeAccessPermission. Most are permissions are part of the System.Security.Permission namespace. The standard permissions of the Runtime Security Policy are shown in Table 3.2.

Table 3.2   Standard Permissions in .NET

MANAGED CLASS	DESCRIPTION
DirectoryServicesPermisson	Permission to access System.DirectoryServices
DnsPermission	Permission to access DNS servers
EnvironmentPermission	Permission to access environment variables
EventLogPermission	Permission to access event logs
FileDialogPermisson	Permission to access files or folders through dialog boxes
FileIOPermisson	Permission to access specific files and folders
IsolatedStorageFilePermission	Permission to access isolated storage
MessageQueuePermission	Permission to access remote message queues
OleDbPermission	Permission to access the OLE DB managed provider
PerformanceCounterPermission	Permission to access performance counter
PrincipalPermission	Permission to access the current principal
PrintingPermission	Permission to print
ReflectionPermission	Permission to access metadata
RegistryPermission	Permission to access registry
SecurityPermission	A set of generic permissions—see Table 3.3
ServiceControllerPermission	Permission to access Windows services
SocketPermission	Permission to access a socket
SQLClientPermission	Permission to access Microsoft SQL managed provider
UIPermission	Permission to access GUI or clipboard
WebPermission	Permission to the System.Net.WebRequest

The SecurityPermission aggregates several permissions and identifies the applicable permission using the SecurityPermissionFlag. The SecurityPermissionFlag, a bitwise flag, is a member of the SecurityPermission class. Table 3.3 lists its possible values.

Table 3.3 Possible Values for SecurityPermissionFlag

SECURITY PERMISSION FLAGS	DESCRIPTION
AllFlags	Unrestricted
Assertion	Permission to assert
ControlAppDomain	Permission to manage application domains
ControlDomainPolicy	Permission to set domain policy
ControlEvidence	Permission to submit and alter evidence
ControlPolicy	Permission to manipulate security policy
ControlPrincipal	Permission to access current principal
ControlThread	Permission to control advance thread operations
Execution	Permission for code to execute
Infrastructure	Permission to insert new components into the common language runtime infrastructure
NoFlags	Permissions not granted
RemotingConfiguration	Permission to configure remoting channels and types
SerializationFormatter	Permission to serialization services
SkipVerification	Permission to skip code verification of an assembly
UnmanagedCode	Permission to interface with unmanaged code

Permission sets are clusters of permissions and are applied to code groups. Permission sets remove the drudgery of assigning individual permissions to each and every assembly. Through a code group, a permission set is assigned to assemblies of similar functionality or trust. The permissions of related assemblies can be adjusted simply by updating the permission set. Compare this to individually updating the permissions of each assembly, surely a time-consuming and error-prone process. Permission sets are not universal, but are specific to policy levels. .NET provides predefined permission sets, called named permission sets, such as the Internet named permission set. These permission sets contain the File Dialog, Isolated Storage File, Printing, Security, and User Interface permission. By default, each policy level starts with the same assortment of named permission sets. See Table 3.4 for the list of named permissions sets.

Permission sets can be listed using either Mscorcfg or Caspol. With Capsol, use the policy level attribute to list permission sets of a specific policy level: (en)terprise, (m)achine, (u)ser, (a)ll.

```
caspol-en -listpset
caspol-m -listpset
```

It is often helpful to extract the permission set and permissions assigned to a code group. In Mscorcfg, select the target code group and choose Edit Code Group Properties from the right pane. In the resulting dialog box, switch to the Permission Set property sheet to view the permission set and permissions of that group (see Figure 3.7). In addition, the permissions of a code group can be listed programmatically. There is no command in Caspol to list only the permissions of a code group.

Table 3.4 The Named Permission Sets

PERMISSION SET	DESCRIPTION
Nothing	No permissions
Execution	Permissions that allow assembly execution[1]
Internet	Limited permissions granted to Internet applications
LocalInternet	Limited permissions granted to Intranet applications
Everything	All permissions, except skip verification
FullTrust	All permissions
SkipVerification	Permission to skip verification

[1] Consult the knowledge base or MSDN to ascertain the permissions of any named permission set.

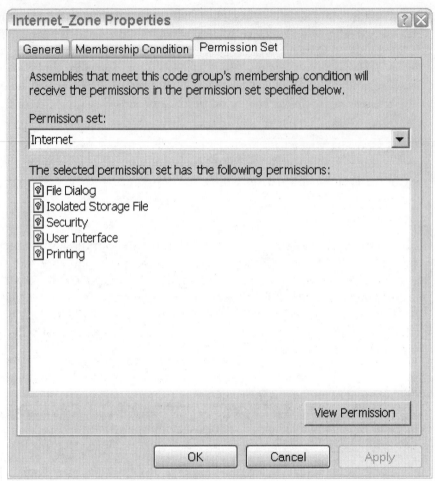

Figure 3.7 Permissions of the Internet Code Group using Mscorcfg.

Code Groups

Code groups are the pivotal components within runtime security policy. They categorize and set permissions on assemblies. When viewed in their entirety, code groups form the security policy of the enterprise, machine, user, and application domain. Editing code groups changes security policy. If the Runtime Security policy were a building, adding or deleting code groups would add or remove bricks from the security infrastructure. As mentioned earlier, code groups consist of three parts:

Membership condition. Membership condition determines which assemblies are members of a specific code group. Defined by evidence, code groups offer a single membership condition.

Permission set. A permission set is the array of permissions assigned to a code group. Permissions cannot be assigned directly to a code group, but only assigned as part of a permission set. Of course, an individual permission can be assigned to a code group by creating a permission set with only that permission.

Attributes. Code groups support attributes that are modifiers of the Runtime Security Policy. The two most important attributes are the LevelFinal and Exclusive attributes—both are described shortly.

Zones

Enterprise and User policy levels start with a single code group, the All_Code group. The membership condition of Enterprise::All_Code and User::All_Code, as the names imply, is all assemblies and grants members full trust. The level::code group is the idiom used to name a code group in the context of a policy level. Heavy lifting for the Runtime Security Policy is accomplished at the machine level, which is the only policy level that begins with multiple code groups. For this reason, Machine level policy sets the default policy. Machine level code groups are separated into zones based on proximity. Closer assemblies are granted higher trust then distant assemblies. Applications installed on the local hard drive are fully trusted, but remotely executing applications are only partially trusted. These are the default code groups within Machine level policy:

NOTE Native code is an exception and is not trusted regardless of location.

All_Code. This code group includes all assemblies and grants the Nothing permission set.

My_Computer_Zone. Assemblies installed on the local machine are members of this zone and granted FullTrust permissions and have unlimited access to securable resources and tasks.

LocalIntranet_Zone. Intranet-based assemblies are members of this zone and assigned the LocalIntranet permission set, which limits access to securable resources. The most notable restriction is that intranet assemblies are not granted access to the standard file system; but permission is granted to Isolated File Storage.

Internet_Zone.   Internet-derived assemblies are members of this zone and are assigned the Internet permission set. Internet assemblies are less trusted then intranet applications. For example, an Internet assembly is not granted any access to the file system, including no rights to Isolated File Storage.

Restricted_Zone.   Assemblies originating from a restricted zone, as defined by Internet Explorer, are members of this zone. Restricted assemblies are not trusted and are assigned the Nothing permission set, which grants no permissions to securable resources or operations.

Trusted_Zone.   Assemblies originating from a trusted zone, as defined by Internet Explorer, are members of this zone. Trusted assemblies are fully trusted and are granted the FullyTrusted permission set.

Code Group Hierarchy

The Runtime Security Policy offers multiple code groups arranged in a tiered and tree structure. First, policy levels represent tiers of code groups. Second, within a policy level, code groups are organized in trees. A code group tree comprises a parent group and one or more child groups (descendents). The best examples of code trees are found in Machine level policy. The All_Code group contains five child groups, one of them is the My_Computer_Zone tree, which contains two child groups: Microsoft_Strong_Name and ECMA_Strong_Name. Figure 3.8 presents the My_Computer_Zone tree.

Code group trees factor mightily in the algorithm for assigning permission to assemblies. Assemblies can belong to more than one code group; the permissions of an assembly are the union of permissions granted those code groups and the intersection of rights granted at each policy level. Determining the permissions granted to an assembly, requires the Security Manager to evaluate or walk through each code group tree, beginning at the Enterprise level. The Machine, User, and Application Domain levels, in that order, are evaluated next. Within a code group tree, the parent group is evaluated first, followed by all descendants. Evaluation traverses a code group tree, with the assembly collecting permissions until the membership condition fails on a particular code group. When a membership test fails, the Security Manager starts anew at the foot of another branch. Code groups further down the tree are not tested and their permissions are omitted. If the present code group tree is fully evaluated, testing continues with the next code group tree. When the process is complete, the permissions granted an assembly represent the union of permissions from all code groups of which it is a member.

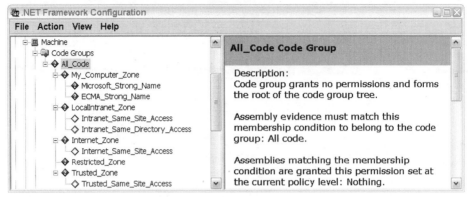

Figure 3.8 Machine level policy code group tree.

We have been discussing code groups. The following program enumerates each policy level and reports the code groups contained within them. Policy-Heirarchy, as an attribute of the SecurityManager class, returns a collection of policy levels. PolicyLevel and CodeGroup classes are abstractions of a policy level and a code group, respectively. RootCodeGroup is an attribute of the PolicyLevel class, and returns the top group of that policy. Children is an attribute of the CodeGroup class, and returns a list of child groups for the current code group.

```
using System;
using System.Security;
using System.Collections;
using System.Security.Policy;
namespace Donis
{
    public class CodeGroup
    {
        static public void Main()
        {
            IEnumerator policies=
                SecurityManager.PolicyHierarchy();
            while (policies.MoveNext())
            {
                PolicyLevel policy = (PolicyLevel)
                policies.Current;
                Console.WriteLine("\n"+policy.Label);
                System.Security.Policy.CodeGroup root=
                    policy.RootCodeGroup;
                IList children=root.Children;
                EnumCodeGroup(children, 1);
```

```
            }
        }
        static public void EnumCodeGroup(IList children, int depth)
        {
            foreach(System.Security.Policy.CodeGroup child in
                children)
            {
                string spacer=new string(' ', (depth*5));
                Console.WriteLine(spacer+child.Name);
                IList grandchildren=child.Children;
                if(grandchildren.Count!=1)
                    EnumCodeGroup(grandchildren, depth+1);
            }
        }
    }
}
```

Policy Levels

The Runtime Security Policy partitions code groups into rings of security called policy levels; there are Enterprise, Machine, User, and Application domain policy levels. This is depicted in Figure 3.9. Different realms of an enterprise often require unique security considerations and are administered by disparate users. The security policy for a specific machine may be inadequate as a enterprise policy. Furthermore, the policy of a specific user may not be appropriate for the shared users of a machine. The person administering user policy is likely not the same individual responsible for administering the enterprise policy. Policy levels mirror the real-world model, where there are realms of security and tiered administration. Assemblies are granted the *intersection* of permissions from the different policy levels. Conversely, within a policy level, an assembly is granted the permissions of every code group of which it is a member. Restated, permissions within a policy level are combined as a *union*.

NOTE

To be granted to an assembly, the permission must be granted at every policy level.

These are the four policy levels:

- Enterprise level is the outermost ring of security policy. The membership condition of Enterprise level code groups are applied to all assemblies throughout the enterprise. Qualifying assemblies are granted the applicable permissions, regardless of their location in the enterprise. Enterprise level defaults to one code group, which is the All_Code group, and every assembly is a member. The Enterprise::AllCode group grants FullTrust to all assemblies. Obviously, granting full trust to all assemblies in the enterprise is not a great idea. The permissions granted to assemblies at the Enterprise level are refined at the Machine, User, and Application domain levels. Enterprise level policies can be configured by enterprise administrators.

- Machine level is the default policy and is applied to assemblies on the local computer. At this level, code groups are organized in zones, as described earlier in the "Code Group" section. This level can be configured by enterprise or local administrators.

- Within the User Level, code groups are applied to assemblies of a particular user session. Similar to the Enterprise level, this level begins with one group—the All_Code group. The User::AllCode group grants FullTrust to member assemblies. This level can be configured by administrators and the current user.

- Application Domain level policy is optional and is set by the related host.

Permissions granted at an outer ring, or senior policy level, cannot be expanded upon in a lower-level policy; but can be restricted. If an assembly is denied access to printing at the Enterprise level, this denied right cannot be overridden at the Machine level. Conversely, if all access is granted to a particular file at the Machine policy level, that access can be refined to write-only access at the User level. In this way, lower-level policies refine the higher-level policies and permissions granted to assemblies.

Applications are deployed in different enterprises, deployed on various machines, or run within a variety of user contexts. Each of these represents a potentially dissimilar configuration of the Runtime Security Policy, and the assembly must be prepared to deal with these differences. To plug as many security holes as possible, developers must test assemblies against as many configurations as practically possible.

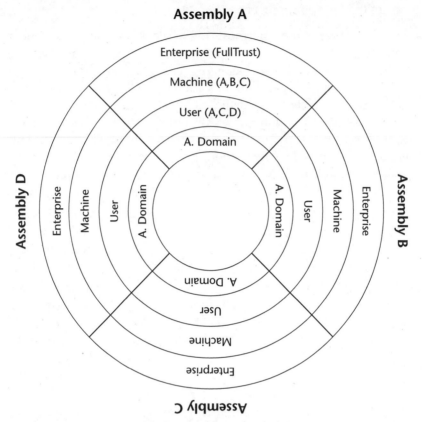

Figure 3.9 Rings of the .NET security policy. The parentheses represent permissions granted at each policy level. Assembly A would be granted permissions A and C.

Policy Level Modifiers

LevelFinal and Exclusive are attributes of code groups and modify the behavior of the Runtime Security Policy and, more precisely, policy levels. LevelFinal prevents policy evaluation beyond the current policy level—only policies of that level or higher apply. If stipulated at the Machine level, policies stated in User level are ignored. This is an effective tool for preventing lower-level policies from overriding or otherwise changing the present policy. Administrators might use LevelFinal to prevent users from revising the policies on critical applications. The Exclusive attribute instructs the Runtime Security Policy to ignore other policy levels and groups, in favor of using a single code group that exclusively sets policy for its member assemblies. Members of a code group, with the Exclusive attribute set, garner the partitions exclusively granted in that code group.

Refining the Runtime Security Policy

This chapter has documented how an assembly is granted specific permissions as dictated by the Runtime Security Policy. The assembly must run within this security envelope or suffer security exceptions. Assemblies adopt one of three strategies at run time for living within this security envelope.

First, they can accept the policy and run "as is"—this is called security neutral code.

Second, they can rebel. They can list required permissions for successful execution and demand that they be provided, and if they are not provided, refuse to execute. This is the classic, "If you won't play by my rules, I'll take my ball and go home" approach.

Third, an assembly can refuse permissions that it is otherwise granted. Why? Unnecessary permissions are potential security holes.

As a developer, security neutral code is easier to write because it requires no intervention. Implicitly accepting the Runtime Security Policy shifts the responsibility for security and code safety to administrators managing the Runtime Security Policy. Sometimes, intervention is required. If an application does not run correctly without certain permissions, those permissions can be demanded. The required permissions form the basis of an agreement between assembly and the Security Manager, and must be provided before the assembly is allowed to execute.

Importantly, an assembly cannot expand upon the permissions granted to it at run time. The assembly can express an opinion, refuse to run, refine, or accept the granted permissions. Imagine the anarchy if assemblies could influence their own permissions and thereby set security policy.

Security Neutral Code

Security neutral code assumes that the security policy is adequate for execution. This type of assembly expresses no opinion on the soundness of the the Runtime Security Policy, does not attempt to refine the Runtime Security Policy, and does not protect others from breaches of the security policy. Security neutral code is easy to implement—you do nothing. At run time, the assembly is granted the appropriate permissions, as determined by the security policy, and operates within the constraints of those grants. If security is breached, a security exception is raised and, typically, the application is terminated.

There are three areas of concern with security neutral code:

- User experience
- Downstream problems
- Correctness

Unsatisfactory user experiences can be by-product of security neutral code. Security neutral assemblies, particularly lowly trusted assemblies, are prone to raising security exceptions. Few rights are granted lowly trusted assemblies, and the potential for security infractions are much greater when compared to a fully trusted assembly. Security infractions are manifested as security exceptions, which definitely do not improve the user experience. Figure 3.10 is a security exception raised in security neutral code—this is not something most users would appreciate.

Security neutral code does not protect downstream assemblies from landmines in the security policy. When Assembly A calls in to Assembly B and Assembly B calls into Assembly C, both Assembly A and B are considered downstream of Assembly C. Assembly C is the upstream assembly. Downstream assemblies sometimes cannot predict or manage the security requirements as required for the upstream assembly. In these circumstances, the upstream assembly might consider exempting downstream assemblies from the troublesome security policy. (Exempting an assembly downstream from having a certain permission is called an assert and is discussed in the Chapter 4, "Code Access Security.") The problem is that security neutral code never exempts downstream assemblies from the security policy, even when appropriate. Assembly C is security neutral. Unbeknownst to Assembly A and B, Assembly C requires a permission to access a specific resource. Since they neither possess nor are exempted from the required permission, when these assemblies call in to Assembly C, a security exception is raised.

An assembly that requires specific permissions to execute correctly should not operate as security neutral code. The assembly should notify the common language runtime of its requisite permissions and refuse to execute without them. Alternately, the assembly may opt to execute but notify the user of the potential problem. Either way, running as security neutral code is not appropriate in this circumstance.

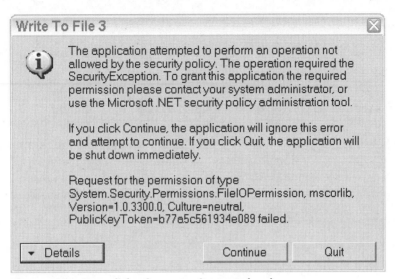

Figure 3.10   Error dialog from security neutral code.

Fully Trusted versus Partially Trusted Assemblies

In .NET, there are two types of assemblies: fully trusted assemblies and partially trusted assemblies. Fully trusted code is granted universal access to secure resources and operations, while partially trusted code runs with a subset of permissions. Fully trusted code run unrestricted and is most often a local application. Partially trusted assemblies allow potentially unsafe programs to run safely within boundaries set by the security policy. Examples of partially trusted code are Internet and intranet applications.

Strongly named assemblies are implicitly available to fully trusted code. Partially trusted code must receive an explicit grant to access a strongly named assembly. Strongly named assemblies are public and shared, thereby requiring an extra layer of protection. Strongly named assemblies can relax this requirement. The AllowPartiallyTrustedCallers attribute grants partially trusted assemblies access to a strongly named assembly.

```
[assembly: AssemblyKeyFile("mykey.key")]
[assembly: AssemblyKeyName("")]
[assembly: AllowPartiallyTrustedCallers]
```

Strongly named assemblies that relax the security policy with the AllowPartiallyTrustedCallers attribute should be fully tested against malicious code. As always, relaxing the security policy might inadvertently open a security hole.

Refining the Runtime Security Policy

Assemblies wishing to comment on the security policy use the SecurityAction attribute. SecurityAction expresses an opinion and never causes additional permissions to be granted to an assembly. SecurityAction is an assembly-level attribute and is evaluated at run time. It is a flag with three options:

- RequestMinimum
- RequestRefused
- RequestOptional

RequestMinimum names specific permissions necessary to execute the assembly correctly. Without these permissions, the assembly will not run correctly and will opt not to execute. Any attempt to load the assembly without the stipulated permissions will cause a policy exception. WriteToFile is an application that is granted low trust but minimally requests full trust permissions. Attempts to run the assembly will result in an error (see Figure 3.11).

This is the attribute that requested full trust permissions as a minimum requirement for executing the WriteToFile application.

```
[assembly: PermissionSetAttribute(SecurityAction.RequestMinimum,
    Name = "FullTrust")]
```

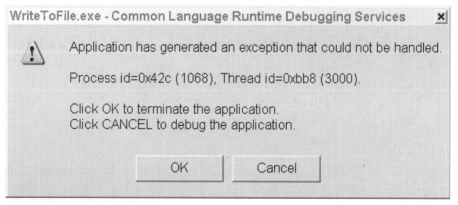

Figure 3.11 This error dialog results from an attempt to load an assembly with inadequate permissions.

Assemblies use RequestRefused to repudiate permissions that would otherwise be granted. Denying permissions that are not needed closes potential security holes that can be exploited by malicious code. This is especially important because of differences between traditional Win32 and .NET security. Making a blind request for a basket of permissions in Win32 is rarely successful. Therefore, in the Win32 environment, developers request only the permissions needed and do not grab for everything hoping to get something. If any permission is denied, all access is denied. However, in .NET a security grab might work. The caller is granted some permission even if other permissions are denied. RequestRefused prevents the granting of permissions that would otherwise be harmful to the assembly. The following attribute refuses file input/output permission.

```
[assembly: FileIOPermission(SecurityAction.RequestRefuse)]
```

Optional permissions, when omitted, affect noncritical operations of the assembly. Unlike minimal permissions, optional permissions are not required for the assembly to run correctly. The following code indicates that File Input/Output Permission is optional for proper execution of an assembly.

```
[assembly: FileIOPermission(SecurityAction.RequestOptional,
    Unrestricted=true)]
```

Runtime Security Policy in Practice

WriteFile.exe, WriteFile2.exe, and WriteFile3.exe are instances of the same application and each can write to the fa.txt, fb.txt, and fc.txt files. WriteFile and WriteFile2 are strongly named assemblies, while WriteFile3 is not. The applications present the same window (see Figure 3.12), which contains three buttons, one for writing to each text file. The programs are executed remotely from a file share (g:) and are therefore considered intranet applications. Of course this presents a challenge, based on default policy, Intranet-based assemblies cannot write to a local hard drive. New permissions, and possibly groups, are required to augment the Runtime Security Policy and accommodate this behavior. Code groups (G1, G2, G3, G4, and G5) and permission sets (P1, P2, P3, and P4) have been added to the Runtime Security Policy for the purpose of granting file access to the WriteToFile assemblies. Adjustments of this sort are typical in the daily administration of the Runtime Security Policy.

Figure 3.12 WriteToFile, WriteToFile2, and WriteToFile3 are applications that present three buttons—one each for writing to File A (fa.txt), File B (fb.txt), and File C (fc.txt).

Table 3.5 describes the code groups added to the default security policy:

Permissions P1, P2, P3, and P4 grant varying degrees of permission to access fa.txt, fb.txt, and fc.txt files. Table 3.6 describes the added code groups:

WriteToFile and WriteToFile2 share the same strong name, which is input as evidence to the G2 code group. As mentioned previously, WriteToFile3 does not have a strong name. Figure 3.13 sketches the relationships between the added code groups and permission sets.

Let us examine how the new policy is applied to WriteToFile.exe and WriteToFile3.exe.

Security Policy for WriteToFile

Determining the Runtime Security Policy applicable to an assembly begins by exploring each policy level. Within each policy level, the code group hierarchy and trees must be evaluated. Policy evaluation begins at the enterprise policy level with the root group, usually All_Code, and proceeds to the child objects, then grandchild objects, and so on.

Table 3.5 Description of Code Groups Added to the Default Security Policy

NAME	LEVEL	PERMISSIONS	PERMISSION DESCRIPTION
P1	Enterprise	FileIO	c:\data\fa.txt : read, write, append
			c:\data\fb.txt : read, write, append
P2	Machine	FileIO	c:\data\fa.txt : read, write, append
			c:\data\fb.txt : read
P3	Machine	FileIO	c:\data\fc.txt : read, write, append
P4	Machine	FileIO	c:\data\fb.txt : write, append

Table 3.6 The Added Code Access Groups[2]

G	LEVEL	PATH	MEMBERSHIP CONDITION	P
G1	Enterprise	All_Code::G12	URL: file://g:*	P1
G2	Machine	All_Code:: LocalInternet_Zone::G2	Strong name	P2
G3	Machine	All_Code:: LocalInternet_Zone::G2::G3	URL: file:// g:\writetofile.exe	P3
G4	Machine	All_Code:: LocalInternet_Zone::G2::G4	URL: file:// g:\writetofile3.exe	P4
G5	Machine	All_Code:: LocalInternet_Zone::G2::G5	URL: file:// g:\writetofile2.exe	P4

[2] Double colons are used to delineate parent and child groups.

At the Enterprise policy level, WriteToFile belongs to the All_Code group. The membership condition of Enterprise::All_Code group is all code and therefore includes WriteToFile. All_Code grants the FullTrust permission set. Next, we evaluate the G1 group. Since the program resides at the g:\ share, it also belongs to the G1 code group. This group grants the P1 permission set. Enterprise level grants WriteToFile the following permission sets: FullTrust (. P1. FullTrust grants universal permission, which makes P1 is irrelevant. An assembly cannot receive more than universal permissions—it is all-inclusive. Thus, at the Enterprise policy level, WriteToFile is granted universal permissions. Figure 3.13 depicts permissions granted at each policy level.

At the Machine policy level, WriteToFile belongs to the All_Code group. At this level, All_Code grants the Nothing permission set. As an intranet application, WriteToFile is also a member of the LocalInternet_Zone group, which grants the LocalIntranet permission set. In addition, WriteToFile has the required strong name and is thus a member of the G2 code group, which grants the P2 permission set. Finally, WriteToFile belongs to the G3 group and receives the P3 permission set. The membership condition of G3 is the URL path "file://g:\ WriteToFile.exe". Permission sets granted to WriteToFile at the Machine policy level are: Nothing $\cup$ Intranet $\cup$ P2 $\cup$ P3.

At the User policy level, there is a single code group, All_Code, which grants the FullTrust permission set. Therefore, at the User policy level, WriteToFile receives universal permissions.

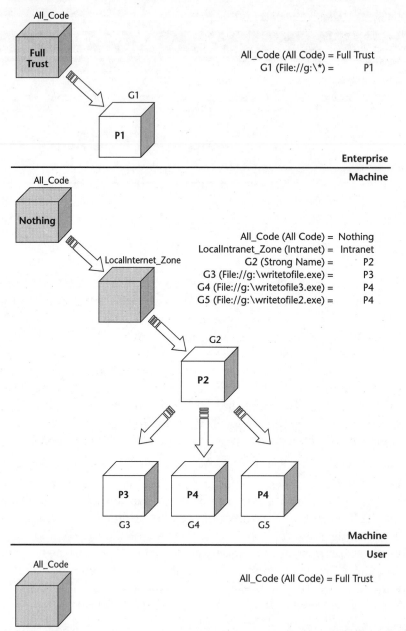

All_Code (All Code) = Full Trust
G1 (File://g:*) =   P1

Enterprise

Machine

All_Code (All Code) = Nothing
LocalIntranet_Zone (Intranet) = Intranet
G2 (Strong Name) =   P2
G3 (File://g:\writetofile.exe) =   P3
G4 (File://g:\writetofile3.exe) =   P4
G5 (File://g:\writetofile2.exe) =   P4

Machine

User

All_Code (All Code) = Full Trust

Figure 3.13 At each policy level, permissions are granted to the WriteToFile sample application.

Intersect the permission sets granted at Enterprise, Machine, and User policy level to determine the permissions granted to WriteToFile.

Enterprise	FullTrust
Machine	Nothing $\cup$ Intranet $\cup$ P2 $\cup$ P3
User	FullTrust

Intersection	Intranet $\cup$ P2 $\cup$ P3

Decompose the permission sets Intranet, P2, and P3, to discover that WriteToFile is granted the following permissions:

DNS File Dialog Printing Reflection Security
Event Log User Interface
Environment Variables Isolated Storage File FileIO

The FileIO permission of the P2 and P3 permission sets grant read, write, and append access to fa.txt and fc.txt files, while only read access is granted to fb.txt. The first and third button of WriteToFile successfully update fa.txt and fb.txt. However, clicking the second button results in the exception illustrated in Figure 3.14.

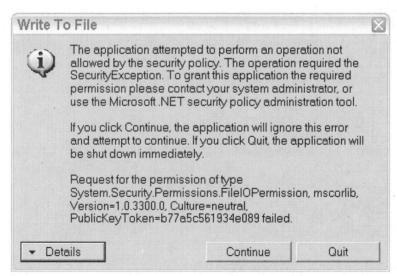

Figure 3.14 This error is displayed when the second button is clicked.

Security Policy for WriteToFile3

WriteToFile3 raises an exception when writing to fa.txt, fb.txt, or fc.txt. Why? Without a strong name, the assembly fails the membership test for code group G2. This prevents the descendents of G2 from being evaluated—extrapolation of a code group tree stops at the first failure. Lacking the permissions of G2 to G5, WriteToFile3 is granted only intranet permissions and no FileIO rights, which causes the exception.

Resolving Assembly Permissions

Resolving the permissions granted to an assembly yields valuable information, including confirmation of our calculations as related to WriteToFile and WriteToFile3. Mscorcfg provides this functionality, while Caspol offers this feature but only within the context of permission sets. Security Permission is a .NET tool available on this book's companion Web site. It lists the permissions granted to a particular assembly. You provide the full path of an assembly, and the program details the permissions. Expanded details of a permission can be ascertained by double-clicking on the permission item (see Figures 3.15 and 3.16).

In the program, Resolve_Click is a button handler and resolves the permissions of an assembly. The targeted assembly is loaded using Assembly.LoadFrom, whereupon the permissions sets granted to the assembly are extracted by calling SecurityManager.ResolvePolicy. The subsequent for loop iterates the individual permissions. IPermission.ToXml returns a SecurityElement object. Security element methods are used to extract the name of the permission, which is then added to the Permissions list box.

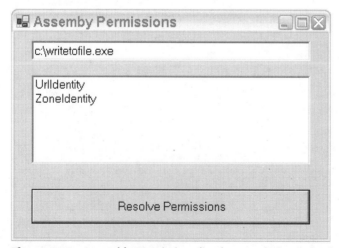

Figure 3.15 Assembly Permissions list the permissions of WriteToFile.exe.

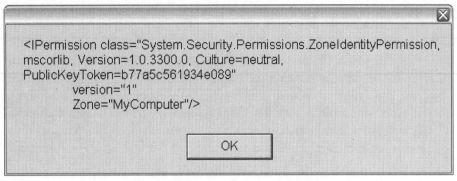

Figure 3.16 The expanded details of the FileIO permission.

The OnDoubleClick handler copies the permissions from the permission set into a permission array. The details of the selected permission are then displayed in a message box.

```
PermissionSet pset;
private void Resolve_Click(object sender, System.EventArgs e)
{
    if(Filename.Text.Length>0)
    {
        Assembly a=Assembly.LoadFrom(Filename.Text);
        pset=SecurityManager.ResolvePolicy(a.Evidence);
      Permissions.Items.Clear();
        foreach(IPermission p in pset)
        {
            SecurityElement se=p.ToXml();
            string attrib=se.Attribute("class");
            string [] values=attrib.Split(',');
            string [] names=values[0].Split('.');
            string name=names[names.Length-1];
            string permission=name.Remove(name.Length-10, 10);
            Permissions.Items.Add(permission);
        }
    }
}
public void OnDoubleClick(Object o, EventArgs e)
{
    IPermission [] p=new IPermission[pset.Count];
    pset.CopyTo(p,0);
    string name=
        p[((ListBox)o).SelectedIndex].ToString();
    MessageBox.Show(name);
}
```

What's Next?

This chapter explained the Runtime Security Policy. The Runtime Security Policy is not alone in waging the battle against malicious code. Code access security is a fellow soldier in the perpetual security battle, where the goal is to protect securable resources. Code access security and the Runtime Security Policy work together to erect an impenetrable security fortress that protects assemblies from malfeasance.

The Runtime Security Policy distributes permissions to assemblies at run time. When code attempts to access a securable resource, code access security enforces the security policy by demanding appropriate permissions before allowing access to a securable resource or performing a security task. It intersects the required permissions and the permissions granted by the Runtime Security Policy. If a required permission is granted, the code is allowed to proceed. If it is not present, code access security raises a security exception to prevent the offending code from proceeding.

The next chapter provides a detailed explanation of code access security.

Code Access Security

C ode access security acts as the security police of .NET. The primary responsibility of the Code Access Security objects is preventing interlopers of low trust from stealing the identity of higher-trusted code to improperly manipulate sensitive or dangerous resources.

When uncovered, interlopers are arrested. Actually, an exception is thrown, which is equally unpleasant. Interlopers launch luring or other attacks, which code access security targets, intercepts, and eradicates. Sensitive resources are guarded by code access security through a series of demands that ensure that callers possess permissions to sensitive resources and are not relying on the permissions of the called function. Demands trigger a stack walk that confirms the permissions granted to each caller (function) and limits access to those resources. If a function on the call stack is not granted the requested permission, a security exception is raised and the operation is aborted.

The Runtime Security Policy and code access security are collaborators, and together are largely responsible for protecting sensitive resources in the .NET operating environment. The Runtime Security Policy is the governing body of the .NET security apparatus, setting the precepts by which assemblies and components must abide.

Assemblies run locally are implicitly trusted to be safe, law-abiding citizens, while code of unknown origin is partially trusted, subjected to extra scrutiny, and granted limited permissions. Code access security enforces the permissions granted by the Runtime Security Policy. Permissions granted to an assembly at run time are enforced by code access security during execution whenever a sensitive resource is requested. If the request belies current security policy, code access security fires an exception to ring the alarm. This differs from traditional Win32 security, but the growing pervasiveness of component development necessitates a new model that protects resources from belligerent callers.

Code access security addresses some of the legitimate concerns presented when assembling applications from loosely coupled components. Constructing a cohesive application from disparate components is becoming more commonplace—especially for Web-based applications. Components are snapped together to erect fully functional applications from loosely coupled components. Reduced development time, improved robustness from using tested third-party components, and fusing the technical prowess of developers, separated geographically or otherwise, into a common solution are some of the compelling reasons for the rapid adoption of this programming methodology. It represents the inevitable and natural evolution of object-oriented programming. COM (Common Object Model) developers embraced this approach to Windows programming years ago. In addition, other initiatives, such as CORBA (Common Object Request Broker Architecture), have helped popularize the component development of applications on other platforms, while simultaneously introducing an assortment of new security concerns.

Luring attacks are a potential security hazard for applications consisting of components. A luring attack occurs when a low-trusted component, granted limited rights, tricks higher-trusted components, with imperious rights, to act on its behalf. In this way, the component with limited permissions commandeers the permissions of a trusted component and can improperly access sensitive resources using hijacked permissions. Sharing a security context between an application and its components, which is common in the native Win32 operating environment, invites luring attacks.

Security was of lesser concern when applications used only known or local components. This is the archetype of a single-vendor solution common to Win32 programming, and the security model reflected the intrinsic safeness of this approach. In traditional Win32 security, a process assimilates the user context of the access token inherited from the host application. Threads, the basic units of execution, then borrow the user context from the process or parent application. When a library is loaded into an application, components from the library run on threads of the application. Thus, the application, any threads, and components loaded from a library share the same security context. (We are ignoring impersonation and other methods for temporarily changing the security context.) Shared security context is not a problem when vendors employ private or local libraries exclusively. Single-vendor solutions, although safe, lack the unprecedented flexibility offered in .NET, where loosely coupled components are the emerging standard.

In an environment where loosely coupled components are the norm, how does an application distinguish between trusted and untrusted components? Code access security and the Runtime Security Policy jointly provide the solution. Based on evidence, assemblies, applications, and libraries are separately categorized and granted permission based solely on their identity and location—libraries do not implicitly share the security context of the parent application. There is no shared security context. Code access security grants or denies access to protected resources based on individual merits.

.NET gives each application and library a separate security context—there is no shared identity. Combined with demands and stack walks, which are the favorite tools of code access security, protecting assemblies against attacks is easier.

Demand is the pivotal command in code access security. Before attempting to access a sensitive resource, demand is invoked to confirm that every caller (function) in the call stack has the required permissions for the protected resource. Instead of making every caller responsible for checking security policy, the common language runtime performs a stack walk on behalf of everyone. If the permission is confirmed for all callers, the resource can then be accessed safely. Demands either enforce or refine the Runtime Security Policy and never expand upon the granted permissions.

As noted, a demand forces a stack walk. When function FuncA calls function FuncB, then FuncB calls FuncC, and finally FuncC calls FuncD, a ladder called the stack is built in which each rung is a stack frame that contains state information related to that function. Demand asks code access security to climb the stack ladder, identifying each function within a stack frame and testing for the required permissions for using a sensitive resource. If a function does not have the requested permission for the protected resource, the demand fails and the code is tossed off the ladder.

Assert is the reverse of a demand and exempts callers from having specific permissions. Trusted code can vouch for upstream callers by short-circuiting the stack walk, thereby shielding those callers from a demand. This allows lower-trusted code to successfully call higher-trusted code, even without the appropriate permission grants. When code asserts, it assumes the responsibility of protecting against malicious callers. Since the stack walk is stopped prematurely, asserts can open security holes, so they should be used sparingly. FuncA calls function FuncB, and FuncB reads the sensitive resource R1; FuncB, but not FuncA, has the required permission P1 that grants access to R1. When FuncA calls FuncB, a security exception is raised, because FuncA does not possess permission P1. FuncB could assert permission P1 and short-circuit the stack walk. This would allow FuncA to call FuncB with impunity. FuncA is then responsible for protecting the sensitive resource R1 from malicious callers.

Code access security and traditional Win32 security sometimes overlap. The two security models are not mutually exclusive. Access to a file may be granted by the operating system but denied by code access security. Win32 security uses access tokens, privileges, and access control entries to grant or deny access to a securable resource or task, while .NET uses evidence, permissions, code groups, and the Runtime Security Policy. .NET adds additional safeguards against deleterious code.

Overview of Code Access Security

Code access security enforces the Runtime Security Policy by demanding appropriate permissions when a protected resource is targeted. Enforcement is not isolated to the immediate caller but is enforced on the extended chain of callers. Modifiers such as Assert change the behavior of a stack walk. Code access security is meant to refine or fine-tune the Runtime Security Policy, but used incorrectly it can create holes that dangerous code can exploit.

This chapter shows how to explicitly invoke code access security. There is an alternative. Security neutral code, as discussed in Chapter 3, "Runtime Security Policy," accepts security defaults from the Runtime Security Policy. This alternative also accepts the default implementation of code access security, as provided in managed classes of the base class library (BCL). Managed classes, such as StreamWriter, are wrappers of sensitive resources and invoke the Demand method to test callers for needed permissions. In security neutral code, implicit demands enforce the Runtime Security Policy. This is part of the default security policy and applied implicitly whenever a managed class that wraps a sensitive resource is used.

StreamWriter is an excellent example of a managed wrapper and contains an implicit demand that protects file resources.

```
StreamWriter myfile=new StreamWriter(@"c:\data\fb.txt", true);
```

Let us follow the trail of managed functions from the StreamWriter constructor forward. StreamWriter.StreamWriter, the constructor, calls StreamWriter.Create-File, which creates a FileStream object. To protect the file resource, the FileStream constructor immediately invokes a demand confirming all callers are granted the FileIOPermission for the named file. The following IL code (abbreviated for brevity) is from the Filestream constructor. See Figure 4.1.

```
.method public hidebysig specialname rtspecialname
        instance void  .ctor(native int handle,
                             valuetype System.IO.FileAccess access,
                             bool ownsHandle,
                             int32 bufferSize,
                             bool isAsync) cil managed
{
  .permissionset demand = (3C 00 50 00 65 00 72 00 6D 00 69 00 73 00 73 00    // <.P.e.r.m.i.s.s.
                           69 00 6F 00 6E 00 53 00 65 00 74 00 20 00 63 00    // i.o.n.S.e.t. .c.
                           6C 00 61 00 73 00 73 00 3D 00 22 00 53 00 79 00    // l.a.s.s.=.".S.y.
                           73 00 74 00 65 00 6D 00 2E 00 53 00 65 00 63 00    // s.t.e.m...S.e.c.
                           75 00 72 00 69 00 74 00 79 00 2E 00 50 00 65 00    // u.r.i.t.y...P.e.
                           72 00 6D 00 69 00 73 00 73 00 69 00 6F 00 6E 00    // r.m.i.s.s.i.o.n.
                           53 00 65 00 74 00 22 00 0D 00 0A 00 20 00 20 00    // S.e.t."........
                           20 00 20 00 20 00 20 00 20 00 20 00 20 00 20 00    // . . . . . . . .
                           20 00 20 00 20 00 20 00 20 00 76 00 65 00 72 00    // . . . . .v.e.r.
                           73 00 69 00 6F 00 6E 00 3D 00 22 00 31 00 22 00    // s.i.o.n.=.".1.".
                           3E 00 0D 00 0A 00 20 00 20 00 20 00 3C 00 49 00    // >........<.I.
                           50 00 65 00 72 00 6D 00 69 00 73 00 73 00 69 00    // P.e.r.m.i.s.s.i.
                           ...)                                               // >........
  // Code size       362 (0x16a)
  .maxstack  4
  .locals (int32 V_0,
           bool V_1)
  IL_0000:  ldarg.0
  IL_0001:  call       instance void System.IO.Stream::.ctor()
  IL_0006:  ldarg.2
  IL_0007:  ldc.i4.1
  IL_0008:  blt.s      IL_000e
  IL_000a:  ldarg.2
  IL_000b:  ldc.i4.3
  IL_000c:  ble.s      IL_0023
  IL_000e:  ldstr      "access"
  IL_0013:  ldstr      "ArgumentOutOfRange_Enum"
  IL_0018:  call       string System.Environment::GetResourceString(string)
  IL_001d:  newobj     instance void System.ArgumentOutOfRangeException::.ctor(string,
                                                                               string)
  IL_0022:  throw
  IL_0023:  ldarg.s    bufferSize
  IL_0025:  ldc.i4.0
  IL_0026:  bgt.s      IL_003d
  IL_0028:  ldstr      "bufferSize"
  IL_002d:  ldstr      "ArgumentOutOfRange_NeedPosNum"
  IL_0032:  call       string System.Environment::GetResourceString(string)
  IL_0037:  newobj     instance void System.ArgumentOutOfRangeException::.ctor(string,
```

Figure 4.1   A view from ILDASM of an implied demand within a managed class.

Assemblies that are not security neutral explicitly call Demand, Assert, and other security commands to refashion security policy. Developers who alter the security policy wield a two-edge sword: one edge sharpens security policy, while the other can open security holes. For this reason, whether or not to alter security policy is always an important decision. Some common reasons for altering the policy are to:

- Exempt callers from unknown permissions
- Refuse granted permissions
- Limit access to a base class
- Restrict callers to fully trusted code
- Protect the interface of a class
- Provide expanded access to unmanaged code
- Protect previously unprotected sensitive resources

Code access security is implemented using imperative or declarative syntax. Imperative syntax involves custom attributes, while declarative syntax relies on the methods of permission objects. Isolated storage is typical of resources protected in .NET. For declarative security, use the IsolatedStoragePermission-Attribute. The IsolatedStoragePermission object is used to imperatively protect the sensitive resource.

Declarative Security

Declarative code access security is declared using custom permission attributes. When applied to a method, declarative security affects the decorated method and callers. Affixed to a class, the command applies to all methods of the class or limits inheritance. For example, denying a permission to a class prevents all methods of that class from using that permission. As an assembly declaration, declarative security refines the Runtime Security Policy with the SecurityAction enumerated value: SecurityAction.RequestMinimal, Security-Action.RequestRefused, or SecurityAction.RequestOptional. This is discussed in Chapter 3, "Runtime Security Policy."

Declarative access security is planned and coded at design time, which limits flexibility. Declarative commands are represented as flags within the Security-Action enumeration:

SecurityAction.Demand.   This performs a stack walk searching for specific permissions.

SecurityAction.LinkDemand.   This initiates a single-level stack walk that inspects the immediate caller for a required permission.

SecurityAction.InheritanceDemand.   This checks derived classes for required permissions.

SecurityAction.Assert.   This successfully concludes the stack walk at the current frame.

SecurityAction.Deny.   This denies the indicated permission to the current method and downstream functions.

SecurityAction.PermitOnly.   This allows the current method and downstream functions to access only resources identified by the command.

The following program demonstrates the declarative approach to code access security.

```
// Financial.dll ( Fully Trusted )

using System;
using System.IO;
```

```csharp
using System.Reflection;
using System.Security;
using System.Security.Permissions;

[assembly: AssemblyKeyFile("mykey.key")]
[assembly: AllowPartiallyTrustedCallers]

namespace Donis
{
    [FileIOPermission(SecurityAction.Assert, All =
        @"c:\accounting.txt")]
    public class Financial
    {
        public string GetData()
        {
            return Calculate();
        }

        public string Calculate()
        {
            return DateTime.Now.ToLongTimeString()+
                " Confidential financial data";
        }

        public void SaveData()
        {
            StreamWriter file=new
                StreamWriter(@"c:\accounting.txt", true);
            file.WriteLine(Calculate());
            file.Close();
        }
    }
}


// Wrapper.dll ( Fully Trusted )

using System;
using System.Windows.Forms;
using System.IO;
using System.Security;
using System.Reflection;
using System.Security.Permissions;

[assembly: AssemblyKeyFile("mykey.key")]
[assembly: AllowPartiallyTrustedCallers]

namespace Donis
{
    public class Wrapper
    {
```

```
        public Wrapper()
        {
            f=new Financial();
        }

        [UIPermission(SecurityAction.Demand,
            Window=UIPermissionWindow.AllWindows)]
        public void Display()
        {
            MessageBox.Show(f.GetData());
        }

        public void Save()
        {
            f.SaveData();
        }

        Financial f;
    }
}
```

The preceding code lists two libraries, each with a single class. Financial.dll contains the financial class, which performs calculations, saves information to the local drive, and returns financial data to callers. Wrapper.dll contains a wrapper class, which abstracts the details of the financial class—this is the class that clients are expected to use. Both assemblies are strongly named, installed in the GAC, and allow partially trusted callers. The financial class writes to the local drive, requiring the FileIOPermission, which it asserts to exempt callers. This is necessary since partially trusted callers are expected. The Wrapper.Display method invokes MessageBox.Show. User interface components require the UIPermission attribute. A demand on the UIPermission attribute is added to the Display method to test for that permission and avoid unexpected security exceptions.

This is the client code:

```
// Client.exe ( Partially Trusted )
using System;
using System.IO;
using System.Security;
using System.Security.Permissions;
namespace Donis
{
    class Client
    {
```

```
[UIPermission(SecurityAction.Deny,
    Window=UIPermissionWindow.AllWindows)]
public static void Main()
{
    Wrapper w=new Wrapper();
    w.Save();
    Console.WriteLine("\nFinancial data saved.");
    w.Display();
}
}
}
```

In the client code, an instance of the wrapper is created, which is used to save and display the current financial data. The client executes from a file share and is therefore partially trusted and is not granted the FileIOPermission. The assert in the financial component prevents a security exception on this permission and allows the client application to call Wrapper.Save successfully. Client is also a console application and denies the UIPermission permission to prevent downstream functions from accessing the user interface. This causes the Wrapper.Display method to throw a security exception. Figure 4.2 is the exception from the program.

SECURITY ALERT

Custom attributes are preserved in the metadata of an assembly and can be read using reflection. Imperative code access security, described with custom attributes, is also visible through reflection. Malicious code can leverage knowledge gained through reflection to identify weaknesses in the security design of an assembly.

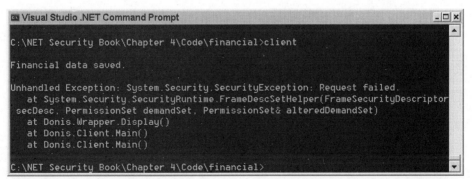

Figure 4.2   In this result of running client.exe, an exception is raised when the Message-Box.Show method is invoked.

Imperative Security

Enforcing code access security at run time requires the imperative syntax, which depends on security objects instead of custom attributes. At run time, you define an instance of a security object, typically a permission object, and call Demand or another security method. Code access security is deployed at run time, where current conditions can be accessed and security adjusted. Compared to declarative security, set at compile time, imperative security is more flexible. Methods are the smallest unit of declarative security, while imperative security can be assigned to lines of code and is therefore more granular.

In the following code, the declarative attributes have been removed from the Wrapper.Display method and replaced with permission objects and the imperative syntax.

```
//      [UIPermission(SecurityAction.Demand,
Window=UIPermissionWindow.AllWindows)]
public void Display()
{
    UIPermission ui=new UIPermission(UIPermissionWindow.AllWindows);
    try
    {
        ui.Demand();
        MessageBox.Show(f.GetData());
    }
    catch(SecurityException ex)
    {
        Console.WriteLine(ex.Message);
    }
}
```

The revised Display method creates an instance of the UIPermission object. In the following try block, the AllWindows permission is demanded. If the stack walk is successful, a MessageBox is displayed. If an exception is raised, output is redirected to the console window. This demonstrates the flexibility of using imperative code access security.

Exceptions from declarative code access security are raised in the caller, which limits options for handling the exceptions. Offending code is not presented with an opportunity to proactively react to an exception or plot an alternative. Security exceptions linked to imperative security are raised within the source, offering considerable more flexibility. In the previous client code, the exception was trapped and output redirected to the console window. This was not possible in the declarative approach.

Reflection is an often-mentioned shortcoming of declarative security. Malicious code can use reflection to unearth the security specifics of an assembly. However, imperative code access security is not impervious to data mining for security specifics.

SECURITY ALERT

Source code from managed languages is compiled into Intermediate Language (IL) and preserved in an assembly—this includes instructions from imperative code access security. Reading the IL code of an assembly is a mundane task that is easily accomplished programmatically or by using one of many publicly available tools, such as ildasm. Reading the imperative security commands evident in IL code could be the first step in planning a security attack. Some would find reading IL code easier than deciphering the metadata of an assembly, where declarative code access security is persisted. Finding the imperative security commands in the following IL code is not difficult.

```
.method public hidebysig instance void FuncB(string info) cil managed
{
  // Code size       27 (0x1b)
  .maxstack  3
  .locals init (class
       [mscorlib]System.Security.Permissions.FileIOPermission V_0)
  IL_0000:  ldc.i4.s   15
  IL_0002:  ldstr      "C:\\donis.txt"
  IL_0007:  newobj     instance void [mscorlib]System.Security.Permis-
sions.FileIOPermission::
       .ctor(valuetype[mscorlib]
System.Security.Permissions.FileIOPermissionAccess, string)
  IL_000c:  stloc.0
  IL_000d:  ldloc.0
  IL_000e:  callvirt   instance void [mscorlib]
System.Security.CodeAccessPermission::Deny()
  IL_0013:  ldarg.0
  IL_0014:  ldarg.1
  IL_0015:  call       instance void CAS.Sample::FuncA(string)
  IL_001a:  ret
} // end of method Sample::FuncB
```

Stack Walk

It is hard to review code access security without repeatedly mentioning stack walks. In this context, a stack walk protects a sensitive resource. Stack walks are common to declarative and imperative security. Starting at the current frame, a stack walk inspects the stack, confirming that each caller has permissions to the protected resource. This prevents luring attacks, where callers trick higher-trusted code into performing unauthorized tasks or manipulating sensitive resources.

The IStackWalk interface is a contract for security objects that implement a stack walk and defines related commands, such as Assert, Demand, Deny, and PermitOnly. Permission objects inherit and implement the IStalkWalk inter-face, which is further explored in Chapter 8, "Customizing .NET Security." Alternately, custom attributes for code access security permissions rely on the SecurityAction enumeration to control the stack walk.

What is a stack? Stacks consist of stack frames that are akin to rungs on a lad-der. As code enters or exit functions, the stack grows or shrinks, respectively. Stack frames are cached in memory as last in/first out (LIFO) structures. Stack walks climb the stack ladder, examining each stack frame sequentially, begin-ning with the bottom rung or current frame. It is never safe to hop around on a ladder. Each stack frame, beginning with the current frame, contains a pointer to the next stack frame, which greatly simplifies the challenge of walk-ing the stack. Stack frames contain additional information, including local variables, parameters, and code pointers. (For a detailed explanation of the stack, stack frame, and stack walks, consult MSDN.) The stack frame is basi-cally the state object for a function.

Stack walks are an expensive, but necessary evil. Without stack walks and the ability to check the security of each caller, it is difficult to detect and guard against malicious code. Security modifiers can mitigate the overhead related to the security stack walk. Security modifiers, such as Assert, are discussed in detail later in this chapter.

SECURITY ALERT

Stack walks do not cross process or machine boundaries. Win32 processes do not share memory, and walking across process boundaries, although not impossible, is expensive. The challenge of following a stack trail across machine boundaries is more daunting. For this reason, other security verification techniques are employed in Web-based applications and Web services. (Even if the Web application existed on the same server, a stack walk initiated by the Web service would be ineffectual. The Web service and Web application would exist in different application domains, which is a process within a process.) Attempting to use code access security in these situations causes unexpected results. Function FuncA on Machine MA calls FuncB on Machine MB. FuncB is a Web method within a Web service and calls FuncC, which calls FuncD. FuncB, FuncC, and FuncD reside on Machine MB, which is the Web server. FuncD demands a stack walk, checking for permission P1. Everyone has

permission P1 except FuncA. FuncA is remote code and is not fully trusted on the Web server. One might expect that the appearance of a remote function might make the stack walk fail. The stack walk will test FuncB and FuncC successfully and stop at the machine boundary. Since the local functions were validated, the stack walk ends successfully, and the operation is allowed to proceed despite the fact that the code originated from lower-trusted code without the required permission. See Figure 4.3.

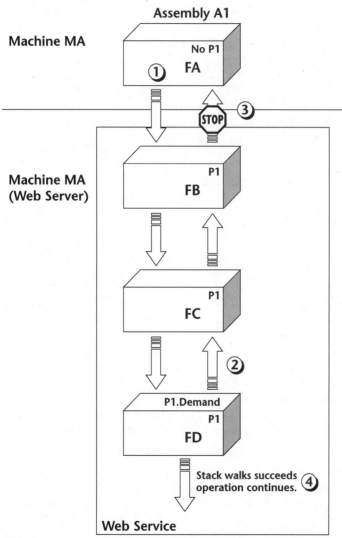

Figure 4.3 A stack walk from client application to Web service.

Demand and Link Demand

Demand and LinkDemand enforce or refine the Runtime Security Policy through stack walks. Before accessing a security-sensitive resource, a demand is called to guard access to the protected resource. During the stack walk, each caller is inspected for the demanded permission or permission set. If a caller is not granted the requested permission, a System.Security.SecurityException object is thrown and the stack walk is aborted. Exception handling can be used to trap the security exception, and the program can either attempt to recover or gracefully exit. When compared to a security neutral assembly, where the exception would detonate the application, this is an appealing alternative.

Demand triggers a complete stack walk, while LinkDemand checks only the most immediate stack frame. LinkDemand tests one caller, not the entire stack. Demands do *not* inspect the permissions of the source function. Only the callers are checked for the demanded permission. The following code demonstrates this fact.

```
using System;
using System.Security;
using System.Security.Permissions;
class Starter
{
    public static void Main()
    {
        FileIOPermission p =
            new FileIOPermission(
            FileIOPermissionAccess.AllAccess,
            @"C:\test.txt");
        p.Demand();
    }
}
```

The preceding application is run as an intranet application and not granted access to the FileIOPermission permission. Despite this, the demand in Main does not cause a security exception. Demands do not inspect the current function. However, the following code will cause an exception.

```
using System;
using System.Security;
using System.Security.Permissions;
class Starter
{
    public static void Main()
    {
        FuncA();
    }
```

```
public static void FuncA()
{
    FileIOPermission fp =
        new FileIOPermission
        (FileIOPermissionAccess.AllAccess,
        @"C:\test.txt");
    fp.Demand();
}
}
```

In this version, Main calls FuncA, which demands the FileIOPermission permission. Neither FuncA nor Main has the permission; but the exception is raised because of Main. Main is in the call stack of FuncA, making it susceptible to the demand. Figure 4.4 is the stack trace of the exception.

Link demands offer performance advantages over standard demands. Since a link demand does not trigger a complete stack walk, performance is improved. This command only verifies the permissions granted the immediate caller. Callers of the caller are not checked, making security breaches easier to plan and execute. The caller is responsible for enacting adequate security controls for the remainder of the stack.

The extent of a stack walk is the primary difference between demand and link demand. FuncA calls FuncB, which then calls FuncC. Finally, FuncC calls FuncD, where the SocketPermission is demanded. A regular demand would start at the stack frame of FuncD and walk to FuncA, confirming the availability of that permission. A demand link would start at FuncD and finish at FuncC—inspecting a single stack frame or caller. There is a performance gain, but protection against a luring attack is limited. Link demand basically secures a single method or interface.

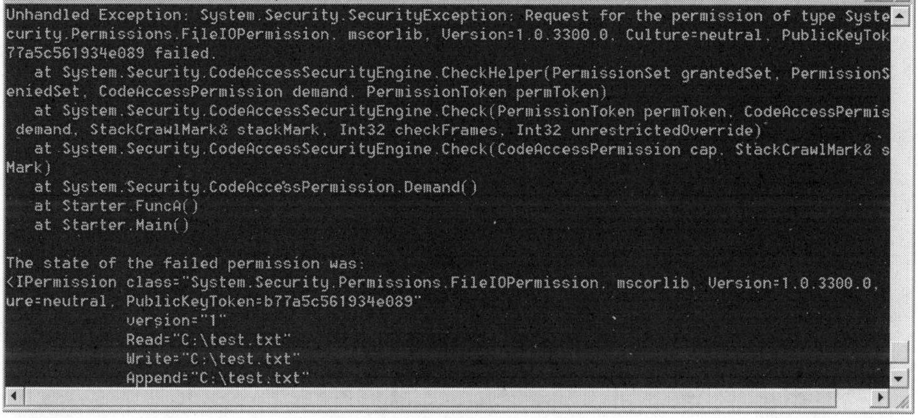

Figure 4.4 Stack trace from a security exception.

Link demands are tested at just-in-time compilation and when invoking a function through reflection. A stack walk is not incurred on each instance of a function call bound to a link demand. This drastically reduces costs, but is less secure than a full demand. As indicated, the caller is responsible for adding additional security, if needed. This shifts some of the responsibility from the source function to the caller.

Reflection is a powerful tool in .NET, with many capabilities, including support of late-binding and subsequent runtime invocation of functions. Link demand is triggered twice when using reflection to execute a function with this attribute. First, a link demand is prompted when reflection binds to the object. Second, when the reference is used to invoke a function, link demand is again engaged. Since binding and invocation can be performed by different code, the second link demand is imperative.

Combining code access security and code identity security (discussed in the next chapter) addresses some of the concerns related to link demands. Security concerns are lessened if link demands are used with known callers.

LinkDemand can be described in the declarative syntax.

SECURITY ALERT

Assuming "the other guy did it" is never a good approach to security. Because of link demand and other modifiers to the stack walk, full protection is never guaranteed. Functions needing that level of protection should demand it. Never assume that a downstream function has commanded a full stack walk.

Managed wrappers for API engines are one place where link demands are helpful. XYZ Company sells stock trade analysis software directly to consumers but also encourages value added retailers (VARs) to leverage this product as third-party solutions. To that end, XYZ Company promotes a library that offers an API interface to its software, which has been migrated to .NET. The API library is not intended for direct use, but is exposed through other libraries that hide some of the minutia. Only code from XYZ Company is allowed to access the API library directly. For the API library, a LinkDemand could restrict immediate callers to components housed in other XYZ Company assemblies. These friendly components would then set security policy for outside components.

This is a review of the differences between demand and link demand:

- Demands are set using imperative or declarative syntax and evaluated at run time or load time, respectively. Link demand is described only with declarative syntax and affirmed at just-in-time compilation and reflection.

- Each time a function is called that contains a demand, a stack walk is initiated. However, the limited stack walk from a link demand is usually performed only once.

- Link demands provide minimal protection from luring attacks.

Inheritance Demand

Inheritance demand grants inheritance privileges to a derived class or method, based on listed permissions.

Base classes can restrict derived classes to classes granted certain permissions. Classes not granted the prerequisite permissions are unable to inherit the base class. A class that is a wrapper for a sensitive resource prevents lesser-trusted classes from inheriting the base class and inappropriately gaining access to that resource.

Inheritance demand can also limit the overriding of functions from a base class. The inheritance demand attribute stipulates the permissions required of a derived class that wants to override a specific method of the base class. A derived class without the stated permission would be unable to override the decorated method. Code not granted the required permission can inherit the base class, but will be unable to override the designated function.

Inheritance demand is limited to the declarative syntax and indicated with the SecurityAction.InheritanceDemand enumeration. Inheritance demands propagate from the base class to the most derived class. Child classes inherit inheritance demand from the base class, which is then inherited by the grandchild class, and so on. Here is some sample code:

```
// COrange Assembly ( Library )

using System;
using System.IO;
using System.Net;
using System.Net.Sockets;
using System.Security.Permissions;
using System.Security;

[SocketPermission(SecurityAction.InheritanceDemand, Unrestricted=true)]
public class COrange
{
    TcpClient socket;
    NetworkStream n;

    public COrange()
    {
```

```
            socket=new TcpClient("localHost", 50000);
            n=socket.GetStream();
        }

        public void ReadFromSocket()
        {
            StreamReader s=new StreamReader(n);
            string input=s.ReadLine();
            Console.WriteLine(input);
        }
    }
}


// CPear Assembly ( Library )

using System;
using System.Security;
using System.Net.Sockets;
using System.Net;
using System.Security.Permissions;

public class CPear: COrange
{
    public CPear()
    {
        Console.WriteLine("C'tor of CPear");
    }
}


// CApple Assembly ( Library )

using System;
using System.Net;
using System.Net.Sockets;
using System.Security.Permissions;
using System.Security;

[assembly: SocketPermission(SecurityAction.RequestRefuse,
    Unrestricted=true)]

public class CApple: CPear
{
    public CApple()
    {
        Console.WriteLine("C'tor of CApple");
    }
}


// Client Assembly ( Executable )

using System;
```

```
class Starter
{
    public static void Main()
    {
        CApple obj=new CApple();
        obj.ReadFromSocket();
    }
}
```

COrange is a wrapper for a socket client. The constructor initializes the socket client, while the ReadFromSocket method reads data from the socket. To access any socket, which is a sensitive resource, the derived classes should possess the socket permission. To enforce this, the inheritance demand of the socket permission is added to the COrange class as a declarative attribute and makes the permission mandatory for derived classes. CPear is the child class of COrange. CApple is derived from CPear and is the grandchild of COrange. The inheritance demand of the socket permission propagates from the parent to any descendants, including CApple. For this reason, when the socket permission is refused in the CApple assembly, CApple is prevented from inheriting from CPear, and an exception is raised.

Demand and link demand are offered to tighten security. As usual, the devil is in the details. Faulty implementation can open more security holes than it closes. Following are two additional alerts that should be considered when using demand or link demand.

SECURITY ALERT

Casting between a base and derived class is one way to skirt security defenses. Implementing consistent security across a class hierarchy is the best defense against this type of attack. Security within a class hierarchy and associated instances is only as strong as the weakest link. Hiding classes (private) of inferior security, when compared with others in the hierarchy, is another alternative. The accompanying code exploits the security loophole that casting between classes can open. COrange class is the base class of CPear. CPear is the parent of CApple. A link demand of the FileIO-Permission is attached to the CPear class, which requires immediate callers to have this permission. In the test application, the link demand is avoided by initializing a base class with a derived object. When CPear.FuncA is called, it succeeds, although the FileIOPermission is not granted to the test assembly. Make the CApple class private or add LinkDemand of the FileIOPermission to the class to prevent this problem.

```
// Orange Assembly ( library )

using System;
using System.Security;
using System.Security.Permissions;
```

```
public class COrange
{
     public virtual void FuncA()
     {


     }
}


[FileIOPermission(SecurityAction.LinkDemand, All = @"c:\cat.txt")]
public class CPear: COrange
{
     public override void FuncA()
     {
          Console.WriteLine("should be secure");
     }
}


public class CApple: CPear
{


}


// Test Assembly ( Executable )

using System;
using System.Security;
using System.Security.Permissions;

[assembly: FileIOPermission(SecurityAction.RequestRefuse,
     Unrestricted=true)]

class Starter
{
     public static void Main()
     {

          CPear p=new CApple();
          p.FuncA();
     }
}
```

SECURITY ALERT

■■■■ Managed classes often wrap sensitive resources with access protected by demand or link demand. Placing the demand in the constructor of the managed class seems like a logical solution. However tempting, this does not work. Constructors are called once for each instance, not whenever the object is used. Every method is potentially an entry point, providing access to the sensitive resource, and should be evaluated, and proper security should be applied. If not, security holes may appear.

The ensuing code demonstrates the importance of plugging every entry point. COrange is a wrapper for a low-level input/output stream. The stream is hypothetical, but useful for this example. COrange class is adorned with the SuppressUnmanageCodeSecurity attribute to make the class available to partially trusted code. To protect the sensitive resource, the constructor is adorned with the FileIOPermission attribute and demands this permission from the instance creator.

The CPear class has a single method. CPear.YouDoIt is a static method, with COrange as the sole parameter. YouDoIt calls COrange.WriteToFile. Importantly, CPear exists in an assembly where the FileIOPermission is denied and the COrange.WriteToFile should fail.

The Test application, a fully trusted assembly, creates an instance of COrange, and calls WriteToFile. The COrange instance is passed as a parameter into CPear.YouDoIt method. The call should fail, but works. However, the demand in the constructor has already been used and is not very helpful now. A demand in the WriteToFile method would solve the problem.

```csharp
// Orange Assembly ( library )

using System;
using System.Security;
using System.Security.Permissions;
using System.IO;

[SuppressUnmanagedCodeSecurity()]
public class COrange
{
    [FileIOPermissionAttribute(SecurityAction.Demand,
        Unrestricted=true)]
    public COrange()
    {

    }

    public void WriteToFile()
    {
        Console.WriteLine("Write to IO worked.");
    }
}

// Pear Assembly( library )

using System;
using System.Security;
using System.Security.Permissions;
```

```
[assembly: FileIOPermission(SecurityAction.RequestRefuse,
    Unrestricted=true)]

public class CPear
{
    static public void YouDoIt(COrange obj)
    {
        obj.WriteToFile();
    }
}

// Test Assembly ( Executable )

using System;
using System.Security;
using System.Security.Permissions;

class Starter
{
    public static void Main()
    {
        COrange o=new COrange();
        o.WriteToFile();
        CPear.YouDoIt(o);
    }
}
```

Assert

Asserts relax code access security and allow downstream code to exempt callers from the normal security check of a demand. Asserts are the antithesis of demands. Functions use demands to protect sensitive resources from lower-trusted callers, while asserts exempt callers from having permissions that would otherwise be required. Higher-trusted code can vouch for the safeness of lower-trusted code by using an Assert command. However, trust can always be abused. Every assert is potentially an entry point for a luring attack.

Only permissions presently granted can be asserted. Letting code assert any permission, even a permission that is not granted, would give lower-trusted assemblies the ability to adversely affect the Runtime Security Policy. An attempt to assert a permission that is not granted is simply ignored.

Since asserts can adversely affect security edicts, administrators can limit access to the Assert command by using the security permission. "Assert any permission that has been granted" is a flag that can be set with this permission. See Figure 4.5. One possibility is limiting asserts only to fully trusted assemblies. Asserting, when the Assert permission is not granted, will cause an exception. When asserting, nest the command in a try block to handle an exception gracefully and prevent unplanned program interruption.

When considering demands and asserts, stack walks can travel three different paths.

- Each stack frame on the stack has the requested permission. The stack walk succeeds, access to the sensitive resource is granted, and execution continues.

- The stack walk proceeds until a stack frame is found not to have the requested permission. The stack walk fails, a security exception is raised, and execution changes.

The stack walk proceeds until an assert is located in a stack frame. The stack walk is stopped, access to the sensitive resource is granted, and execution continues. Figure 4.6 illustrates the three paths.

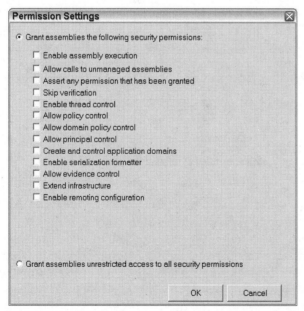

Figure 4.5 This illustrates the Security Permission from the mscorcfg tool.

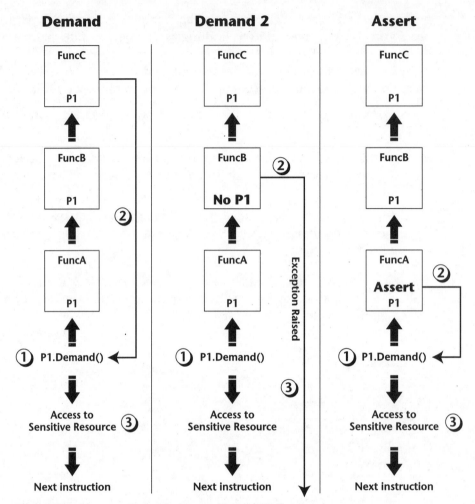

Figure 4.6 Three scenarios for a security stack walk.

Asserts are available in either declarative or imperative syntax. For declarative syntax, use the SecurityAction.Assert flag. Alternately, the Assert command can be called on a permission object when using imperative syntax. An assert exempts a demand for a permission and subsets of that permission. Subsets of a permission can be confirmed using the Permission.IsSubsetOf method. For example, a directory permission extends to any subdirectory. This code uses the IsSubsetOf method.

```
using System;
using System.Security;
using System.Security.Permissions;
class Starter
{
```

```
public static void Main()
{
    FileIOPermission fp =
        new FileIOPermission(FileIOPermissionAccess.AllAccess,
        @"C:\");
    FileIOPermission fp2 =
        new FileIOPermission(FileIOPermissionAccess.AllAccess,
        @"C:\wiley");
    FileIOPermission fp3 =
        new FileIOPermission(FileIOPermissionAccess.AllAccess,
        @"e:\");
    if(fp2.IsSubsetOf(fp))
        Console.WriteLine("fp2 is a subset of fp");
    else
        Console.WriteLine("fp2 is not a subset of fp.");
    if(fp3.IsSubsetOf(fp))
        Console.WriteLine("fp3 is a subset of fp");
    else
        Console.WriteLine("fp3 is not a subset of fp.");
}
}
```

Do not use asserts indiscriminately. Since asserts loosen security restrictions, add an assert only after careful consideration. When a function asserts, responsibility for protecting the sensitive resource rests solely with the asserting code. Inadequate protection allows lower-trusted code to improperly manipulate a guarded resource and exploit the security hole created by the assert command. Here are some valid reasons for asserting:

- Implicitly unmanaged code (native) or resources are fully protected by the .NET Framework. This is not always necessary—some native code is perfectly safe. Asserting for unmanaged code that is safe poses little risk. However, without reasonable protection malicious programs can compromise even safe code. An example would be a buffer overflow attack. Validating parameters is typically a minimal precaution with safe code and is effective against buffer overflow attacks.

- Code that fully abstracts a dangerous resource can consider asserting the related permission. Protecting direct and indirect access to the resource is important. For example, abstracting a resource does not necessary prevent a denial of service attack. Defend against this and other potential security attacks before exempting callers from security checks.

- Permissions are often not predictable. Callers are sometimes unable to ascertain the proper permissions required to make a call. When this occurs, the source code might consider asserting a concealed permission.

- If callers are limited to fully trusted assemblies, asserts on frequently used and protected resources are safe and can improve performance. Asserts can improve performance, but should not be the sole consideration when deciding whether to use the command.

- Managed wrappers of native code, when the callers is not expected to have unmanaged code permission, is another place where asserts are useful.

Deny

Deny allows functions to voluntarily reject permissions that would otherwise be granted. Rejecting permissions in a function narrows the securable resources available to the present function and upstream callers. Functions invoke the deny method to deny called code access to sensitive resources. FuncA calls FuncB. FuncB calls FuncC. FuncA denies the socket permission, preventing FuncB and FuncC from accessing a socket.

Denying optional permission removes unneeded permissions that called code can exploit. In addition, code may want to limit the activities of upstream code. Preventing called code from accessing the local file system might be one possibility and is easily accomplished by denying the FileIOPermission.

Upstream code can circumvent a deny with an assert of the same permission. The assert short circuits the stack walk, making the deny unreachable. Administrators can prevent this possibility by removing the assert permission.

Deny is available in either declarative or imperative syntax. With a permission attribute, use the SecurityAction.Deny flag to deny access to a resource protected by a permission or permission set. Permission objects offer the Deny method. The deny applies to the named permission and any subset therein.

```
using System;
using System.Security;
using System.Security.Permissions;
using System.IO;
class Starter
{
    public static void Main()
    {
        CBanana b=new CBanana();
        b.FuncA();
    }
}
public class CBanana
{
    public void FuncA()
```

```
    {
        FileIOPermission fp =
            new FileIOPermission(
            FileIOPermissionAccess.AllAccess, @"C:\test.txt");
        fp.Deny();
        CApple a=new CApple();
        a.FuncB();
    }
}
public class CApple
{
    public void FuncB()
    {
        StreamWriter s=new StreamWriter(@"c:\test.txt", true);
        s.WriteLine("writing stuff...");
        s.Close();
    }
}
```

In the preceding code, an exception is raised in Main when CBanana.FuncA is called. FuncA explicitly denies the FileIOPermission permission for the test.txt file. The function then calls CApple.FuncB, which attempts to write to the file using the StreamWriter class. The implicit demand embedded in the StreamWriter class triggers a stack walk for the FileIOPermission and an exception is raised because of the Deny.

PermitOnly

PermitOnly is the reverse of Deny. Deny details permissions for protected resources that cause a stack walk to fail. PermitOnly articulates permissions that alone will cause a stack walk to succeed. Often, it is easier to stipulate allowable resources as opposed to denied resources. PermitOnly lists resources that code or upstream callers are allowed to access; all other resources are implicitly denied. This prevents callers from manipulating resources not protected by the permissions stated in the PermitOnly command.

PermitOnly is available in either declarative or imperative syntax. With a permission attribute, use the SecurityAction.PermitOnly flag to permit access to only the designated resources. Permission objects offer the PermitOnly method. PermitOnly applies to the named permission and any subset therein.

```
using System;
using System.Security;
using System.Security.Permissions;
using System.IO;
```

```
class Starter
{
    public static void Main()
    {
        CBanana b=new CBanana();
        b.FuncA();
    }
}
public class CBanana
{
    public void FuncA()
    {
        FileIOPermission fp =
            new FileIOPermission(
            FileIOPermissionAccess.AllAccess, @"C:\dog.txt");
            fp.PermitOnly();
        CApple a=new CApple();
        a.FuncB();
    }
}
public class CApple
{
    public void FuncB()
    {
        StreamWriter s=new StreamWriter(@"c:\cat.txt", true);
        s.WriteLine("scratch scratch...");
        s.Close();
    }
}
```

The preceding code raises an exception in Main. CBanana.FuncA permits access to dog.txt and no other file. When FuncA calls CApple.FuncB, there is an attempt to write to cat.txt and a demand occurs for that file. Since access is permitted to only dog.txt, the demand fails and an exception is thrown.

ReverseAssert, ReverseDeny, RevertPermitOnly, and RevertAll

Assert, Deny, and PermitOnly can be undone or removed from a stack frame. ReverseAssert, ReverseDeny, and RevertPermitOnly reverse an Assert, Deny, or PermitOnly, respectively. After reversing the command, that command can be restated with the same or other permissions. RevertAll provides a single method to reverse the collective commands as compared to calling the revert functions individually.

Only a single Assert, Deny, or PermitOnly can be outstanding at any moment. A second Assert, Deny, or PermitOnly will not supersede the previous method but will raise an exception. If there is an outstanding assert for FileIOPermission, asserting on SocketPermission will raise an exception. Even if asserting a different permission, a second assert will not work. To effect multiple permissions, create a permission set of those permissions and invoke Assert, Deny, or PermitOnly on the permission set.

Demands cannot be reversed. There is nothing to be reversed, because demands are evaluated immediately. Each demand is independent, and a demand can be called repeatedly in the same function. Use a permission set to demand more than one permission.

Within a stack frame, this is the order of priority:

1. Deny

2. PermitOnly

3. Assert

The reverse functions are static functions of the CodeAccessPermission class and are available only imperatively. The following code illustrates how to group permissions in a permission set, reverse a security command, and properly reissue a security command.

```
using System;
using System.Security;
using System.Security.Permissions;
using System.IO;
class Starter
{
    public static void Main()
    {
        CBanana b=new CBanana();
        b.FuncA();
    }
}
public class CBanana
{
    public void FuncA()
    {
        FileIOPermission fp =
            new FileIOPermission(
            FileIOPermissionAccess.AllAccess, @"C:\cat.txt");
        SecurityPermission sp=
            new SecurityPermission(
            SecurityPermissionFlag.Assertion);
        PermissionSet ps=new PermissionSet(
```

```
                        PermissionState.Unrestricted);
            ps.AddPermission(fp);
            ps.AddPermission(sp);
            try
            {
                ps.Deny();
                CApple a=new CApple();
                a.FuncB();
            }
            catch(SecurityException ex)
            {
                Console.WriteLine(ex.Message+" caught.");
                CodeAccessPermission.RevertDeny();
                sp.Deny();
                CApple a=new CApple();
                a.FuncB();
            }
        }
    }
    public class CApple
    {
        public void FuncB()
        {
            StreamWriter s=new StreamWriter(@"c:\cat.txt", true);
            s.WriteLine("scratch scratch...");
            s.Close();
        }
    }
}
```

Most of the relevant code is in CBanana.FuncA. A file and socket permission are created and then combined into a permission set, which is then denied. Since the FileIOPermission is not granted, calling CApple.FuncB raises an exception and execution continues in the catch block. In the catch block, the deny is reverted, and then the socket permission is denied. FuncB is then called successfully, because the FileIOPermission is no longer denied.

Unmanaged Code

Unmanaged code, such as Win32 APIs, COM objects, and functions published by native DLLs, are dangerous and protected by the UnmanagedCode flag of the security permission. The common language runtime abstracts the native operating system, making issues related to unmanaged code pervasive.

Several BCL classes are solely wrappers for native resources—the managed class for a Socket is one such example. Managed classes that aggregate native resources demand a specialized permission assigned to that resource. Implicit demands guarding unmanaged code are part of the default Runtime Security Policy and grant fully trusted assemblies access to native code and resources. Partially trusted code, such as assemblies in the Internet and Intranet zones, are not granted unmanaged code permissions.

Access to unmanaged code is frequently overlooked and obscured by managed classes such as the Registry managed class. The complete abstraction of native code contributes mightily to the portability of the .NET framework. Native code is directly accessible through the Platform Invoke Model or COM Interoperability Services, and requires the unmanaged code permission.

Direct access to native code should be sequestered in a single class, making management of unmanaged code easier. With native code in a single class, asserting the unmanaged code permission is simpler. Spreading native code across several classes makes it harder to manage native code as a unit.

The .NET Framework views native code as universally dangerous and grants access only to fully trusted assemblies. There are exceptions where native code or resources can be safely exposed, even to partially trusted assemblies. Assert the unmanaged code permission using the Security permission object or attribute as demonstrated in the following code.

```
using System;
using System.Security;
using System.Security.Permissions;
[SecurityPermissionAttribute(SecurityAction.Assert, UnmanagedCode=true)]
public class CPear
{
    public void FuncA()
    {
        // Use native resource or command (unmanaged code)
    }
}
public class CGrape
{
    public void FuncB()
    {
        SecurityPermission sp=
            new SecurityPermission(
            SecurityPermissionFlag.UnmanagedCode);
        sp.Assert();

        // Use native resource or command (unmanaged code)
    }
}
```

The SuppressUnmanagedCodeSecurityAttribute is a compromise between asserting and enforcing the unmanaged code permission. The attribute tests the immediate caller for the unmanaged security permission during just-in-time compilation. This is similar to a link demand, and the attribute can be affixed to a class or method.

SECURITY ALERT

Asserting the unmanaged code permission confers broad powers to lower-trusted callers and can lead to unforeseen consequences. Relaxing the unmanaged code permission to permit access to a single native resource opens the door to all native code, including the Win32 API interface. Unmanaged code permission is not granular and denies or grants unfettered access to native code. Malicious code can leverage the expanded access to attack not only the called code but also the .NET Framework. For these reasons, limit the use and duration of asserts for the unmanaged code permission.

Performance Optimizations

Code access security is a performance hit for managed applications. However, compared to the alternative of not securing the application, the impact is acceptable. Demands are the primary reason for most of the overhead. Managing demands while maintaining a reasonable level of security can safely improve performance.

In no particular order, the following is a list of suggestions for improving performance:

- The common language runtime caches the results of previous demands and improves performance by not repeating unnecessary demands. Adding a Deny or PermitOnly to the stack forces a complete stack walk and obviates the demand optimization.

- Asserts, Deny, and PermitOnly are performed faster when made declaratively.

- Demands are faster if done imperatively.

- Demand and then assert any permission required repeatedly in a method. Incur the cost of the demand once to validate all callers, then assert to exempt callers thereafter. This opens a small window of opportunity for malicious code to exploit.

- When appropriate, choose LinkDemand versus Demand.

What's Next

Code access security enforces the Runtime Security Policy and protects sensitive resources from inappropriate access. Applications built from loosely coupled components are becoming more popular and have heightened security concerns, such as luring attacks. Code access security attempts to address the following and other security issues:

- Demand is the primary command of code access security and forces a stack walk to verify the permissions of callers. This prevents highly trusted code from errantly providing lower-trusted callers access to dangerous resources.

- Code access security is coded using custom attributes (declarative) or permission objects (imperative).

- Modifiers, such as Assert, Deny, and PermitOnly, affect the stack walk. Use these commands to refine security policy. However, be careful not to open new security holes.

- Assert a permission to exempt callers from having to be granted a permission.

- An assembly may deny otherwise allowable permissions to downstream assemblies and curtail their available activities.

- Assert the unmanaged code permission to permit access to native libraries, COM objects, or Win32 APIs.

In .NET, code has a security context. In traditional Win32 security, security context is reserved for users, groups, and computers. .NET also supports users and groups as defined in code identity security. Generic and Windows principles are the primary ingredients of code identity security and the focus of the next chapter.

CHAPTER 5

Role-Based Security

I dentity theft is a problem in both the real and the virtual world. Challenging and protecting the identity and role of a user is important in building adequate protection for an application. Effective authentication, impersonation, and authorization of user identity are important tools in protecting against security attacks based on false or shared identities.

Code access security alone is not a universal vaccine inoculating managed applications from all forms of security germs, otherwise known as malicious code. Code access security does not protect against stolen user credentials or luring attacks based on identity.

When addressing the unique security needs of enterprise and Web-based applications, role-based security is more flexible and extensible than traditional Win32 security. Notably, role-based security is not limited to simply the flavors of Windows authentication. In many ways, role-based security is more similar to the COM+ 2.0 security model.

The security requirements of an enterprise or distributed application differ greatly from those of a client-side application. Enterprise applications commonly support multiple users and must often micromanage code access based on user identity. Enterprise applications are sometimes deployed in a heterogeneous environment, which necessitates a solution that is not solely platform specific. Accounting programs used by multinational corporations are representative of enterprise applications and span multiple environments where multiple users in different roles are accessing the disperse components of the application. Each component, such as the inventory, disbursement, or payroll module, can establish its own criteria for user access and may rely on a different security authority. The payroll module would grant access only to payroll clerks, the inventory module could restrict access to buyers and asset managers, while the employee policy module would be accessible to everyone. Instead of granting access once at application startup, the identity of the user is confirmed at various gates within the program that grant access to specific modules. This approach is depicted in Figure 5.1.

Role-based security can handle the arduous requirements of enterprise security, while being nimble enough to handle user profiling. Whether displaying customized content or user-specific menus, the impact of role-based security can extend well beyond security.

Emulating like behavior in Win32 security requires far more effort. This is especially true when attempting to manipulate an access token. Managing an access token is happily abstracted in .NET. The one exception is impersonation, which is discussed later in the chapter. In .NET, determining the username, security context, or role of a user is much simpler.

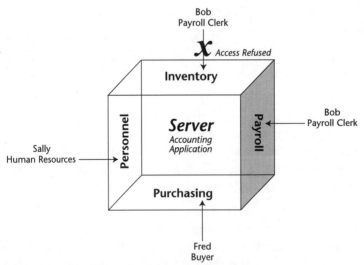

Figure 5.1 Enterprise applications often consist of multiple modules, each setting Its own security policy.

Universally, the three pillars of user security are authentication, impersonation, and authorization. They are also the cornerstones of role-based security.

Authentication is verification of user identity, normally through a form of challenge/response. Users are challenged upon logon to provide two pieces of information, one public and the other private, such as a name and password. The operating environment submits the credentials to a trusted authority that authenticates the user.

There are a variety of authentication schemes. This chapter focuses on generic and Windows authentication. Other methods of authentication, such as Forms and Passport authentication, are discussed in Chapter 6, "ASP.NET Security."

Windows authentication is linked to the access token and security context of the current thread. NTLM and Kerberos are the common authentication schemes in Win32, with the Active Directory and Kerberos Distribution Center (KDC) as the security authorities, respectively. .NET provides managed objects for Windows identities and principals. Alternately, an application can employ generic authentication and not bind to the access token of the underlying thread. The authority for a generic identity is likely a backend database, such as SQL 2000, that maintains the names and passwords of valid users. Generic security is more flexible, particularly in a heterogeneous operating environment, and more extensible than Windows authentication. Both generic identities and principal objects are supported in .NET. Windows authentication is simpler in .NET, because the operating system provides the security infrastructure. However, it is not the best solution in all operating modalities.

Authorization grants or denies an authenticated user access to a securable resource or task. Authentication establishes who the user is, while authorization determines what the user can do. Access can be granted on individual identity or the role the user exists within.

Impersonation prevents shared server identity. Enterprise and Web applications run on servers, where the logon user has enormous privileges. Server code running at the bequest of the client uses the security context of the server, not the client. Therefore, a lesser-trusted client can request that the server application undertake activities that it otherwise would be unable to perform. This is the classic luring attack. Impersonation means that the server adopts the persona of the client, including the security context. Running within the security context of the client prevents the server from being lured by a client into unauthorized activities.

Authentication, impersonation, and authorization help manage user identities and roles. Win32 programmers are probably more familiar with the terms users and groups, such as the Guest user account or Administrators group. Identities and roles are equivalent to user and groups. Identity is the name of an individual user, while a role represents a basket of users operating with a shared security context. Roles equate to clubs, where identities are the members. Instead of coding to specific users, which is not very extensible, using roles adds flexibility and lowers the total cost of administration. Instead of managing specific users programmatically, an application defines acceptable roles. Users are then managed implicitly as they are inserted and deleted from roles. This offers code-free management of users. An identity and its role membership are encapsulated by a Principal object, which defines a security context in the .NET Framework.

Some may recognize the term role from COM+. COM+ marries COM and enterprise development. Enterprise services such as transactions, queued components, object pooling, and role-based security are integral to COM+. Although conceptually similar, roles in .NET and COM+ are implemented entirely differently. .NET developers have the best of both worlds and can use roles from role-based security or COM+. This chapter provides instruction on both.

Securing an application is akin to wrestling with a tiger. Grabbing the cat by the tail is not enough. Binding the legs, securing a muzzle, and using a high-caliber rifle might also be advisable. Role-based security is not offered as an alternative to code access security, but rather as a complement. Effective security programming requires using all available tools to protect your application. Role-based security is one additional tool. With code access security, role-based security, and traditional Win32 security, a developer can erect multiple perimeters around a .NET application to protect it from perpetrators of malicious code.

Finally, .NET offers a PrincipalPermission object as a convenience for those familiar with code access security. Using this object, role-based security is implemented similarly to code access security. Instead of demanding permissions, the PrincipalPermission object demands an identity or role. This allows developers to use techniques learned from code access security for writing role-base security code, making the transition from code access security to role-based security easier. That was awfully nice of Microsoft.

Policy Defaults

In .NET, the current principal sets the security context. A Windows principal is associated with the present active token, while a generic principal is independent of Windows security. If not set explicitly, what is the default principal of role-based security policy? The default is a generic principal that is anonymous (no name). To change the default policy object, use AppDomain.SetPrincipalPolicy. SetPrincipalPolicy is ignored if the principal object is set explicitly or the default principal object has already been established.

SetPrincipalPolicy is an instance method of the AppDomain class. An AppDomain object can be obtained with the AppDomain.CurrentDomain property or by calling the Thread.GetDomain method; both are static. PrincipalPolicy is the sole argument of the SetPrincipalPolicy method. PrincipalPolicy is an enumeration with three values.

WindowsPrincipal.   This sets the default principal to a Windows principal object created from the access token of the underlying thread.

UnauthenticatedPrincipal.   This sets the default principal of the thread to an anonymous generic principal.

NoPrincipal.   By default the thread is not assigned a principal object.

The following program switches between the three security policy options.

```
using System;
using System.Security;
using System.Security.Principal;
using System.Threading;
class Starter
{
    public static void Main()
    {
        Thread.GetDomain().SetPrincipalPolicy(
            PrincipalPolicy.WindowsPrincipal);
        IPrincipal p=Thread.CurrentPrincipal;
        PrincipalType(p);
        Console.WriteLine(p.Identity.Name);
        Thread.GetDomain().SetPrincipalPolicy(
            PrincipalPolicy.UnauthenticatedPrincipal);
        p=Thread.CurrentPrincipal;
        PrincipalType(p);
```

```
        Console.WriteLine(p.Identity.Name);
        Thread.GetDomain().SetPrincipalPolicy(
            PrincipalPolicy.NoPrincipal);
        p=Thread.CurrentPrincipal;
        PrincipalType(p);
        Console.WriteLine(p.Identity.Name);
    }
    public static void PrincipalType(IPrincipal p)
    {
        if(p is WindowsPrincipal)
            Console.WriteLine("\nWindows Principal");
        else if(p is GenericPrincipal)
            Console.WriteLine("\nGeneric Principal");
        else
            Console.WriteLine("\nNo principal");

    }
}
```

This program changes the default policy to Windows, to generic, and finally to no principal. Each policy change is recorded in the console window. Unfortunately, this program does not work. Look at the results of the program in Figure 5.2.

The default principal is set to a Windows principal and never changed despite subsequent calls to SetPrincipalPolicy. The problem is the Thread.Current-Principal property, which is used in multiple places in the application. CurrentPrincipal returns and pins the principal of the thread, which is necessary to provide a definitive principal. Subsequent calls to SetPrincipalPolicy are ineffective, since an explicit principal has already been created and returned—it is too late to affect default policy.

The revised version of the program spawns multiple threads. Each thread tests a specific default policy and then is discarded. New threads start without an explicit principal. That resolves the mentioned problem, and our program now works perfectly. This is the new program. The results are shown in Figure 5.3.

Figure 5.2 The results of the policy program.

```
using System;
using System.Security;
using System.Security.Principal;
using System.Threading;
class Starter
{
    static private PrincipalPolicy policy;
    public static void Main()
    {
        policy=PrincipalPolicy.WindowsPrincipal;
        Thread t=new Thread(new ThreadStart(SetPolicy));
        t.Start();
        t.Join();
        policy=PrincipalPolicy.UnauthenticatedPrincipal;
        t=new Thread(new ThreadStart(SetPolicy));
        t.Start();
        t.Join();
        policy=PrincipalPolicy.NoPrincipal;
        t=new Thread(new ThreadStart(SetPolicy));
        t.Start();
    }
    static public void SetPolicy()
    {
        string principal;
        Thread.GetDomain().SetPrincipalPolicy(policy);
        IPrincipal p=Thread.CurrentPrincipal;
        if(p is WindowsPrincipal)
            principal="Windows Principal";
        else if(p is GenericPrincipal)
            principal="Generic Principal";
        else
            principal="No principal";
        Console.WriteLine("\n"+principal);
        if(p!=null)
            Console.WriteLine("Identity name:
                "+p.Identity.Name);
        else
            Console.WriteLine("No principal object");
    }
}
```

Figure 5.3 The corrected results of the revised program.

Identity

Identities identify a specific user and method of authentication and the basic element of role-based security. There are different types of identity objects: Windows, Generic, Passport, and so forth. All identity objects implement the IIdentity interface. These are the members of the interface:

AuthenticationType. The authentication protocol used to validate the user-name, which returns a string, such as NTLM or PassPort, and is initiated by the authentication authority.

IsAuthenticated. A boolean that confirms whether the user identity has been authenticated.

Name. The name of the user.

Generic Identity

Generic identities represent users that exist independent of Windows authentication. This is useful in a variety of circumstances.

- This flexibility is invaluable in an enterprise application that has Windows and non-Windows users, where there may be islands of security not entirely compatible with each other. Generic identities are useful in bridging security islands created by incompatible security models that sometimes exist in a heterogeneous operating environment.

- With Active Directory hosting the security database, there is an issue of scaling to millions of users. This is more likely with a Web application and is revisited in Chapter 6, "ASP.NET Security." Vast numbers of users are common with Web applications. If there is the potential for that many users, generic identities are a reasonable alternative.

- Firewalls can pose a problem with Windows authentication. Let's assume that Company A purchases Company X and attempts to integrate the myriad of computer systems that exist between the two companies and that are separated by firewalls. Passing access tokens through firewalls can be problematic. Generic identities packaged in XML envelopes successfully navigate firewalls.

The GenericIdentity managed class is a wrapper for a generic identity and little more than an implementation of the IIdentity interface. GenericIdentity inherits only the IIdentity interface and does not contribute any additional methods or properties. Therefore, IIdentity fully describes a GenericIdentity object.

GenericIdentity Constructors

Generic identity offers a one- and two-argument constructor. The one-argument constructor sets the name of the identity object, while the two-argument constructor sets both the name and the authentication type. Name and authentication type are read-only properties of the generic identity object and must be initialized at object creation using the constructor. A security identity can be replaced, but it cannot be modified.

```
using System;
using System.Security;
using System.Security.Principal;
using System.Threading;
class Starter
{
    public static void Main()
    {
        GenericIdentity g=new GenericIdentity("Doe, John",
            "Custom Authentication");
        GenericPrincipal p=new GenericPrincipal(g, null);
        Thread.CurrentPrincipal=p;
        Console.WriteLine(Thread.CurrentPrincipal.Identity.Name);
        Console.WriteLine(
            Thread.CurrentPrincipal.Identity.AuthenticationType);
    }
}
```

Windows Identity

A Windows identity is an abstraction of the access token of a Windows authenticated user and is implemented in the WindowsIdentity class. WindowsIdentity is a managed class and inherits, implements, and extends the IIdentity interface. Unlike the GenericIdentity class, it is more than a mere implementation of the IIdentity interface and offers several additional members specific to Windows identities.

WindowsIdentity implements standard identity members, such as the Name property. The Name property of WindowsIdentity adheres to the "domain\username" format—for example "DONIS\GEARHEAD". The AuthenticationType property should be "NTLM" or "Kerberos," the standard authentication methodologies for Windows operating systems.

IIdentity is the core interface of WindowsIdentity, which it extends with the following members:

IsAnonymous.   Boolean value that is true if the account is an anonymous account.

IsGuest. Boolean value that is true if the account is a guest account.

IsSystem. Boolean value that is true if an account is the system account.

Token. Handle to the access token of the Windows authenticated user.

GetAnonymous. Static method that returns a WindowsIdentity object of an anonymous user.

GetCurrent. Static method that returns the Windows identity of the current operating system thread.

Impersonate. Impersonates the specified user. Impersonation is explained in detail later in the chapter.

WindowsIdentity is not described with a default constructor. The default constructor is a no argument constructor. Minimally, a WindowsIdentity must be initialized to an access token requiring at least a one-argument constructor. For this reason, all WindowsIndentity constructors have at least one parameter, which is a token handle.

WindowsIdentity Constructor

The WindowsIdentity class has four overloaded constructors. Each constructor accepts an access token as the first parameter. The name of user is extracted from the access token. Therefore, the symbolic name of the user is not accepted as a parameter.

public WindowsIdentity(IntPtr TokenHandle).

This is the signature for the one-argument constructor of the Windows-Identity class. TokenHandle is the handle to an access token that belongs to an authenticated Windows user. Extract the access token from another WindowsIdentity object or create using the unmanaged API LogonUser or equivalent call. LogonUser is further elaborated on in the section pertaining to impersonation.

public WindowsIdentity(IntPtr TokenHandle, string Type).

This is the two-argument constructor of the WindowsIdentity class: TokenHandle is the handle to an access token. Type is the authentication method used to authenticate the user, such as "NTLM."

public WindowsIdentity(IntPtr TokenHandle, string Type, Windows-AccountType AccountType).

This is the three-argument constructor of the WindowsIdentity class. TokenHandle is the handle to an access token. Type is authentication method. WindowsAccountType defines the user type: WindowsAccount-Type.Anonymous, WindowsAccountType.Guest, WindowsAccount-Type.Normal, or WindowsAccountType.System.

public WindowsIdentity(IntPtr TokenHandle, string Type, Windows-AccountType ccountType, bool IsAuthenticated).

This is the four-argument constructor of the WindowsIdentity class. TokenHandle is the handle to an access token. Type is the authentication type. WindowsAccountType defines the user type. The fourth parameter, IsAuthenticated, is true if the user is authenticated.

Principal

Windows authenticated users are often members of groups. Common groups are Administrators, Guests, and Power Users, and a user can belong to multiple groups simultaneously. Group membership is recorded in the security identifier (SID) of the access token. WindowsPrincipal is a managed class and abstracts the security context of a Windows authenticated user, including group membership. Like the GenericPrincipal class, this class offers an implementation of the IPrincipal interface.

The most important member is the IsInRole member, which tests a user's membership in a group. For the purposes of a Windows identity, a role and a group are synonymous. IsInRole is offered in three flavors:

bool IsInRole(int RID). RID is a fragment of a SID and identifies membership in a group. A SID is a variable-length structure and can include one or more RIDs.

bool IsInRole(string role). Role is the symbolic name of the group, such as "*domain*\Administrator."

bool IsInRole(WindowsBuiltInRole). WindowsBuiltInRole is an enumeration of standard groups. The available selections are: AccountOperator, Administrator, BackupOperator, Guest, PowerUser, PrintOperator, Replicator, SystemOperator, and User.

The following sample code tests for membership in the Administrators group. First, membership is tested using the string name of the group. Second, WindowsBuiltInRole.Administrator determines membership. Either approach returns the same results.

```
using System;
using System.Security.Principal;
using System.Threading;
public class Starter
{
        public static void Main()
        {
                AppDomain.CurrentDomain.SetPrincipalPolicy(
                    PrincipalPolicy.WindowsPrincipal);
```

```
WindowsPrincipal wp=(WindowsPrincipal)
        Thread.CurrentPrincipal;
if(wp.IsInRole(@"BUILTIN\Administrators"))
        Console.WriteLine(
            "{0} is an administrator.",
            wp.Identity.Name);
if(wp.IsInRole(
            WindowsBuiltInRole.Administrator))
        Console.WriteLine("{0} is an administrator.",
            wp.Identity.Name);
    }
}
```

Principal Permission

PrincipalPermission and PrincipalPermissionAttribute classes enforce role-based security using the syntax of code access security. However, Principal-Permission classes are not derived from the managed CodeAccessPermission class. Code access security methods Assert, Deny, and others are not available through principal permission objects.

Demand is the pivotal method of the PrincipalPermission class. There is an important difference between a demand on a principal versus a code access security object. A demand on a code access security object performs a stack walk. A demand on a principal object does not trigger a stack walk.

SECURITY ALERT

The demand of a PrincipalPermission object does not perform a stack walk. Princi-palPermission.Demand checks the role of the current function only. Do not rely on this demand to prevent luring attacks.

In the following code, the Auditor role is demanded in the Dog.Barking method. Main, the caller of the Barking method, executes in the security context of an Accountant. Despite this, the demand does not throw an exception in Main. The demand simply checks the role of the Barking method, which passes, and then continues execution. Main is never checked. Demand does not perform a stack walk. More important, the two functions share a thread and security context. To successfully test the security context of the client, Dog.Barking should call the demand on the principal permission object prior to updating its security context. Basically, move the demand from the end of the routine to the beginning.

```
using System;
using System.Security.Principal;
using System.Threading;
using System.Security.Permissions;
public class Starter {
        public static void Main() {
```

```
                    GenericIdentity identity=new
                        GenericIdentity("John");
                    GenericPrincipal principal=new
                        GenericPrincipal(identity,
                        new string [] {"Accountant"});
                    Thread.CurrentPrincipal=principal;
                    Dog Fido=new Dog();
                    Fido.Barking();
                }
        }
        class Dog{
            public void Barking() {
                    GenericIdentity identity=new
                        GenericIdentity("Sally");
                    GenericPrincipal principal=new
                        GenericPrincipal(identity,
                        new string [] {"Auditor"});
                    Thread.CurrentPrincipal=principal;
                    PrincipalPermission perm = new
                        PrincipalPermission(null, "Auditor");
                    perm.Demand();
                }
        }
```

Imperative

Imperative use of the PrincipalPermission object supports the demanding of a specific role or user at run time.

```
PrincipalPermission perm = new
    PrincipalPermission(null, "Auditor");
```

PrincipalPermission offers three overloaded constructors:

- PrincipalPermission(PermissionState state)
- PrincipalPermission(string identity, string role)
- PrincipalPermission(string identity, string role, bool authentication)

A null identity or role is different from an empty identity or role. The Null role or identity is a wildcard; otherwise any role or identity is acceptable. An empty identity or role translates into an identity or role with no name, which is different from an anonymous user. The previous sample code demands any user in the auditor group. The following code creates a user named "Bob Jones" of any group.

```
PrincipalPermission perm = new
    PrincipalPermission("Bob Jones", null);
```

Declarative

The principal permission object is also available as a custom attribute. The attribute can be applied to classes and member functions. Within the principal attribute, name identifies a specific user, while role stipulates a group. Name or role can be used independently or together. A null Name or Role is a wild-card for any user or group, respectively.

In the following code, a principal permission attribute is applied to the Dog class.

```
using System;
using System.Security.Principal;
using System.Threading;
using System.Security.Permissions;
public class Starter {
      public static void Main() {
         GenericIdentity identity=new
             GenericIdentity("John");
         GenericPrincipal principal=new
             GenericPrincipal(identity,
             new string [] {"Accountant"});
         Thread.CurrentPrincipal=principal;
         Dog Fido=new Dog();
         Fido.Barking();
      }
}
[PrincipalPermissionAttribute(SecurityAction.Demand, Role="Accountant")]
class Dog {
     public void Barking() {
         GenericIdentity identity=new
             GenericIdentity("Sally");
         GenericPrincipal principal=new
             GenericPrincipal(identity,
             new string [] {"Auditor"});
         Thread.CurrentPrincipal=principal;
         // do something...
     }
}
```

In the above code, callers must be members of the Accountant role to call methods of the Dog class.

CallContext

CallContext is a logical abstraction of thread local storage (TLS), which is use-ful when passing data, including the security context, between threads within the same or a different application domain. System.Runtime.Remoting.Messaging is the namespace where the CallContext managed class resides.

CallContext manages a data store of thread static data. Similar to thread local storage, the CallContext facilitates writing and reading of thread-specific data. Information stored in the CallContext is available to all functions sharing a thread context and stack. Unlike thread local storage, the CallContext supports the remoting of data between different threads residing in disparate application domains. CallContext records information in named slots, where internally the data is stored in a hash table. Each slot can contain separate objects. Using the LogicalCallContext class, the CallContext can propagate objects between threads within the same or a different application domain. This is particularly useful in a remoting scenario. Importantly, only objects that implement ILogicalThreadAffinative can be replicated between threads.

Assume that FuncA and FuncB execute on Thread One. FuncA inserts an object in the "Banana" slot of the Call Context for later retrieval by FuncB. FuncC, running on a different thread, would be prevented from accessing the "Banana" slot of the mentioned CallContext unless the aggregated object implements the ILogicalThreadAffinative interface. This is illustrated with Figure 5.4.

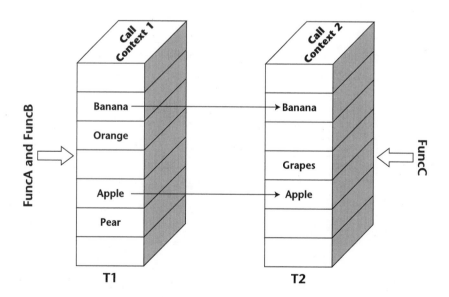

**Banana and Apple inherit the interface
ILogicalThreadAffinative**

Figure 5.4 Between threads, objects that implement ILogicalThreadAffinative are copied to the CallContext of the new thread.

The most important methods of the CallContext class are SetData, GetData, and FreeNamedDataSlot. SetData records data in a named slot of the CallContext, GetData retrieves data from a slot, and FreeNamedDataSlot relinquishes a data slot. Here is some sample code:

```
using System;
using System.Security.Principal;
using System.Threading;
using System.Security.Permissions;
using System.Runtime.Remoting.Messaging;
public class Starter
{
        public static void Main()
        {
           CallContext.SetData("TestData", 100);
           Apple myapple=new Apple();
           myapple.Peel();
           Thread t=new Thread(new ThreadStart(Thread2));
           t.Start();
           t.Join();
           CallContext.FreeNamedDataSlot("TestData");
        }
      public static void Thread2()
      {
          try
          {
              int data=(int)
                  CallContext.GetData("TestData");
              Console.WriteLine("Thread2: The data is {0}",
                  data);
          }
          catch(SystemException)
          {
              Console.WriteLine(
                  "Thread2: CallContext.GetData failed");
          }
      }
}
class Apple
{
      public void Peel()
      {
          try
          {
              int data=(int)
                  CallContext.GetData("TestData");
              Console.WriteLine("Peel: The data is {0}",
                  data);
          }
          catch(SystemException)
```

```
            {
                Console.WriteLine(
                    "Peel: CallContext.GetData failed");
            }
        }
    }
```

In Main, CallContext.SetData places an integer value into the named data slot "TestData." Next, Apple.Peel is invoked and the integer value is retrieved using CallContext.GetData. Since Main and Peel share a thread context, the operation is successful. After invoking Apple.Peel, Main spawns Thread2 as a thread and waits for its completion. An integer value does not inherit from the ILogicalThreadAffinative. Therefore, "TestData" data is not copied into the logical context of Thread2, and the attempt to retrieve the related named slot from that thread will raise an exception. Fortunately, there is a try...catch block protecting the code. Finally, back in Main, the data slot is released with Free-NamedDataSlot.

Propagating Principals

Use the CallContext to cache and propagate the security principal of callers. The called function retrieves the principal from the CallContext and impersonates the caller to prevent a luring attack based on a shared security context. If the CallContext does not contain the security principal of the caller, the called function should impersonate a user with limited rights, most probably the anonymous account.

SECURITY ALERT

It is imperative to implement a strategy to prevent luring attacks based on shared identity. Client impersonation is the most common method of attacking this problem. There are many techniques for implementing impersonation, some which use the CallContext. Impersonation is discussed further later in this chapter.

The methods CallContext.SetData and CallContext.GetData are sufficient for passing a security principal between functions sharing the same thread context. However, if the caller and called functions are on different threads, a wrapper class must be created for the principal object, and the wrapper should inherit ILogicalThreadAffinative.

Fortunately, the .NET Framework automatically replicates the principal between threads executing within the same application domain. That is right—you do nothing. If the caller sets the security principal, that principal is implicitly available to the called function, even if it runs on a different thread.

The called function has the right to override the inherited security context and set the security context to something different. Look at the following code.

```
using System;
using System.Security.Principal;
using System.Threading;
class Starter {
    static public void Main()
    {
            GenericIdentity identity=new
                GenericIdentity("John");
            GenericPrincipal principal=new
                GenericPrincipal(identity, new string[]
                {"Accountant"});
            Thread.CurrentPrincipal=principal;
            principal=(GenericPrincipal)
                Thread.CurrentPrincipal;
            Console.WriteLine(
                "Main: Identity is {0} and he"+
                "is {1}an accountant.",
                principal.Identity.Name,
                principal.IsInRole("Accountant")?"":"not ");
            Thread t2=new Thread(new
                ThreadStart(Starter.Thread2));
            t2.Start();
            t2.Join();
    }
    static public void Thread2()
    {
            GenericPrincipal principal=(GenericPrincipal)
            Thread.CurrentPrincipal;
            Console.WriteLine(
                "Thread2: Identity is {0} and he is"+
                " {1}an accountant.",
                principal.Identity.Name,
                principal.IsInRole("Accountant")?
                    "":"not ");
    }
}
```

Main creates a GenericPrincipal for John the Accountant and then updates the current principal with the new principal. The output from Main lists John and Accountant as the current principal. Notice there is no reference to the Call-Context in the Main method or a wrapper class to propagate the principal. Main then spawns Thread2. The thread retrieves the current principal and outputs the relevant data to the screen, which will be John the Accountant again. The security principals are passed implicitly between threads of the same application domain. Thread2 is automatically using (impersonating) the security context of Main. There is no need to explicitly call CallContext.GetData and

CallText.SetData. As mentioned previously, Thread2 can ignore the implied security context and set the security principal explicitly to something else.

CallContext and Remoting

When collaborating functions exist in separate application domains, the security principal has to be explicitly passed between the two threads. This is done with the logical call context, and the .NET Framework provides important assistance. There is a LogicalCallContext managed class.

In a remoting scenario, the client and server likely reside in separate application domains. The .NET Framework automatically copies slots from the Call-Context of the originating thread into the destination thread. Only entries in the CallContext that are derived from ILogicalThreadAffinative are copied across application domains, while other entries are localized.

There are four basic steps to propagating the security principal from a remoting client to a server:

1. In a separate assembly, create a wrapper class for the principal object. The wrapper class should inherit the ILogicalThreadAffinative interface.

2. In the client routine, invoke CallContext.SetData and cache the caller's security principal.

3. In the server, invoke CallContext.GetData to retrieve the security principal of the caller.

4. When performing tasks on behalf of the client, the server should use the credentials of the client.

In the following example, ForeignPrincipal is a wrapper class for a principal object. The ForeignPrincipal class inherits the ILogicalThreadAffinative interface, offers a one-argument constructor for initializing the internal principal, and exposes a principal property for extracting the internal security principal. It is housed in a separate assembly, making it equally accessible to client and server applications. The assembly also contains the interface of the server class. This is useful since the client will access the server component through an instance of the server interface. Sharing the server interface while hiding the server component provides a layer of protection similar to that of COM.

```
using System;
using System.Security.Principal;
using System.Runtime.Remoting.Messaging;
using System.Reflection;
using System.Security.Permissions;
[assembly: AssemblyKeyFile("mykey.snk")]
```

```
[assembly: AssemblyVersion("3.0.0.0")]

[Serializable()] public class ForeignPrincipal
                : ILogicalThreadAffinative
{
        public ForeignPrincipal(IPrincipal _principal)
        {
                pprincipal=_principal;
        }
        private IPrincipal pprincipal;
        public IPrincipal principal
        {
                get
                {
                        return pprincipal;
                }
        }
}
public interface IServer
{
        void DoSomething();
}
```

Next is the client code, which starts by creating a security principal. This principal explicitly sets the security context of the client. Next, a ForeignPrincipal object is created and initialized using the present security context of the thread. The ForeignPrincipal object is then inserted into CallContext of the client. Finally, a channel is opened to the server and the DoSomething method is called on the server component. The ForeignPrincipal object will be copied from the client to the CallContext of the server thread.

```
using System;
using System.Security.Principal;
using System.Threading;
using System.Runtime.Remoting;
using System.Runtime.Remoting.Channels;
using System.Runtime.Remoting.Channels.Tcp;
using System.Runtime.Remoting.Messaging;

public class Client {
        static public void Main() {
                GenericIdentity identity=new
                    GenericIdentity("Alice");
                GenericPrincipal principal=new
                    GenericPrincipal(identity,
                    new string[] {"Auditor"});
                Thread.CurrentPrincipal=principal;
                ForeignPrincipal fp=new
                    ForeignPrincipal(Thread.CurrentPrincipal);
                CallContext.SetData("ClientContext", fp);
```

```
            TcpChannel channel=new TcpChannel();
            ChannelServices.RegisterChannel(channel);
            IServer server=(IServer) Activator.GetObject(
                    typeof(IServer),
                    "tcp://127.0.0.1:4000/TheServer");
            server.DoSomething();
        }
    }
```

The server code follows. Most of the code in Main of the remoting server focuses on preparing for a remoting conversation with a client. However, the server also sets the appropriate security context. In our example, the server executes as a generic administrator. In the DoSomething function, the ForeignPrincipal object of the client is downloaded from the CallContext. The principal property of that class updates the current principal of thread. The server is now impersonating the client and can safely perform tasks on behalf of that user.

```
using System;
using System.Security.Principal;
using System.Security.Permissions;
using System.Threading;
using System.Runtime.Remoting;
using System.Runtime.Remoting.Channels;
using System.Runtime.Remoting.Channels.Tcp;
using System.Runtime.Remoting.Messaging;
using System.Reflection;
[assembly: AssemblyKeyFile("mykey.snk")]
[assembly: AssemblyVersion("2.1.0.0")]

class Starter
{
    static public void Main()
    {
        GenericIdentity identity=new
            GenericIdentity("Generic");
        GenericPrincipal principal=new
            GenericPrincipal(identity,
            new string[] {"Administrator"});
        Thread.CurrentPrincipal=principal;
        principal=(GenericPrincipal)
            Thread.CurrentPrincipal;
        Console.WriteLine(
            "Main: Identity is {0} and he"+
            " is {1}an administrator",
            principal.Identity.Name,
            principal.IsInRole("Administrator")?
              "":"not ");
        TcpChannel channel=new TcpChannel(4000);
        ChannelServices.RegisterChannel(channel);
        RemotingConfiguration.RegisterWellKnownServiceType(
```

```
                          typeof(Server),
                          "TheServer",
                          WellKnownObjectMode.SingleCall);
            System.Console.WriteLine("<enter> to exit");
            System.Console.ReadLine();

        }
    }

    public class Server
                    : MarshalByRefObject, IServer
    {
        public void DoSomething()
        {
            ForeignPrincipal fp=(ForeignPrincipal)
                    CallContext.GetData("ClientContext");
            Thread.CurrentPrincipal=fp.principal;
            Console.WriteLine("Doing something for {0}.",
                    Thread.CurrentPrincipal.Identity.Name);
            Console.WriteLine("Something...");
        }
    }
```

The CallContext is an excellent tool for copying the security context between methods during a function call, even when they reside in different application domains. This is an ideal strategy for generic principals, which are not necessarily linked to an access token or Windows authentication.

Impersonation

A WindowsIdentity is essentially a wrapper for an access token and abstracts a Windows authenticated user. The WindowsIndentity object is used to initialize a WindowsPrincipal object, which is the security context of the user. To prevent luring attacks, the server should impersonate the security context of the client. Allowing the client to pilfer the security context of a higher-trusted server opens the door to malicious manipulation. While impersonating the client, the server masks its own security context in favor of the client context. The server performs the task requested by the client, then undoes the mask and reacquires its original security context.

To impersonate a client, the server masks its access token with that of the client. This requires acquiring the access token of the client. Unfortunately, the .NET Framework Class Library (FCL) does not offer managed classes for manipulating an access token. To create or otherwise manage an access token requires interoperability services of .NET and making calls to unmanaged code. LogonUser is the security API and unmanaged call that is needed to authenticate the client and create the access token. That newly created access token is used to create a WindowsIdentity. The server then impersonates the client by calling WindowsIdentity.Impersonate. The impersonate method returns a WindowsImpersonationContext object, which is used to undo impersonation when necessary.

Steps the server application takes to impersonate the client include:

1. The server obtains client credentials via the CallContext or some other mechanism.

2. The credentials of the client is challenged using LogonUser. If successful, an access token representing the security context of the client is returned.

3. Create a WindowsIdentity object from the access token of the client.

4. Call the WindowsPrincipal.Impersonate method to mask the security context of the server and to impersonate the client. This method returns a WindowsImpersonationContext object.

5. After completing the client request, use WindowsImpersonationContext .Undo to reverse impersonation and unmask the security context of the server.

This code demonstrates the steps necessary to impersonate a client:

```
using System;
using System.Security;
using System.Security.Principal;
using System.Threading;
using System.Runtime.InteropServices;
using System.Text;
abstract class Win32Api
{
        [DllImport("Advapi32.dll")]
        public static extern bool LogonUser(
                string Username,
                string Domain,
                string Password,
                System.Int32 dwLogonType,
                System.Int32 dwLogonProvider,
                ref IntPtr phToken);
        [DllImport("Advapi32.dll")]
        public static extern bool GetTokenInformation(
                IntPtr TokenHandle,
                int TokenInformationClass,
                ref int TokenInformation,
                System.Int32 TokenInformationLength,
                ref System.Int32 ReturnLength);
        [DllImport("Kernel32.dll")]
        public static extern bool CloseHandle(
```

```
                    IntPtr hObject);
        public const int LOGON32_LOGON_NETWORK=3;
        public const int LOGON32_PROVIDER_DEFAULT=0;
        public const int TOKEN_TYPE=8;
}


class Starter
{
    public static void Main()
    {
            IntPtr pToken=IntPtr.Zero;
            bool resp=Win32Api.LogonUser("John", "",
                    "test",
                    Win32Api.LOGON32_LOGON_NETWORK,
                    Win32Api.LOGON32_PROVIDER_DEFAULT,
                    ref pToken);
            if(resp==false)
            {
                    Console.WriteLine("Logon to user
                    failed.");
                    return;
            }
            int nType=0, bytes=0, TOKEN_TYPE = 4;
            string prefix="";
            Win32Api.GetTokenInformation(pToken,
                    Win32Api.TOKEN_TYPE,
                    ref nType, TOKEN_TYPE, ref bytes);
            if(nType==0)
                    prefix=" not";
            Console.WriteLine(
                "John's token is {0} an"+
                " impersonation token.",
                prefix);
            WindowsIdentity newidentity=new
                    WindowsIdentity(pToken);
                    Console.WriteLine("Before impersonation
                    {0} ", WindowsIdentity.GetCurrent().Name);
            WindowsImpersonationContext
                    wic=newidentity.Impersonate();
            Console.WriteLine("During impersonation
                    {0} ", WindowsIdentity.GetCurrent().Name);
            // Do something...
            Console.WriteLine("Doing something for John");
            wic.Undo();
            Console.WriteLine("After undoing impersonation
                    {0} ", WindowsIdentity.GetCurrent().Name);
            Win32Api.CloseHandle(pToken);
    }
}
```

The Win32Api type is an abstract class that wraps three unmanaged calls. First, a reference to LogonUser is defined. This is the API that will authenticate and create an access token for the user. Second, GetTokenInformation is defined, and this API is used to query information pertaining to the access token. Third, the CloseHandle is used to properly close the access token returned from LogonUser.

In Main, an access token is defined and initialized to null. LogonUser is then called to create an access token from the credentials of the client user. (Since it is irrelevant to the implementation of impersonation, the way that the credentials are acquired is not demonstrated here.) GetTokenInformation is invoked to confirm that the client token is an impersonation token. Next, a WindowsIdentity is created from the access token of the client and then impersonated. The client task is performed and, afterward, WindowsImpersonationContext.Undo is called to reverse impersonation, and the server application reassumes its security context. Finally, CloseHandle is called to relinquish the access token of the client.

What's Next

The next chapter is the first of three chapters on advanced topics: ASP.NET, cryptography, and customizing code access security. ASP.NET is the first advanced chapter. ASP.NET and Web development employ different security models than other types of applications. There are many differences:

- Windows authentication is almost never appropriate with an Internet application. Forms, Passport, and other types of authentication are more appropriate in a Web scenario.

- ASP offers new concepts that are not applicable elsewhere, such as URL authorization and the worker process security context.

- A Web application is often the middle tier in an n-tiered solution and must function both as a client and a server. This mandates unique security considerations.

- The important role of configuration files in ASP.NET is hard to overemphasize. Pertaining to security, the administrator's configuration file (machine.config) and Web developer's configuration file (web.config) are important tools for securing a Web application.

In the next chapter, alternate authentication strategies are defined and demonstrated. URL authorization and other security concepts unique to ASP.NET are explored. Configuration files are dissected as they pertain to .NET security.

.NET is fully Web integrated. ASP.NET is an integral part of the philosophy of delivering solutions to clients anywhere, anytime, on any platform. But this new openness requires strident security measures. When conducting an open house, some security is prudent, particularly when some guests are hackers with less than laudable objectives, and critical resources are potentially exposed. The next chapter builds on role-based security to erect the appropriate protections for a Web-based application.

CHAPTER 6

ASP.NET Security

A SP.NET security protects the most sensitive resource of a Web application, the Web server. The paradigmatic Web server hosts several applications and users that potentially number from a scant few to several thousands. The Web server also taps into other sensitive resources, such as back-end database servers. For this reason, breaches in Web security can have an adverse impact on a variety of users, the local server, and other referenced servers. As a propellant that can quickly propagate an attack to a larger audience, Web servers are popular targets of security attacks. Effective Web security protects not only the Web server, but also users, from perpetual attacks. As a Web site administrator or developer, what resource is more critical than the user?

Web applications exist in a public or semipublic forum. Conversations held in public are inherently more susceptible to security attacks compared to a private conversation conducted in a backroom that has no windows and is held behind locked doors. There is a constant tussle between good and evil for control of your Web application. It is an understatement to say that Web applications are under continued attack. For this reason, the Internet is uncompromising on Web applications with inadequate security. Web applications should always assume that someone is listening to, attempting to modify, or otherwise adversely affecting services, conversations, or worse.

In .NET, ASP.NET security is the electrified fence surrounding a Web application. However, it is not the only security perimeter. Win32 operating system and IIS (Internet Information Services) security are also working to secure the ASP.NET Web application. Since a Web application must endure attacks from various sources, it is only fair to have many defenders. A multitier approach to security is warranted in such a competitive environment.

Because of this, do not assume that ASP.NET is the origin of every security error. Actually, ASP.NET is a last, but capable, line of defense. Figure 6.1 is a Web application security error reported by IIS. The error was caused because a user authenticated in IIS was not granted file access to a requested resource. Since the request was denied at IIS, it was never forwarded to ASP.NET.

Authentication, impersonation, and authorization are the major components of ASP.NET security. Authentication is the consulting of a trust authority to verify the credentials of the client. Credentials are submitted by the user and usually consist of a username and a password. Depending on configuration settings, the user is authenticated by the Win32 operating system, IIS, or ASP.NET. Impersonation occurs when ASP.NET impersonates an authenticated user during a request. Once a user is authenticated and a proper security context is adopted, authorization allows or denies access to specific resources, such as a Web site or page.

Authentication, impersonation, and authorization can be configured in the machine.config and web.config configuration files. There is one machine.config file per machine, and multiple web.config files. Both types of files host a myriad of tags that configure the security perimeter surrounding an ASP.NET application. This is convenient, because ASP.NET security can be updated without altering the code of the relevant Web application. Tags in both configuration files are well formed. For example, the tags are case sensitive.

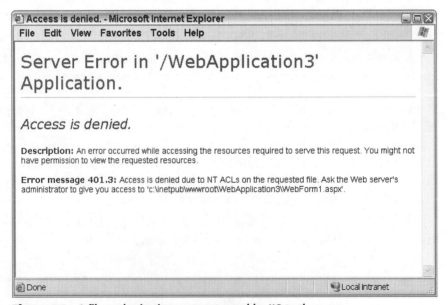

Figure 6.1   A file authorization error returned by IIS to the user.

Implementing ASP.NET security requires a core understanding of ASP.NET processing. Without this understanding, a developer is largely navigating in the dark.

ASP.NET Pipeline

From the moment a request originates and the response is delivered, there is a pipeline that processes the incoming requests and generates the outgoing response. The pipeline is an ordered sequence of steps that flows from the client application, through IIS, and finally to ASP.NET. Documenting the steps in the pipeline helps us identify the role of each player and subsequently plot an impenetrable security strategy (Figure 6.2).

1. On a remote machine, the client makes an HTTP request for an ASP.NET Web page or resource, using a browser, thin client, or other client-side interface. Security starts at the origin. Internet Explorer and other browsers offer security options. Any competent thin client also offers security parameters.

2. The request enters the server machine at Port 80, the default port of HTTP.

3. IIS performs a variety of security checks, including *file authorization*. If the security checks fail, IIS returns an error page to the user, and progression through the pipeline halts. Notably, ASP.NET never gets the requests. If the security check is successful, based on the security settings of ASP.NET, the security context of an anonymous or named authenticated user is forwarded to ASP.NET.

4. In ASP.NET, the request first flows through a series of modules. Second, the request is parsed and processed at the endpoint of the pipeline, which is the page handler. The handler creates a response that is returned through the pipeline to the client. Some of the modules are related to security, such as the FileAuthorizationModule and WindowsAuthenticationModule modules, and apply a security algorithm to the incoming request. If the request is rejected, an error page is returned to the client and progression through the pipeline halts.

   In the page handler, where the bulk of the application logic resides, role-based security and other developer-initiated security checks are applied to the request. If the security checks fail, an error page is returned. Otherwise, the requested page is parsed and a response is returned to the client.

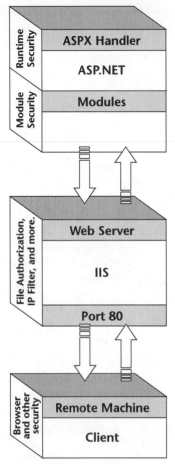

Figure 6.2 The ASP.NET pipeline.

IIS Security

IIS security is an extensive topic worthy of a dedicated book. This section focuses on the aspects of IIS that affect ASP.NET. For completeness, I would recommend reading a book focused solely on IIS.

Two primary responsibilities of IIS are authenticating and creating access token for users of client applications. Depending on ASP.NET security settings, IIS will deliver the resulting access token to ASP.NET. The conditions whereupon an access token is forwarded to ASP.NET are explained later in this chapter. ASP.NET offers a variety of authentication techniques including Basic, Digest, and Integrated Windows Authentication.

Select an authentication strategy from the Authentication Method property page. These are the steps for selecting a authentication method:

1. Open IIS from the Administrative Tools folder in the Control Panel.

2. Select the target Web site or Web application and choose Properties from the context-sensitive (right-click) menu. The Properties dialog box appears.

3. Switch to the Directory Security tab.

4. Click the Edit button in the Anonymous Access and Authentication Control group box. The Authentication Methods dialog box appears. See Figure 6.3.

   The Authentication Methods dialog box offers an assortment of authentication strategies.

Figure 6.3   Select the appropriate authentication method in the Authentication Methods dialog box.

Basic Authentication

Basic authentication locally presents the client with a login form locally, where the credentials are entered. If the client resides on the server machine or within the same domain, a login dialog box may not be presented. Credentials acquired from the dialog box are transformed using Base64 encoding and then transferred to IIS for authentication at the Web server. IIS authenticates the user with the submitted credentials. The user should map to a valid Windows account.

Basic authentication is inherently less secure than other authentication techniques. Base64 encoding is easily deciphered, and exposing the credentials of Basic Authentication is trivial. Combining Basic authentication and SSL/TLS (Secure Sockets Layer/Transport Layer Security) heightens security appreciably, but may cause performance concerns.

Digest Authentication

Similarly to Basic authentication, Digest authentication presents a login form to the client. The credentials are sent to IIS and authenticated on the Web server. However, Digest authentication uses cryptographic algorithms instead of Base64 encoding to protect the credentials before transmission. Digest authentication is only an option on domain servers. In addition, SSL/TLS can be used with Digest authentication to make it even more secure.

Integrated Windows Authentication

Integrated Windows authentication is standard Win32 authentication using NTLM or Kerberos. Like Digest authentication, Integrated Windows authentication is quite secure; but transmits an access token instead of credentials consisting of a username and password. Integrated Windows authentication is preferred when all potential users have Windows accounts. Integrated Windows authentication has difficulty crossing firewalls and proxies, probably limiting its usefulness to intranets.

Anonymous Access

Anonymous access asks IIS *not* to authenticate the client and to use the anonymous user. If necessary, ASP.NET is now responsible for authenticating the user.

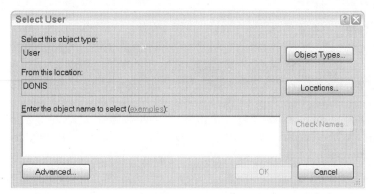

Figure 6.4 From this dialog box, change the account assigned to the Anonymous user.

Anonymous users initially map to the IUSR_*Machine* account, which is created when is IIS is installed and has limited permissions. However, anonymous users do not irrevocably map to IUSR_*Machine*. Open the Select User dialog box to map a different user account to the anonymous user. In the Authentication Methods window (see Figure 6.3), choose the Browse button in the Anonymous Access group box. To change the assignment, enter a user account in the resulting dialog box. Anonymous users subsequently will map to the newly selected user account. The Select User dialog box is shown in Figure 6.4.

Delegation

Delegation permits a server to present an impersonated token or security context to another server, such as a data server, for authentication. There are single- and multi-hop tokens. Single-hop tokens can be presented to one server. Multi-hop tokens can be presented to a chain of servers. Multi-hop tokens are more flexible than single-hop tokens.

In IIS, several factors affect the level of delegation supported. These are some of the items that affect delegation:

- Basic authentication supports delegation.
- Digest authentication does not support delegation.
- Integrated Windows authentication has NTLM and Kerberos support. NTLM does support delegation, while Kerberos supports delegation.
- When IIS is allowed to control the password of the authenticated account, the resulting access token does not support delegation.

Configuration Files

ASP.NET places most security settings in configuration files. The machine .config file is found in the \%system%\Microsoft.Net\Framework*version*\config directory and applies to the entire machine. Web.config files are valid at the Web site directory, Web application directory, and any Web application subdirectory. The configuration files form a security hierarchy with machine.config at the pinnacle and web.config files completing the lower tiers.

The closest configuration file affects ASP.NET Web resources. Visual Studio .NET automatically creates a web.config file for each Web application. If there is no applicable web.config file, the machine.config contains the default security settings. Figure 6.5 is an example of a configuration hierarchy and shows its impact on Web applications.

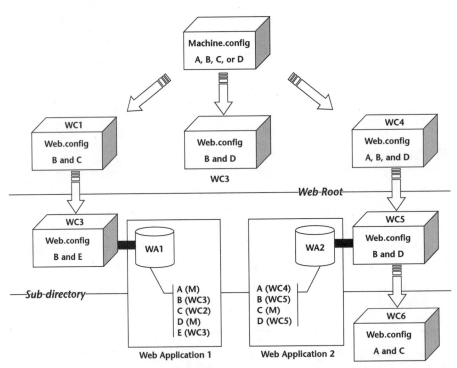

Figure 6.5 Security settings of Web Application 1 and 2 are assembled from a variety of configuration files.

web.config configuration files normally affect all pages in the same directory. Use the <location> tag to influence specific pages in the current or other sub-directory. The <location> tag can be applied to a single page or several pages in a subdirectory. The <location> tag allows a developer or administrator to jump to a specific level in the hierarchy (only descendants) and logically insert configuration tags. In addition, applying different security settings to pages in the same directory requires the <location> tag. These are different scenarios for using the <location> tag. For example, an ISP (Internet service provider) could use the location tag to disable impersonation on all member sites. A Web developer may want to set new defaults for Web pages within a site.

Settings in a local web.config file override the same settings in a <location> tag. The allowOverride attribute of the <location> tag can prevent local overrides. Set allowOverride to false to prevent overrides from a local web.config file.

NOTE

In some .NET documentation and help files, *<instruction>* is referred to as an element, not a tag. This book uses the term tag, because it is a more common phraseology.

This is an example of the <location> tag:

```
<configuration>
    <location path="Sample" allowOverride="false">
        <system.web>
        <identity impersonate="false"/>
                                                        </system.web>
    </location>
</configuration>
```

The local web.config file attempts to override the preceding location tag by explicitly enabling impersonation in the following example:

```
<identity impersonate="true"/>
```

Figure 6.6 is the error page generated because of the attempted override.

NOTE

When one is debugging an ASP.NET Web application, the error for an invalid attempt to override a <location> tag is vague and misleading.

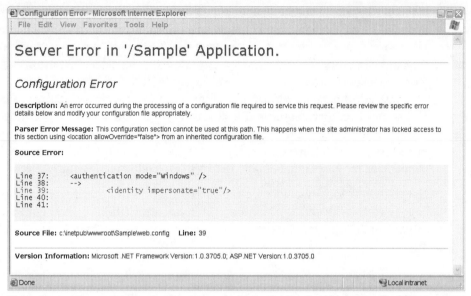

Figure 6.6 The error page that is returned when a lower-tiered web.config file attempts to override a <location> tag.

Changes to both the machine.config and web.config are immediately reported to the common language runtime. The affected Web applications are shut down, configuration files are reloaded and reapplied, and applications are restarted. Developers are informed of the application's restart in the Application_Start and Application_End event handlers in the Global.asax file.

Configuration files are packed with sensitive data, including security settings, SQL connection strings, and other general configuration data. Any interested party could download web.config files found in Web application directories. Unfortunately, a hacker could be the interested party. Information gained from the web.config file could be used to circumvent security or otherwise disrupt a Web site.

The HttpHandler section of the machine.config file prevents downloading of configuration and other sensitive files. To prevent downloading, files with the .config extension are assigned to the HttpForbiddenHandler handler. This handler will return an error page on an attempted download of a configuration file. Figure 6.7 is the HttpHandler section from a machine.config file.

```
<httpHandlers><!--<add verb="*" path="*.vsdisco" type="System.Web.Services.Discovery.
    <add verb="*" path="trace.axd" type="System.Web.Handlers.TraceHandler"/>
    <add verb="*" path="*.aspx" type="System.Web.UI.PageHandlerFactory"/>
    <add verb="*" path="*.ashx" type="System.Web.UI.SimpleHandlerFactory"/>
    <add verb="*" path="*.asmx" type="System.Web.Services.Protocols.WebServiceHandler
    <add verb="*" path="*.rem" type="System.Runtime.Remoting.Channels.Http.HttpRemoti
    <add verb="*" path="*.soap" type="System.Runtime.Remoting.Channels.Http.HttpRemot
    <add verb="*" path="*.asax" type="System.Web.HttpForbiddenHandler"/>
    <add verb="*" path="*.ascx" type="System.Web.HttpForbiddenHandler"/>
    <add verb="*" path="*.config" type="System.Web.HttpForbiddenHandler"/>
    <add verb="*" path="*.cs" type="System.Web.HttpForbiddenHandler"/>
    <add verb="*" path="*.csproj" type="System.Web.HttpForbiddenHandler"/>
    <add verb="*" path="*.vb" type="System.Web.HttpForbiddenHandler"/>
    <add verb="*" path="*.vbproj" type="System.Web.HttpForbiddenHandler"/>
    <add verb="*" path="*.webinfo" type="System.Web.HttpForbiddenHandler"/>
    <add verb="*" path="*.asp" type="System.Web.HttpForbiddenHandler"/>
    <add verb="*" path="*.licx" type="System.Web.HttpForbiddenHandler"/>
    <add verb="*" path="*.resx" type="System.Web.HttpForbiddenHandler"/>
    <add verb="*" path="*.resources" type="System.Web.HttpForbiddenHandler"/>
    <add verb="GET,HEAD" path="*" type="System.Web.StaticFileHandler"/>
    <add verb="*" path="*" type="System.Web.HttpMethodNotAllowedHandler"/>
</httpHandlers>
```

Figure 6.7   The HttpHandlers section from a machine.config file.

ASPNET User

ASP.NET Web applications borrow the security context of the ASP.NET worker process, which is the ASPNET user. The ASPNET user is created when ASP.NET is installed. Web applications, when launched as application domains in the worker process, inherit the security context of the worker process (ASPNET). Web applications running with the limited permissions granted to the ASPNET user account are inherently less vulnerable to security attacks. Web developers, as needed, can expand the repertoire of permissions granted to their Web application. First, reclassify the ASPNET user account. Second, change the user account assigned to the ASP.NET worker process. Third, use impersonation to change the security context of the Web application. Let us examine these three methods for modifying the default security context of a Web application.

First, open the Computer Management tool of the Control Panel to reclassify the ASPNET user account. Find the Users folder in the Local Users and Group item. From this folder, the ASPNET user profile can be updated, including changing group membership. The full name of the ASPNET user account is aspnet_wp account. Tools such as User Accounts use the long name of user accounts rather than the short name, such as ASPNET (Figure 6.8).

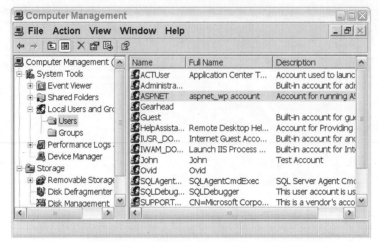

Figure 6.8 Modify the ASPNET user account in the Computer Management tool.

Second, changing the security context of the worker process changes the default security context of the Web application. This is done in the <processModel> tag located in the machine.config file. The <processModel> tag configures the ASP.NET worker process, including setting the username and password associated with this process.

These special user accounts are available: *Machine* maps to the ASPNET user account and *System* maps to the LocalSystem user account. LocalSystem is the true underlying security context of the ASP.NET worker process. Passwords managed by ASP.NET are often marked as AutoGenerate. This prevents changes to the password that would break the ASP.NET worker process. This is an example of the <processModel> tag found in the machine.config file:

```
<processModel enable="true" timeout="Infinite" idleTimeout="Infinite"
    shutdownTimeout="0:00:05" requestLimit="Infinite"
    requestQueueLimit="5000" restartQueueLimit="10"
    memoryLimit="60" webGarden="false" cpuMask="0xffffffff"
    userName="machine" password="AutoGenerate" ogLevel="Errors"
    clientConnectedCheck="0:00:05"
    comAuthenticationLevel="Connect"
    comImpersonationLevel="Impersonate"
    responseRestartDeadlockInterval="00:09:00"
    responseDeadlockInterval="00:03:00" maxWorkerThreads="25"
    maxIoThreads="25" />
```

The userName and password attributes of the <processModel> tag are the credentials assigned to the worker process. By default, the userName is Machine, which is the ASPNET user account. Changing the username and password attribute updates the security context of the ASP.NET worker process and Web applications that have impersonation disabled.

SECURITY ALERT

Beta versions of ASP.NET defaulted the security context of the ASP.NET worker process to the LocalSystem user account instead of ASPNET. LocalSystem is a potent account with considerable privileges, unlike the ASPNET user account. Granting Web applications extraordinary permission by default is potentially dangerous. For this reason, deploying Web applications in many beta versions of ASP.NET is not inherently secure. The security context of the ASP.NET worker process, and therefore Web applications, was changed to the ASPNET user account in the release version. Therefore, granting greater powers to Web applications requires a conscious decision from an administrator or developer. This is a much more prudent approach.

Impersonation is the preferred strategy for assigning the appropriate security context to an ASP.NET Web application and is explained in the next section.

ASP.NET Impersonation

Using impersonation, ASP.NET impersonates an authenticated user through IIS. Impersonation assigns ASP.NET Web applications a security context independent of the ASP.NET worker process. The impersonated user context masks the identity of the worker process, which is typically ASPNET. The <identity> tag configures impersonation, and the impersonate attribute enables or disables impersonation. The userName and password attribute are optional and offer credentials of the specific user to impersonate.

Before impersonating the named user, the user is authenticated by IIS. If authenticated, IIS creates a token for the impersonated user, which is given to ASP.NET. An anonymous user is impersonated if user credentials are not submitted with the <identity> tag and no authentication is performed.

Impersonation is disabled by default, as defined in the machine.config file. web.config files are created without an <identity> tag, while the following tag is placed in the machine.config file. This tag sets the default of no impersonation and offers no credentials.

```
<identity impersonate="false" userName="" password="" />
```

Adding an <identity> tag to a web.config file with the impersonate attribute set to true enables impersonation in pages in the scope of that configuration file. If impersonation is enabled without explicit credentials (no name or password attribute), ASP.NET accepts the security context from IIS. As discussed earlier in the chapter, anonymous requests are forwarded from IIS as the IUSR_*Machine* account.

Submit credentials with the <identity> tag to impersonate a specific user. The following tag enables impersonation and submits the credentials of a user named FWilson. Assuming that FWilson is authenticated, access is granted to related pages.

```
<identity impersonate=true username="machine\FWilson"
    password="secret">
```

WindowsIndentity.GetCurrent returns the current Windows user and is useful for testing the result of an identity tag. This Response.Write code displays the security context of the current ASP.NET page:

```
Response.Write("<H2>"+
    System.Security.Principal.WindowsIdentity.GetCurrent().Name
    +"</H2>");
```

Table 6.1 shows the results of testing various <identity> tags with the preceding Response.Write code.

The smallest configurable unit of security affected by the <identity> tag is a page. All code in a page shares a security context when impersonation is enabled and the same credentials are submitted with each request, which is not always desirable. This is the classic ASP model.

One solution is to segment code of different security contexts into separate pages. This approach maintains the existing model and is simple, but is somewhat cumbersome. A more granular approach to ASP.NET impersonation is simply to use role-based security. Disable impersonation at the page level with the <identity> tag, which is the default. Enable and disable impersonation within the page programmatically with the WindowsIdentity.Impersonate and WindowsImpersonationContext.Undo methods, as described in Chapter 5, "Role-Based Security."

Table 6.1 Test Results from Various <identity> Tags

RESPONSE.WRITE("<H2>"+ SYSTEM.SECURITY.PRINCIPAL.WINDOWSIDENTITY.GETCURRENT().NAME +"</H2>");	
IDENTITY TAG	**RESPONSE.WRITE**
<identity impersonate="false" />	DONIS\ASPNET
<identity impersonate="true" />	DONIS\IUSR_DONIS
<identity impersonate="true" username="Ovid" password="1234" />	DONIS\Ovid

Authentication

Authentication validates credentials of the user against a trust authority. The trust authority could be IIS, Active Directory, ASP.NET, or another chosen credentials agent. ASP.NET supports four different authentication modes defined by the <authentication> tag. The authentication tag can be inserted in the machine.config or web.config file. Only the root web.config file can contain an <authentication> tag. ASP.NET offers Windows, Forms, and Passport authentication. Within the <authentication> tag, indicate the desired type of authentication in the mode attribute.

Windows Authentication

Authentication mode defaults to Windows authentication in ASP.NET. Windows authentication is enabled in the machine.config file. In this mode, ASP.NET imports the authenticated user from IIS. As reviewed earlier, IIS employs various authentication schemes, including Integrated Windows, Basic, Digest, and Certificate Authentication. The following tags request the authenticated user from IIS and impersonate that security context in ASP.NET

```
<authentication mode="Windows" />
<identity impersonate="true" />
```

The resulting authentication model is identical to classic ASP security and requires no coding.

Forms Authentication

Forms authentication presents a login form to unauthenticated users requesting a secured page. The user is authenticated using credentials input into the login form. If authenticated, the user is then forwarded to the originally requested page. Forms authentication is perfect for Web sites offering restricted instead of confidential data, such as a membership site. This type of authentication is also ideal for user profiling.

When using Forms authentication, ASP.NET is responsible for authenticating the user. For that reason, anonymous access should be enabled in IIS and all users forwarded into ASP.NET without authentication being performed. ASP.NET then denies access to anonymous users with an <authorize> tag. This restricts access to only users authenticated by Forms authentication.

Forms authentication starts when a secured page is requested. Previously authenticated users are forwarded to the requested page. Unauthenticated users are forwarded to a login page for authentication, which usually contains a username and password text box. When the form is submitted, the credentials are captured and authentication performed.

If authentication fails, an error page is returned to the user. If it is successful, the RedirectFromLoginPage method is called to load the secured page, while simultaneously creating a cookie containing the users credentials. The cookie is cached on the client machine and attached to future requests for the secured Web page. Assuming that the cookie is valid and active, additional queries skip the login page and jump immediately to the requested page. The flow of Forms authentication is depicted in Figure 6.9.

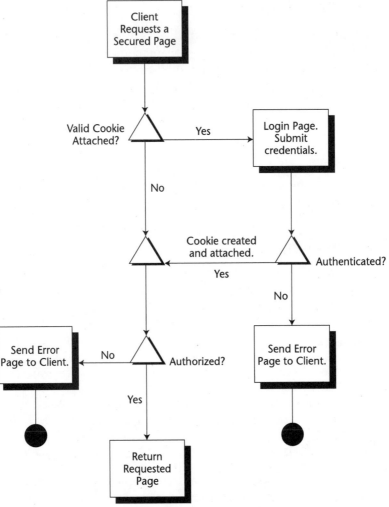

Figure 6.9 The process flow of Forms authentication.

The RedirectFromLoginPage method is a static method of the FormsAuthentication class. The FormsAuthentication class is found in the System.Web.Security namespace.

```
public static void FormsAuthentication.RedirectFromLoginPage(
    string userName, bool createPersistentCookie)
```

Username is the GenericIdentity of the Web application. The next parameter, createPersistentCookie, determines if a cookie persists across sessions. To disable or invalidate a cookie, call the FormsAuthentication.SignOut method. After invoking this method, the user is forced to the login page when the secured page is requested again.

```
public static void FormsAuthentication.SignOut()
```

Setting the authentication mode to "Forms" enables Forms authentication, the details of which are described within the <forms> tag. These details include identifying the login page and timeout duration of the cookie. In addition, the <authorization> tag denies access to anonymous users—only authenticated users are granted access to Web site resources.

These are the typical tags in a web.config file to configure Forms Authentication:

```
<authentication mode="Forms">
    <forms loginURL="mylogin.aspx" />
</authentication>
<authorization>
    <deny users="?">
</authorization>
```

Most of the attributes for the <forms> tag are omitted in the previous example. The machine.config file contains the default attributes of the <forms> tag. This is the <forms> tag in the machine.config file:

```
<forms name=".ASPXAUTH" loginUrl="login.aspx" protection="All"
    timeout="30" path="/">
```

Credentials in web.config File

Instead of a database or other repository, user credentials can be added to the web.config file. Insert the <credentials> tag inside the <forms> paired tag and add the username and password of each user. Each user is added with an <user> tag. This is an example of credentials in a web.config file:

```
<forms loginUrl="MyLogin.aspx">
    <credentials passwordFormat = "Clear">
        <user name="FWilson" password="1234"/>
        <user name="DMarshall" password="5678"/>
    </credentials>
</forms>
```

The <credentials> tag defines a block of credentials to be used with Forms authentication. The attribute passwordFormat states the format of each password. Clear means clear text, which is the easiest to input, but is the least secure format. MD5 and SHA1 are the other password formats and apply a hashing algorithm to each password. For comparison, the later password formats require inputting the hashed password into the web.config file. The <user> tag offers the name and password attribute.

FormsAuthentication.Authenticate method accepts the credentials of a user and authenticates them against the credentials in the <credentials> block. If the credentials are authenticated, Authenticate returns true.

```
public static bool Authenticate(string ,string password)
```

Cookie Security

An authentication cookie manifested in Forms authentication is an abstraction of the credentials of a user and should be considered a sensitive resource. The Protection attribute of the <forms> tag specifies the type of encryption and validation on the cookie. Encryption applies a cryptographic algorithm to the cookie to disguise the contents. Validation hashes the cookie to prevent undetected changes. The choices for the Protection attribute are Encryption, Validation, All, or None. Encryption or Validation enforces encryption or validation on the cookie. The All option applies both encryption and validation to the cookie. None applies neither protection technique to the cookie.

The encryption and validation algorithm applied to the authentication cookie can be configured in the <machineKey> tag. This tag is automatically inserted in the machine.config file and can be added to web.config files on a Web site or in a root directory.

```
<machineKey validationKey="AutoGenerate" decryptionKey="AutoGenerate"
    validation="SHA1"/>
```

The validationKey attribute designates the key value used for hashing algorithms applied to an authentication cookie. AutoGenerate inserts a randomly generated key. The decryptionKey attribute is the key value used for encryption algorithms applied to the authentication cookie. Once again, AutoGenerate inserts a randomly generated key. The validation attribute specifies the encryption algorithm for the cookie. The choices are SHA1, MD5, and 3DES. Cryptography, including many of the terms mentioned in this section, is explained further in the next chapter.

SECURITY ALERT

The Protection attribute of the <forms> tag *only* protects the cookie. To protect the credentials submitted with the form, use HTTPS or encode the username and password using a cryptographic algorithm. In addition, hashing algorithms are useful to protect against tampering. Credentials placed in the web.config file are protected by the passwordFormat attribute in the <credentials> tag.

A Sample Forms Authentication Application

FAExample is an ASP.NET Web application that supports Forms authentication. These are the supporting tags in the web.config file:

```
<authentication mode="Forms">
    <forms loginUrl="MyLogin.aspx">
        <credentials passwordFormat = "Clear">
            <user name="FWilson" password="1234"/>
            <user name="DMarshall" password="5678"/>
        </credentials>
    </forms>
</authentication>
<authorization>
    <deny users="?" />
</authorization>
```

The <authentication> mode tag enables Forms authentication. The <forms> tag names MyLogin.aspx as the login form—see Figure 6.10. The <credentials> tags lists two users: FWilson and Dmarshall. The <authorization> tag denies access to anonymous users.

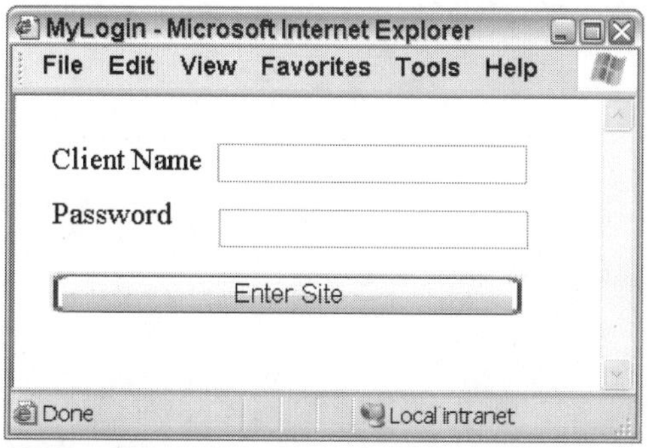

Figure 6.10   A login form used to submit credentials of a user.

NOTE
The default web.config file that Visual Studio .NET generates already contains an <authentication> tag. Modify that tag to support Forms authentication. Adding a second <authentication> tag causes a page exception.

This is the code from the Enter Site button handler of the login form:

```
private void Button1_Click(object sender, System.EventArgs e)
{
    bool resp=FormsAuthentication.Authenticate(
       txtUserName.Text, txtPassword.Text);
    if(resp)
       FormsAuthentication.RedirectFromLoginPage(
           txtUserName.Text, true);
    else
        Server.Transfer("Error.aspx");
}
```

The Authenticate method authenticates the credentials of the user against the credentials stored in the web.config file. Text from the client name and password text boxes are entered as parameters into the Authenticate method. If Authenticate method is successful, RedirectFromLoginPage redirects user to the secured page, as shown in Figure 6.11, and creates a persistent authentication cookie. If the Authenticate method is unsuccessful, Server.Transfer forwards the user to an Error page.

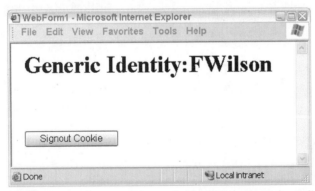

Figure 6.11 The secured page in the FASample Web application.

The secured page displays the GenericIdentity of the Web application. The GenericIdentity was set in the login form. The Signout Cookie button invalidates the cookie, forcing future requests for this page into the login form. Here is the relevant code:

```
private void Page_Load(object sender, System.EventArgs e)
{
    Label1.Text="Generic Identity:"+
        Thread.CurrentPrincipal.Identity.Name;;
}
private void Signout_Click(object sender, System.EventArgs e)
{
    FormsAuthentication.SignOut();
}
```

The page load reads the identity of the current thread and displays it in a label on the form. In the Signout_Click handler, SignOut invalidates the authentication cookie.

Passport Authentication

Passport authentication is centralized authentication and member profiling supported by Microsoft Corporation. Anyone maintaining membership in several different related Web sites may find this service beneficial. People frequenting a variety of Web sites easily amass a coterie of usernames and passwords. Managing assorted credentials can be a logistical nightmare. Replicating the same name and password across several Web sites reduces the administrative hassle, but weakens security. Someone pilfering a shared username and password has great powers. Passport authentication administers shared credentials. Related Web sites, such as an alliance of travel Web sites, can safely share a username and password to encourage traffic between affiliated Web sites.

Vendors deploying Passport authentication subscribe to the Passport Service, where authentication is performed. Member sites, not users, pay for the service. Passport authentication is similar to Forms authentication. When a page secured by Passport authentication is requested, an unauthenticated user is rerouted to a login page supported by the Passport Service. If authenticated, the user is forwarded to the requested page and a cookie containing the credentials is created. When they revisit that Web site or other participating sites, the cookie is attached to the request and access is automatically granted.

Set the authentication mode to "Passport" to enable Passport authentication:

```
<authentication mode="Passport" />
```

The intricacies of Passport authentication are beyond the scope of this book. Passport authentication is a broad and detailed topic and easily warrants several dedicated chapters. For more information on this topic, visit the Passport home page, www.microsoft.com/netservices/passport/.

"None" Authentication

Setting the authentication mode to None improves performance when authentication is not required. A public Web site might use this option. Alternately, None is appropriate when custom authentication is desired. Developers can implement custom authentication by handling the DefaultAuthentication-Module.Authenticate event.

URL Authorization

URL authorization is an array of rules either allowing or denying a user access to a URI. Authorization is undertaken after authentication of the user. Users who are not authenticated are rejected before authorization occurs. Authorization is defined in the <authorization> tag, which can appear in the machine.config file or a web.config file. The default authorization is full access for every user. Based on the default, any user not explicitly denied access to a resource is implicitly granted access. This is the <authorization> tag found in the machine.config file:

```
<authorization>
    <allow users="*"/>
</authorization>
```

The <authorization> paired tags contain an array of <allow> or <deny> tags. The <allow> tag grants access to a Web site or page, while <deny> denies access. The order of the <allow> and <deny> tags are not mandated and is solely determined by the developer. The <allow> and <deny> tags are logically similar to access control entries (ACEs) that protect kernel objects in Win32 security. Guidelines state that Deny ACEs should precede Accept ACEs, and take precedence. There is no similar restriction within the <authorization> tags.

Within the <allow> and <deny> tags, the users or roles attribute identifies a specific role or user. For a Windows identity or principal, the format of user name or role is "domain\username" and simply "username" for a Generic identity or principal. The wildcards * and ? can be substituted for the name. The asterisk means everyone or all users, while the question mark is for anonymous users. The anonymous user wildcard (?) cannot be used with the role attribute. This is an example of the <authorization> tag:

```
<authorization>
    <allow users="mydomain\user1"/>
    <allow users="mydomain\user2, mydomain\user3"/>
```

```
        <allow roles="mydomain\administrator"/>
    </authorization>
```

When authorization is performed, a compilation of the <authorization> tags in the current configuration file and others in the configuration hierarchy are assembled to form a superblock of <allow> and <deny> tags. Tags in the superblock are sequenced by distance from the affected Web site or page, beginning with the tags from the closest configuration file. Once the superblock is assembled, ASP.NET inspects the block, top down. When a match is found, either an <allow> or <deny>, that command is applied and the search is discontinued. A user does not accumulate multiple <allow> and <deny> tags. The first matching <allow> or <deny> command sets the tone of the conversation. Any remaining <allow> or <deny> tags are ignored.

File Authorization

File authorization is performed in ASP.NET when Windows authentication is selected. The security context of the user is compared to the DACL of the file resource to authorize access to the file.

Correct <allow> and <deny> Tag Sequencing Is Important

Inadvertent errors can grant access to improper users and deny access to correct users. Test and retest the validity of these tags. Look at the following authorization block.

```
<authorization>
    <deny users="*" />
    <allow users="FWilson" />
    <deny users="?" />
</authorization>
```

The obvious intent of the preceding <authorization> tag is to grant access to the user FWilson and deny access to everyone else. However, since the <allow> and <deny> tag array first denies access to all users, FWilson is not granted access. Switching the first two tags in the example resolves the problem and grants access to FWilson. This underscores the importance of testing the authorization tags.

The optional verbs attribute of the <authorization> tag highlights a specific action. The choices are GET, POST, and HEAD. This authorization block blocks posts to a page:

```
<authorization>
    <deny verbs="POST" users="*" />
    <deny users="?" />
</authorization>
```

File authorization is only applied to files recognized by ASP.NET. File mapping for ASP.NET is defined in IIS and initialized during the installation of the .NET Framework. ASP.NET files use the ISAPI filter named aspnet_isapi.dll. To view ISAPI mappings for ASP.NET, use the following procedure:

1. Open the Properties on the target Web site.

2. Switch to the Home Directory pane in the Properties dialog box. Click the Configuration button to open application mappings.

   Select an ASP.NET file extension and click the Edit button. The aspnet_isapi.dll file should be listed as the executable.

Figure 6.12 shows the settings from the .aspx file extension, which is an ASP.NET file type.

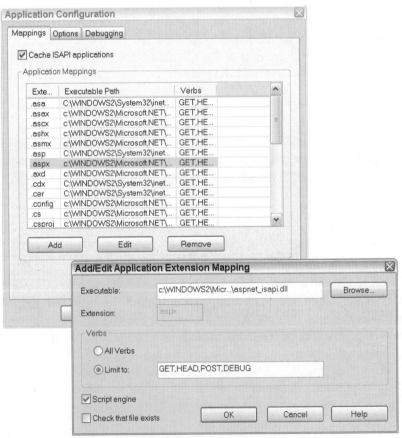

Figure 6.12 Application mapping for an ASP.Net file.

File Authorization in IIS and ASP.NET are separate and independent. File authorization in IIS precedes the handoff to ASP.NET. ASP.NET performs a second File Authorization later with an impersonated token.

Tags Configuration File

The important tags and attributes for ASP.NET security follow.

\<authentication\> tag

- **mode attribute.** Set the authentication mode of ASP.NET: Forms, Windows, Passport, or None (default mode is Windows).

\<authentication\> \<forms\> tag

- **name attribute.** Unique name of authentication cookie (default is ".AUTHASPX").
- **loginUrl attribute.** Login page for gathering credentials. (default is default.aspx).
- **protection attribute.** Protection scheme of authentication cookie: All, Encryption, Validation, or None (default is All).
- **timeout attribute.** Duration of cookie (default is 30 minutes).
- **path attribute.** Path of cookie (default is "/").

\<authentication\> \<forms\> \<credentials\> tag

- **passwordFormat attribute.** Format of user password: Clear, MD5, or SHA-1.

\<authentication\> \<forms\> \<credentials\> \<user\> tag

- **name attribute.** Name of user.
- **password attribute.** Password of user.

\<authorization\> tag

<authorization> <deny> tag

- **users attribute.** List of users affected by tag.
- **roles attribute.** List of roles or groups affected by tag.
- **verbs attribute.** Actions allowed on URI resource: GET, HEAD, and POST.

<authorization> <allow> tag

- **users attribute.** List of users affected by tag.
- **roles attribute.** List of roles or groups affected by tag.
- **verbs attribute.** Actions allowed on URI resource: GET, HEAD, and POST.

<identity> tag

- **impersonate attribute.** Enable or disables impersonation: true or false (default is false).
- **userName attribute.** Name of user to impersonate.
- **password attribute.** Password of user being impersonating.

<location> tag

- **path attribute.** Subdirectory affected by location tag.
- **allowOverride attribute.** Enables or disable ability to override location tag: true or false (default is true).

<machineKey> tag

- **validationKey attribute.** Cryptographic key used to authentication cookie: AutoGenerate or value of key (default is AutoGenerate).
- **decryptionKey attribute.** Cryptographic key used to authentication cookie: AutoGenerate or value of key (default is AutoGenerate).
- **validation attribute.** Validation algorithm applied to authentication cookie: SHA1, MD5, 3DES (default is SHA1).

<processModel> tag (partial list of attributes)

- **userName attribute.**   WindowsIdentity that worker process should emulate.

- **password attribute.**   Password of WindowsIdentity that worker process emulates.

<securityPolicy> tag

<securityPolicy> <trustLevel> tag

- **name attribute.**   Name of trust levels. Full, High, Low, and None trust levels are defined in machine.config (default is Full).

- **policyFile attribute.**   Policy level file associated with trust level.

<trust> tag (partial list of attributes)

- **level attribute.**   Trust level used for the code access security policy: Full, High, Low, None. Except for Full, each level maps to a configuration file containing trust specifics.

What's Next

The next chapter, on cryptography, is about keeping secrets. Cryptography offers a series of techniques to keep secrets hidden and protect against tampering.

The Internet is a public forum where keeping secrets is difficult. Cryptography creates a secure channel in an insecure environment to transfer sensitive data and, when necessary, confirm the identity of the sender or recipient. The Internet is the chosen operating arena of .NET, making cryptography a critical component for deploying secure applications.

Cryptography is a wide stream requiring an ample bridge to cross it. Before wading into cryptography, there is an abundance of terms, concepts, and objects that must be understood. What is symmetric versus asymmetric encryption algorithms? What is a salt value? Why is hashing alone usually not enough to prevent tampering? These and many other questions must be answered before crossing the stream. The next chapter begins by building a bridge of cryptographic terms and concepts. In cryptography, the terms and concepts are sometimes more difficult to grasp than the actual implementation.

Cryptography is unavoidable in .NET. Here are some of the ways cryptography is used in .NET:

- Strong names
- Signed assemblies
- Protecting authentication cookies
- ASP.NET credentials
- Obfuscators

Encryption, hashing, and digital signatures are the three pillars of cryptography and the focus of the next chapter. To provide a broad understanding of cryptography, the Win32 CryptoAPI command set is introduced first. Each of the three pillars is explained fully with the CryptoAPI. You then graduate into .NET Cryptography, with the emphasis on managed providers and the CryptoStream class.

CHAPTER 7

Cryptography

Protecting sensitive data available in a public forum, either transient or persistent, is important, nontrivial, and the role of cryptography. Cryptography protects sensitive data, even when it is transferred through an insecure or public channel. This is especially relevant to .NET, which specializes in Web-enabled enterprise applications built on the public Internet. Financial records, customer data, trade secrets, and human resources databases are a sampling of sensitive data that an application may transmit. Between the sender and recipient, cryptography offers data privacy, data integrity, and confirmation of origination.

Data privacy prevents unattended parties from intentionally or unintentionally viewing private data. This protects sensitive data that is being transferred through unsecure channels. The data is encrypted at the source (location of the sender) using an encryption algorithm and decrypted at the destination (location of the recipient) with a decryption algorithm. The original data is called plaintext and the encrypted transformation is referred to as the cipher text. Anyone intercepting the message would receive cipher text, which is encrypted data, not plaintext. The jumble of bytes received by the interceptor is worthless without knowledge of the security key and encryption algorithm. Cryptography hosts several encryption and decryption algorithms that use either symmetric or asymmetric keys.

Data integrity or validation assures the recipient that the data has not been intercepted and altered between the source and the target. Preventing security attacks based on altered data is an important element of building secure applications. At the target, the recipient must have confidence in the integrity of the data. In cryptography, hashing algorithms ensure the integrity of data. The hashing routines of cryptography create a one-way, fixed-length-encoded representation of variable length data, called a digest. When the data is received, the recipient creates another hash, which is then compared to the original hash. If the hashes match, data integrity is assured.

Authenticating the sender is critical to prevent spoofing of identity. Reliably determining the sender is important before acting upon a request or receipt of data. In a two-way conversation, mutual authentication protects both the sender and recipient. Without authentication, content from a spoofed identity may cause serious security lapses. Cryptography depends on digital signatures, which combines asymmetric encryption algorithms and hash routines to authenticate the identity of the sender or recipient.

Cryptography is not a single entity, but a basket of algorithms, concepts, and objects. Together, these entities offer a cryptographic solution. Correctly leveraging and melding cryptography elements is the difference between a porous solution and an effective security perimeter. For example, hashing alone is probably not an effective security solution. However, combining hashing functions with asymmetric encryption creates a safer method to transmit sensitive data.

This scenario demonstrates the interrelation of cryptographic elements. Jane wants to securely send a confidential data file to John. At the source, Jane encrypts the file to prevent unwanted viewing by unauthorized individuals. John will decrypt the file using a shared secret key to view the confidential data. In addition, a hash of the file is created. The hash is then encrypted and transmitted with the payload. At the destination, John applies a decryption algorithm to the cipher text, while recalculating the hash of the plaintext. The newly created and original hashes are compared. If the hashes are different, John knows the payload has been tampered with while in transmit. To confirm her identity, Jane creates a digital signature, using the hash of the data and the private key of and an asymmetric key pair. John uses Jane's public key to confirm the signature and the sender of the message. Figure 7.1 diagrams the process from Jane's perspective.

Jane [Computer A]

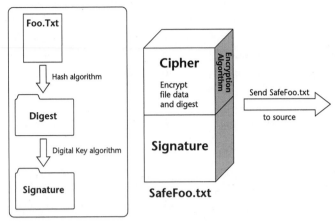

Figure 7.1 On Jane's computer, Foo.txt is encrypted and a signature is generated. Both are sent to the target machine.

Figure 7.2 presents a view from John's computer (target).

The internals of cryptography are complicated, complete with complex mathematical formulas and mind-numbing concepts. In addition, since hackers are busy creating new attacks, cryptography is not static, but is evolving daily, which adds to complexity. For Win32 programmers, the CryptoAPIs largely abstracted the complexity of cryptography.

John [Computer B]

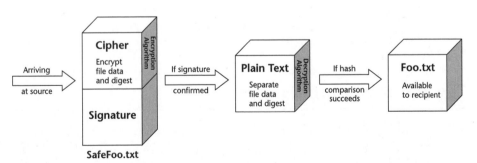

Figure 7.2 On John's target machine, the signature is confirmed, hashes are compared, and then the file is decrypted.

In .NET, the System.Security.Cryptography namespace encapsulates the algorithm and components of cryptography. The objective is to make cryptography widely available as a tool for securing applications. No longer is it necessary to have completed a doctoral program in mathematics to competently use cryptography. Knowledge of certain equations and the internals of specific algorithms, although helpful, is not required.

NOTE Cryptography in .NET is not simply an extension of the CryptoAPI interface. This is further explained later in the chapter.

In the Win32 SDK, the CryptoAPI is the standard interface for cryptography. The interface is used to encrypt and decrypt data, deploy digital signatures, manage X.509 certificates, and hash data. The core of the CryptoAPI is Cryptographic Service Providers (CSP). Each CSP is an implementation of specific cryptographic algorithm. CSPs are extensible. Cryptography vendors can supplement the native CSPs with new providers.

In .NET, cryptography is encapsulated by the System.Security.Cryptography namespace and relies heavily on streams—most notably the CryptoStream class. This namespace offers a variety of CSPs as wrappers of the CryptoAPI or managed providers implemented completely within .NET. Additional providers can be created and then published in a configuration file.

Although the System.Security.Cryptography namespace abstracts much of the unbearable details of cryptography, a basic understanding of related concepts, terminology, and algorithms is essential. Cryptography is about choices, which is only improved with knowledge. Learning the new terms and acronyms in cryptography is a good place to start. Industry pioneers were not advocates of recycling—at least the recycling of terminology. There are many new terms to digest and learn. Actually, *digest* is one of those new terms!

Key Terms of Cryptography

Cryptography is populated with new terms and acronyms largely unfamiliar to anyone working outside this concentration of security. This section lists the most valuable cryptographic terms and their definitions.

Symmetric key.   A symmetric key is a single cryptographic key that represents a shared secret between the sender and recipient. The sender encrypts the message using the symmetric key, and the recipient decrypts the message with the same key. The difficulty is safely sharing the symmetric key, which may require transmitting the key over an insecure channel. Ultimately, the sender and recipient must both acquire the symmetric key before initiating a conversation. Symmetric algorithms are quicker than asymmetric routines. Symmetric algorithms are more convenient for encrypting large amounts of data. Symmetric keys are also used by an individual to encrypt and decrypt data which will not be shared with anyone.

Symmetric keys are also used by an individual to encrypt and decrypt data that will not be shared with anyone. This introduces a problem called key management. Basically, how do you safely store the key used to encrypt? Symmetric keys are used with symmetric encryption for confidentiality.

Symmetric keys are also known as session keys. .NET supports the following symmetric algorithms (which are also called block ciphers):

- DES (Data Encryption Standard algorithm)
- RC2 (Rivest's Cipher algorithm)
- Rijndael (Rijndael Cryptographic algorithm)
- TripleDES (Triple Data Encryption Standard algorithm)

Asymmetric keys. Asymmetric keys are two keys, a public and private key—sometimes referred to as a public/private key pair. Data encrypted with the public key can be decrypted using the private key and with some algorithms, vice versa. Asymmetric algorithms are based on mathematically related, but different keys. Typically, the recipient publishes a public key in a known repository, where senders can acquire the key. The recipient also keeps the private key private and doesn't share it with anyone. Since the public key is meaningless without the matching private key, insecure channels can be used to transmit the public key. Asymmetric keys are preferred when establishing client server connections through an insecure medium, such as the Internet. However, there are drawbacks. First, asymmetric algorithms are slower then symmetric algorithms. Second, asymmetric algorithms cannot be applied to variable-length streams of data. An alternative is using asymmetric keys as a secure channel for transmitting a symmetric key, then using that key to establish secure communication. The sender would encrypt the symmetric key using the public key of an asymmetric public/private key pair, then transmit the cipher text to the recipient. The recipient would decrypt the incoming cipher text using the related private key and obtain the symmetric key. Now, the sender and recipient both have the symmetric key and a secure conversation can begin. Figure 7.3 documents the steps.

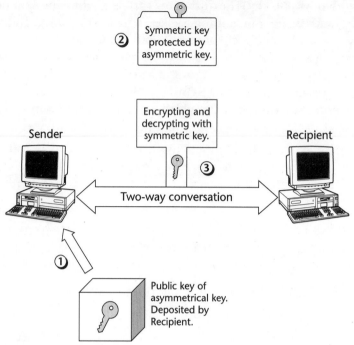

Figure 7.3   Symmetric keys can be shared using asymmetric algorithms.

Asymmetric keys are also called a key-exchange pair. .NET supports the following asymmetric algorithms:

- DSA (Digital Signature algorithm)
- RSA (Rivest, Shamir, Adleman) This algorithm is composed of the intials of the last names of the inventors of the algorithm

Initialization vector.   When using block encryption, each block in a stream is read and then encrypted with the symmetric key. Optionally, block *n* can be encrypted with the symmetric key and the contents of block *n-1*. This technique removes patterns that malicious code can exploit, because two blocks with identical content would render different ciphers. The problem is block 0, which has no preceding data. The initialization vector is a randomly generated block used to encode block 0 and ensure its secrecy.

All of the encryption ciphers that ship with the .NET framework are block ciphers. Block ciphers use initialization vectors (IVs) to ward off what is called block replay. Block ciphers work by taking plaintext in blocks (usually 8 or 16 bytes) and encrypting the blocks. Each encrypted block is XORed with the previous block of cipher text. However, for the first block, there is no previous block. This is where the initialization vector is used; it is this block with which the first encrypted block is XORed.

Cipher. Also known as an algorithm.

Cipher text. Encrypted data is called cipher text, while decrypted data is referred to as plaintext.

Hash and hash-based functions. Hash functions are used for integrity. Using a hash function over some data can prove that the original data hash not been tampered with. If the original data is run through the same hash algorithm as the hash, the resulting hash should be the same. A hash is a fixed length blob derived from variable length data using a hashing algorithm. Hashing is one-way—a hash cannot be reverse-engineered—and collision resistant. Good hashing algorithms make it statistically trivial that any two variable-length inputs result in the same hash. A hash function consumes variable-length data, applies a mathematical formula to the data, and renders a fixed-length representation of the data. .NET supports the following hashing algorithms.

- HMACSHA1 (Hash-based Message Authentication Code using SHA1)
- MACTripleDES (Message Authentication Code using TripleDES)
- MD5 (Message Digest algorithm)
- SHA1 (Secure Hash Algorithm 1)
- SHA256 (Secure Hash Algorithm 256)
- SHA384 (Secure Hash Algorithm 384)
- SHA512 (Secure Hash Algorithm 512)

Digest. A digest is the output from a hash function that was created from variable length input.

Digital signature. Digital signatures are created from asymmetric and hashing algorithms and used to authenticate the sender and prove the data hasn't been tampered with in transit. The recipient creates the digital signature by generating a hash from signature data (plaintext), which is then encrypted with the recipient's private key. The resulting digest is considered the digital signature, which is then appended to the message. The recipient uses the public key to decrypt the digital signature to obtain the hash. The recipient independently calculates the hash of the message, which is compared to the sent hash. If the hashes match, the sender is authenticated and the integrity of the data is proven. The steps are shown is Figure 7.4. If the sender is not the owner of the mathematically related private key or the message has been altered, the comparison fails.

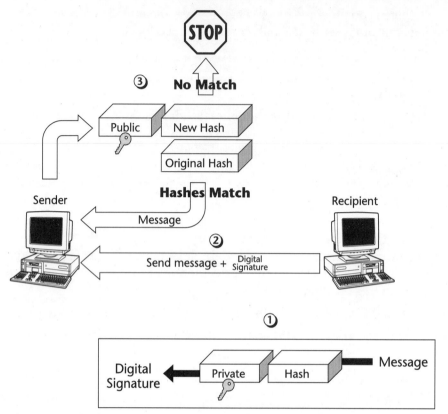

Figure 7.4 The three steps for creating and sending a digital signature with a message.

Key length. Longer keys are more secure than shorter instances. Symmetric keys of the Base Provider are always 40-bit keys, while the Enhanced Provider uses 128-bit keys.

Salt value. Salts are random data combined with plaintext and the session key used to create cipher text. Commonly, salt values are used in password based encryption (PBE) to ward off what is called a dictionary attack. Users typically use weak passwords (such as *password* or *password1*). Some systems run users' passwords through a hash function and store the digest. If attackers gain access to the passwords, they can run each word of a dictionary through the same hash algorithm and compare each result with the hashed password. If they match, the password is found. A salt value wards off this attack by hashing the password and the salt together. This makes the attackers' job much more difficult, if not impossible.

SECURITY ALERT

■■■■ **When encrypting data using a symmetric key, patterns can be detected by observing identically encrypted blocks. Salt values introduce an additional layer of protection against such attacks.**

With a basic understanding of cryptography concepts and definitions, we can now discuss integrating cryptography into Win32 application development. As a precursor to exploring cryptography in .NET, the CryptoAPI of the Win32 SDK is presented first. In the Framework Class Library of .NET, the System.Security.Cryptography is a wrapper for the CryptoAPI and .NET-specific cryptographic routines.

CryptoAPI

The CryptoAPI is the standard interface for Win32 developers using cryptography. It is an extensive interface providing functions for random number generation, encryption and decryption, hashing, digital signatures, certificate management, and much more. The crypto interface is divided into five groupings, excluding subsections. The categories are:

Base cryptography functions. Functions for interfacing with Cryptographic Service Providers (CSP). This includes functions for encrypting, signing, and hashing data.

Certificate and certificate store. Functions to manage certificates, certificate revocation lists (CRL), and certificate trust lists (CTL).

Certificate verification functions. Functions that perform certificate verification through Certificate Trust Lists (CTL) or Certificate Chains.

Message functions. Functions for sending and receiving PKCS #7 (Public Key Certificate Standard) messages. Functionality is grouped into low-level and higher-level simplified functions.

Auxiliary functions. This is a disparate assortment of methods, including routines for managing certificates, extended key usage, PFX blobs, and more.

This book focuses on the Base Cryptography functions, which are further divided into these subcategories:

Cryptographic Service Provider functions. Functions to acquire, enumerate, and set the default CSP. The most important function in this group is the CryptAcquireContext method.

Key generation.   Functions for generating symmetric or asymmetric cryptographic keys. The key routine in this grouping is the CryptGenKey method.

Encoding and decoding certificates.   Functions that encode and decode certificates and related objects. The core function is the CryptEncodeObject method.

Encryption and decryption.   Functions to encrypt plaintext and decrypt cipher text. CryptEncrypt is the key method.

Hashing and digital signatures.   Functions for hashing data and creating a digest. In addition, this interface includes methods for signing and verifying signatures. The most important function is the CryptCreateHash method.

The first task of most cryptographic programs is selecting the desired CSP within the CryptAcquireContext method. Everything else is derived from that fundamental, but important, decision.

Getting Started with CryptoAPI

The CryptoAPI interface is defined in wincrypt.h. It is necessary to include this header in any code that refers to a CryptoAPI function. The Windows.h header file, the standard header file for Win32 programming, automatically includes wincrypt.h. Prior to including wincrypt.h, developers must define the symbol _WIN32_WINNT as greater than or equal to 0x0400, which confirms the presence of a later-generation Win32 operating system that is compatible with the CryptoAPI. In addition, CryptoAPI functions are implemented in the advapi32.dll and implicitly linked into Win32 applications.

The first CryptoAPI instruction in a cryptography routine is typically a call to CryptAcquireContext to acquire a CSP handle, which is used with subsequent cryptography functions. The function also defines the key container that holds the persistent keys of the application. CryptAcquireContext should precede any other CryptoAPI function in the application, as in the following example:

```
BOOL WINAPI CryptAcquireContext(
    HCRYPTPROV *phProv,
    LPCTSTR pszContainer,
    LPCTSTR pszProvider,
    DWORD dwProvType,
    DWORD dwFlags
)
```

The first parameter of CryptAcquireContext is an out parameter and returns a handle to a CSP. Save this handle for later use with other CryptoAPI methods. The second parameter, pszContainer, is the name of the key container that holds the persistent cryptographic keys used by this application. If this parameter is null, a default container is used. The default container is shared among multiple applications and should not be used for storing private keys. The name of the default container is the username of the current security context. The third parameter is the name of the requested CSP. If null, the default CSP is chosen. The dwProvType, the fourth parameter, indicates the provider type. The default type for Windows XP is the Microsoft Strong Cryptographic Provider, which supports encryption, digital signatures, and hashing. The final argument is a disparate assortment of mostly unrelated flags.

When the cryptographic routine finishes, use CryptReleaseContext to release the CSP. It decrements the reference count of the CSP; if the count is zero, the provider is released.

This sample code demonstrates acquiring and releasing a handle of a CSP. The code acquires and releases a handle to an Enhanced CSP.

```
#define _WIN32_WINNT 0x0400
#include <windows.h>
int main()
{
    HCRYPTPROV hProv=NULL;
    CryptAcquireContext(&hProv, NULL, MS_ENHANCED_PROV,
        PROV_RSA_FULL, 0);
    // Cryptography routine
    CryptReleaseContext(hProv, 0);
    return 0;
}
```

Random Number Generation

Initialization vectors, salt values, and keys are sometimes required in cryptographic algorithms. The randomness of these items strengthens the security of the cryptographic algorithm. Functions like rand of the C-runtime library, which is seeded with srand, do not approach the level of randomness sufficient for security and cryptographic routines. In the CryptoAPI, the Crypt-GenRandom method generates a random number that is more appropriate for cryptography, while using an internal seed. Developers can further randomize the results of CryptGenRandom by augmenting the seed with extra programmer-defined bytes.

This is the prototype of CryptGenRandom:

```
BOOL WINAPI CryptGenRandom(
    HCRYPTPROV hProv,
    DWORD dwLen,
    BYTE *pbBuffer
)
```

The first parameter is a handle to a CSP, likely acquired with the CryptAcquire-Context method. The second parameter sets the length, in bytes, of random data returned. The final parameter is an in-and-out buffer. The resulting random value is returned as the out parameter. Optionally, as an in parameter pbBuffer contributes additional seed matter to further randomize the result.

A CSP handle and unique key are the essential ingredients for encryption, decryption, hashing, and digital signature algorithms. The next few pages provide the steps and sample code for each of these algorithms.

Encryption

These are the steps for encrypting plaintext using the CryptoAPI:

1. Request a provider that supports the desired encryption algorithm and key length.

2. Create an exportable symmetric key.

3. Generate an asymmetric key (public/private key pair), which is used to encrypt the symmetric key.

4. Create a key blob from the exportable key, which is then secured with the asymmetric key pair. The symmetric key that is embedded within the key blob can be securely transmitted to the client.

5. Encrypt the document or data using the symmetric key.

6. Persist the key blob and the encrypted data to media accessible to the recipient.

The following sample code demonstrates the steps for encrypting plaintext.

```
#define _WIN32_WINNT 0x0400
#include <windows.h>
int main(int argc, char *argv[])
{
    LPTSTR plaintext=argv[1];
    LPTSTR ciphertext=argv[2];
    HANDLE hPlain=CreateFile(plaintext, GENERIC_READ,
        FILE_SHARE_READ,NULL, OPEN_EXISTING, 0, NULL);
    if(hPlain == INVALID_HANDLE_VALUE)
    {
        MessageBox(NULL, "Invalid Plain Text File", "Error",
            MB_OK);
        return 0;
    }
    DWORD dwPlainSize=GetFileSize(hPlain, NULL);
    BYTE *pPlain=new BYTE[dwPlainSize];
    BOOL bResult=ReadFile(hPlain, pPlain, dwPlainSize, &dwPlainSize,
```

```
        NULL);
    HCRYPTPROV hProv=NULL;
    HCRYPTKEY hCrypt=NULL, hExchange=NULL;
    DWORD dwBlobLen=0;
    CryptAcquireContext(&hProv, NULL, MS_ENHANCED_PROV,
        PROV_RSA_FULL, 0);
    CryptGenKey(hProv, CALG_RC4, CRYPT_EXPORTABLE, &hCrypt);
    CryptGetUserKey(hProv, AT_KEYEXCHANGE, &hExchange);
    CryptExportKey(hCrypt, hExchange, SIMPLEBLOB, 0, NULL,
        &dwBlobLen);
    BYTE *pBlob=new BYTE[dwBlobLen];
    CryptExportKey(hCrypt, hExchange, SIMPLEBLOB, 0, pBlob,
        &dwBlobLen);
    ULONG dwEncryptSize=dwPlainSize;
    bResult=CryptEncrypt(hCrypt, NULL, FALSE, 0, NULL
        &dwEncryptSize, dwPlainSize);
    BYTE *pEncrypt=new BYTE[dwEncryptSize];
    memcpy(pEncrypt, pPlain, dwPlainSize);
    CryptEncrypt(hCrypt, NULL, FALSE, 0, pEncrypt, &dwEncryptSize,
        dwPlainSize);
    DWORD dwTemp=0;
    HANDLE hCipher=CreateFile(ciphertext, GENERIC_WRITE, 0,
        NULL, CREATE_ALWAYS, 0, NULL);
    if(hCipher == INVALID_HANDLE_VALUE)
    {
        MessageBox(NULL, "Invalid File for Encryption", "Error",
            MB_OK);
        return 0;
    }
    WriteFile(hCipher, &dwBlobLen, sizeof(dwBlobLen), &dwTemp,
        NULL);
    WriteFile(hCipher, pBlob, dwBlobLen, &dwTemp,
        NULL);
    WriteFile(hCipher, pEncrypt, dwEncryptSize, &dwTemp,
        NULL);
    delete pPlain;
    delete pBlob;
    delete pEncrypt;
    CloseHandle(hPlain);
    CloseHandle(hCipher);
    CryptReleaseContext(hProv, 0);
    return 0;
}
```

The following separates the code into the six steps for encrypting data.

1. **Request a provider that supports the desired encryption algorithm
   and key length.** In the sample code, the first CryptoAPI method is
   CryptAcquireContext and requests a handle to the Microsoft Enhanced
   Cryptographic Provider. To keep the code simple, our example does not

use a block cipher and extensive error handling. A block cipher, such as DES, encrypts data not as a stream of data, but as a sequence of symmetrical blocks. Block ciphers are more secure than stream ciphers, but performance is slower and code more complex. This section introduces CryptoAPI as a prelude to cryptography in .NET, so block ciphers are not used. The first time this code is run, CryptAcquireContext must be called with the dwFlags parameter set to CRYPT_NEWKEYSET to create a default key container. After creating the key container, you don't have to use the CRYPT_NEWKEYSET parameter again.

```
HCRYPTPROV hProv=NULL;
HCRYPTKEY hCrypt=NULL, hExchange=NULL;
DWORD dwBlobLen=0;
CryptAcquireContext(&hProv, NULL, MS_ENHANCED_PROV,
    PROV_RSA_FULL, 0);
```

2. **Generate an exportable session key.** CryptGenKey creates cryptographic key that is returned as the last parameter. The function can generate symmetric or asymmetric keys. A handle to the CSP is the initial parameter. The encryption algorithm is the next parameter. The sample code chooses CALG_RC4. CALG_RC4 designates a stream cipher, has a 40-bit key length, and is supported by the Enhanced Provider. The third parameter is the type of key. Since the resulting symmetric key is being sent to the client in a text file, the CRYPT_EXPORTABLE flag is necessary.

```
CryptGenKey(hProv, CALG_RC4, CRYPT_EXPORTABLE, &hCrypt);
```

3. **Generate an asymmetric key (public/private key pair), which is used to encrypt the symmetric key.** CryptGetUserKey retrieves the asymmetric key of the current user. The CSP handle is passed as the first argument. The key container contains two private/public key pairs: one for data exchange and another for digital signatures. AT_KEYEXCHANGE requests the data exchange key pair. The handle to the key pair is returned as the last parameter.

```
CryptGetUserKey(hProv, AT_KEYEXCHANGE, &hExchange);
```

4. **Create a key blob from the exportable key, which is then secured with the asymmetric key pair.** CryptExportKey creates a blob that wraps a symmetric key and encrypted with an asymmetric key. The key to be exported is the first parameter. The asymmetric key is the second parameter. The third parameter is the type of blob. SIMPLE_BLOB is a blob that contains a symmetric key. The fourth parameter is an assortment of flags. The final parameter is the output buffer (byte array) for storing the block. CryptExportKey is called twice in the sample code, First to get the size of the blob and second after the buffer is created to actually create the blob.

```
CryptExportKey(hCrypt, hExchange, SIMPLEBLOB, 0, NULL,
    &dwBlobLen);
BYTE *pBlob=new BYTE[dwBlobLen];
CryptExportKey(hCrypt, hExchange, SIMPLEBLOB, 0, pBlob,
    &dwBlobLen);
```

5. **Encrypt the document or data using the symmetric key.** CryptEncrypt encrypts plaintext and creates a cipher. The function starts with a handle to the key to be used in the encryption algorithm. The second parameter is a handle to a hash object, which is used to encrypt and hash data at the same time. The third parameter is a Boolean flag. If true, all input has been encrypted. When encrypting blocks of data, CryptEncrypt may be called multiple times until this parameter is true. The fourth parameter is reserved and not presently used. The fifth parameter is an in-and-out buffer. The buffer contains the incoming plaintext and the resulting cipher. The final parameter is the length of the buffer. The sample code calls CryptEncrypt twice: first, to get the size of the resulting buffer and then to create the cipher.

```
ULONG dwEncryptSize=dwPlainSize;
bResult=CryptEncrypt(hCrypt, NULL, TRUE, 0, NULL,
    &dwEncryptSize, dwPlainSize);
BYTE *pEncrypt=new BYTE[dwEncryptSize];
memcpy(pEncrypt, pPlain, dwPlainSize);
CryptEncrypt(hCrypt, NULL, TRUE, 0, pEncrypt, &dwEncryptSize,
    dwPlainSize);
```

6. **Persist the key blob and the encrypted data to media accessible to the recipient.** In our sample code, the blob length, key blob, and cipher are written successively into a file.

```
DWORD dwTemp=0;
HANDLE hCipher=CreateFile(ciphertext, GENERIC_WRITE, 0,
    NULL, CREATE_ALWAYS, 0, NULL);
if(hCipher == INVALID_HANDLE_VALUE)
{
    MessageBox(NULL, "Invalid File for Encryption", "Error",
        MB_OK);
    return 0;
}
WriteFile(hCipher, &dwBlobLen, sizeof(dwBlobLen), &dwTemp,
    NULL);
WriteFile(hCipher, pBlob, dwBlobLen, &dwTemp,
    NULL);
WriteFile(hCipher, pEncrypt, dwEncryptSize, &dwTemp,
    NULL);
```

Logically, the next step is reversing the process and decrypting the cipher text.

Decryption

These are the steps for decrypting a cipher and recreating the original plaintext.

1. Retrieve the symmetric key used to encrypt the data and the resulting cipher.

2. Request a provider that supports the desired decryption algorithm and key length.

3. Decrypt the cipher text to reformulate the original plaintext.

The following sample code decrypts a cipher created using the encryption sample in the preceding section.

```
#define _WIN32_WINNT 0x0400
#include <windows.h>
int main(int argc, char *argv[])
{
    DWORD dwBlobSize=0, dwTemp=0;
    LPTSTR ciphertext=argv[1];
    LPTSTR plaintext=argv[2];
    HANDLE hCipher=CreateFile(ciphertext, GENERIC_READ,
        FILE_SHARE_READ, NULL, OPEN_EXISTING, 0, NULL);
    if(hCipher== INVALID_HANDLE_VALUE)
    {
        MessageBox(NULL, "Invalid Encrypted Text File", "Error",
            MB_OK);
        return 0;
    }
    BOOL bResult=ReadFile(hCipher, &dwBlobSize, sizeof(dwBlobSize),
        &dwTemp, NULL);
    BYTE *pBlob=new BYTE[dwBlobSize];
    ReadFile(hCipher, pBlob, dwBlobSize,
        &dwBlobSize, NULL);

    DWORD dwEncryptSize=GetFileSize(hCipher, NULL)-dwBlobSize-
        sizeof(dwBlobSize);
    BYTE *pEncrypt=new BYTE[dwEncryptSize];
    ReadFile(hCipher, pEncrypt, dwEncryptSize, &dwEncryptSize, NULL);
    HCRYPTPROV hProv=NULL;
    HCRYPTKEY hCrypt=NULL, hExchange=NULL;
    DWORD dwBlobLen=0;
    DWORD dwPlainSize=dwEncryptSize;
    CryptAcquireContext(&hProv, NULL, MS_ENHANCED_PROV,
        PROV_RSA_FULL, 0);
    CryptGetUserKey(hProv, AT_KEYEXCHANGE, &hExchange);
    CryptImportKey(hProv, pBlob, dwBlobLen, hExchange, 0, &hCrypt);
    CryptDecrypt(hCrypt, NULL, TRUE, 0, NULL, &dwPlainSize);
```

```
BYTE *pPlain=new BYTE[dwPlainSize];
memcpy(pPlain, pEncrypt, dwPlainSize);
CryptDecrypt(hCrypt, NULL, TRUE, 0, pPlain, &dwPlainSize);
HANDLE hPlain=CreateFile(plaintext, GENERIC_WRITE, 0,
    NULL, CREATE_ALWAYS, 0, NULL);
if(hPlain == INVALID_HANDLE_VALUE)
{
    MessageBox(NULL, "Invalid File for Plain text", "Error",
        MB_OK);
    return 0;
}
WriteFile(hPlain, pPlain, dwPlainSize, &dwTemp, NULL);

delete pBlob;
delete pEncrypt;
delete pPlain;
CloseHandle(hCipher);
CloseHandle(hPlain);
CryptReleaseContext(hProv, 0);
return 0;
}
```

The following comments separate the code into the three steps for decrypting a cipher.

1. **Retrieve the symmetric key used to encrypt the data and the resulting cipher.** The sample code used to encrypt the data writes the key blob length, key blob, and cipher to a file. The first step is retrieving this information.

```
HANDLE hCipher=CreateFile(ciphertext, GENERIC_READ,
    FILE_SHARE_READ, NULL, OPEN_EXISTING, 0, NULL);
if(hCipher== INVALID_HANDLE_VALUE)
{
    MessageBox(NULL, "Invalid Encrypted Text File", "Error",
        MB_OK);
    return 0;
}
BOOL bResult=ReadFile(hCipher, &dwBlobSize, sizeof(dwBlobSize),
    &dwTemp, NULL);
BYTE *pBlob=new BYTE[dwBlobSize];
ReadFile(hCipher, pBlob, dwBlobSize,
    &dwBlobSize, NULL);
DWORD dwEncryptSize=GetFileSize(hCipher, NULL)-dwBlobSize-
    sizeof(dwBlobSize);
BYTE *pEncrypt=new BYTE[dwEncryptSize];
ReadFile(hCipher, pEncrypt, dwEncryptSize, &dwEncryptSize, NULL);
```

2. **Request a provider that supports the desired decryption algorithm and key length.** Acquire the handle to a provider that supports the desired

decryption algorithm and key length. In the sample code, the first Cryp-toAPI method is CryptAcquireContext and requests a handle to the Microsoft Enhanced Cryptographic Provider.

```
CryptAcquireContext(&hProv, NULL, MS_ENHANCED_PROV,
    PROV_RSA_FULL, 0);
```

3. **Decrypt the cipher text and regenerate the original plaintext.** Before decrypting the cipher, the key blob must be imported and the symmetric key extracted. CryptImportKey imports a blob and returns a key. The first parameter is a handle to the CSP. The second parameter is a pointer to the blob. The third parameter is the length of the blob. The fourth parameter is the asymmetric key pair used to decrypt the blob. The fifth parameter is an assortment of flags. The final argument is an out parameter and the handle to the imported and now-extracted key. Prior to calling CryptImportKey, CryptGetUserKey is invoked to obtain the asymmetric key pair used in the call. CryptDecrypt decrypts a cipher and returns plaintext. The first parameter is a handle to a cryptographic key. The second parameter is a handle to a hash object. If the plaintext is decrypted and hashed simultane-ously, a handle to the hash object is required. The third parameter is a Boolean flag indicating the final call to CryptDecrypt. The fourth parame-ter is an assortment of flags. The fifth parameter is an in and out buffer. The buffer contains the incoming cipher text and resulting plaintext. The final parameter is the size of the buffer. CryptDecrypt is called twice: first, to get the size of the buffer and second to retrieve the plaintext.

```
CryptGetUserKey(hProv, AT_KEYEXCHANGE, &hExchange);
CryptImportKey(hProv, pBlob, dwBlobLen, hExchange, 0, &hCrypt);
CryptDecrypt(hCrypt, NULL, TRUE, 0, NULL, &dwPlainSize);
BYTE *pPlain=new BYTE[dwPlainSize];
memcpy(pPlain, pEncrypt, dwPlainSize);
CryptDecrypt(hCrypt, NULL, TRUE, 0, pPlain, &dwPlainSize);
```

Hashing

These are steps for employing a hash algorithm to convert variable length data into a digest using the CryptoAPI. The first four steps are identical to the steps for encrypting data.

1. Request a provider that supports the desired hashing algorithm and key length.

2. Create an exportable symmetric key.

3. Generate an asymmetric key (public/private key pair) to encrypt the symmetric key.

4. Create a key blob from the exportable key, which is then secured with the asymmetric key pair. The symmetric key that is embedded within the key blob can be securely transmitted to the client.

5. Specify the hashing algorithm, create the hash object, and calculate the digest.

6. Retrieve the resulting digest.

7. Encrypt the digest to protect it from tampering.

8. Persist the key blob and digest to media accessible to the recipient.

The following sample code illustrates the steps for hashing data.

```
#define _WIN32_WINNT 0x0400
#include <windows.h>
int main(int argc, char *argv[])
{
    LPTSTR plain=argv[1];
    LPTSTR cipher=argv[2];
    HANDLE hPlain=CreateFile(plain, GENERIC_READ, FILE_SHARE_READ,
        NULL, OPEN_EXISTING, 0, NULL);
    if(hPlain == INVALID_HANDLE_VALUE)
    {
        MessageBox(NULL, "Invalid Plain Text File", "Error",
            MB_OK);
        return 0;
    }
    DWORD dwPlain=GetFileSize(hPlain, NULL);
    BYTE *pPlain=new BYTE[dwPlain];
    BOOL bResult=ReadFile(hPlain, pPlain, dwPlain, &dwPlain, NULL);
    HCRYPTPROV hProv=NULL;
    HCRYPTKEY hCrypt=NULL, hExchange=NULL;
    DWORD dwBlob=0;
    CryptAcquireContext(&hProv, NULL, MS_ENHANCED_PROV,
        PROV_RSA_FULL, 0);
    CryptGenKey(hProv, CALG_RC4, CRYPT_EXPORTABLE, &hCrypt);
    CryptGetUserKey(hProv, AT_KEYEXCHANGE, &hExchange);
    CryptExportKey(hCrypt, hExchange, SIMPLEBLOB, 0, NULL, &dwBlob);
    BYTE *pBlob=new BYTE[dwBlob];
    CryptExportKey(hCrypt, hExchange, SIMPLEBLOB, 0, pBlob, &dwBlob);
    DWORD dwEPlain, dwEHash, dwHash, dwEncrypt;
    HCRYPTHASH hHash=0;
    CryptCreateHash(hProv, CALG_MD5, 0, 0, &hHash);
    CryptHashData(hHash, (const unsigned char*) pPlain, dwPlain, 0);
    CryptGetHashParam(hHash, HP_HASHVAL, NULL, &dwHash, 0);
    BYTE *pHash=new BYTE[dwHash];
    CryptGetHashParam(hHash, HP_HASHVAL, pHash, &dwHash, 0);
    dwEPlain=dwPlain;
    dwEHash=dwHash;
```

```
bResult=CryptEncrypt(hCrypt, 0, FALSE, 0, NULL, &dwEPlain,
    dwPlain);
bResult=CryptEncrypt(hCrypt, 0, FALSE, 0, NULL, &dwEHash,
    dwHash);
dwEncrypt=dwEPlain+dwEHash;
BYTE *pEncrypt=new BYTE[dwEncrypt];
memcpy(pEncrypt, pPlain, dwPlain);
memcpy(&(pEncrypt[dwEPlain]), pHash, dwHash);
CryptEncrypt(hCrypt, NULL, FALSE, 0, pEncrypt, &dwEncrypt,
    dwEPlain+dwEHash);
DWORD dwTemp=0;
HANDLE hCipher=CreateFile(cipher, GENERIC_WRITE, 0,
    NULL, CREATE_ALWAYS, 0, NULL);
if(hCipher == INVALID_HANDLE_VALUE)
{
    MessageBox(NULL, "Invalid File for Encryption", "Error",
        MB_OK);
    return 0;
}
WriteFile(hCipher, &dwBlob, sizeof(dwBlob), &dwTemp,
    NULL);
WriteFile(hCipher, pBlob, dwBlob, &dwTemp,
    NULL);
WriteFile(hCipher, &dwPlain, sizeof(dwPlain), &dwTemp,
    NULL);
WriteFile(hCipher, &dwHash, sizeof(dwHash), &dwTemp,
    NULL);
WriteFile(hCipher, &dwEncrypt, sizeof(dwEncrypt), &dwTemp,
    NULL);
WriteFile(hCipher, pEncrypt, dwEncrypt, &dwTemp,
    NULL);
delete pBlob;
delete pEncrypt;
delete pHash;
CloseHandle(hPlain);
CloseHandle(hCipher);
CryptReleaseContext(hProv, 0);
return 0;
}
```

The following explanation dissects the sample code. The explanation of the first four steps is omitted. These steps were explained earlier in the encryption code and somewhat in the decryption code.

1. **Request a provider that supports the desired hashing algorithm and key length.**

2. **Create an exportable symmetric key.**

3. **Generate an asymmetric key (public/private key pair), which is used to encrypt the symmetric key.**

4. **Create a key blob from the exportable key and secured with the asymmetric key.** The symmetric key that is embedded within the key blob can be securely transmitted to the client.

5. **Specify the hashing algorithm, create the hash object, and calculate the digest.** CryptCreateHash creates a hashing object using the stated hashing algorithm. The first parameter is the handle to the selected Cryptographic Provider. The second parameter is the hashing algorithm. The third parameter is the handle to a key for keyed hashing. A keyed hash is a digest created using a hashing algorithm and a shared key. If a keyed hash algorithm is specified in the second parameter, such as HMACSHA1, this parameter would be a handle to a valid key. Otherwise, set this argument to null. The fourth parameter is reserved and not currently used. The final parameter is the handle to the resulting hash object. The sample program requests the CALG_MD5 algorithm, which is the hashing algorithm for MD5. CryptHashData calculates the hash. The function begins with a handle to the hash object. Next is a pointer to plaintext. The size of the data is the following parameter. Microsoft CSPs ignore the final parameter.

```
DWORD dwEPlain, dwEHash, dwHash, dwEncrypt;
HCRYPTHASH hHash=0;
CryptCreateHash(hProv, CALG_MD5, 0, 0, &hHash);
CryptHashData(hHash, (const unsigned char*) pPlain, dwPlain, 0);
```

6. **Return a pointer to the previously calculated digest using CryptGetHashParam.** This is the digest created earlier using CryptHashData. To retrieve the resulting hash, a handle to the hash object is the starting parameter. The type of query is the next parameter. HP_HASHVAL requests the hash digest. The hash digest is copied to the address provided in next parameter. The next parameter is the number of bytes to copy. The final parameter is reserved and not currently used. CryptGetHashParam is called twice: to determine the size of the buffer and then to actually retrieve the digest.

```
CryptGetHashParam(hHash, HP_HASHVAL, NULL, &dwHash, 0);
BYTE *pHash=new BYTE[dwHash];
CryptGetHashParam(hHash, HP_HASHVAL, pHash, &dwHash, 0);
```

7. **Encrypt the digest to protect it from tampering.** Modifying the plaintext and replacing the hash with an updated hash would successfully defeat any protection offered by the original hash. To prevent tampering, the hash should be encrypted. That hash is encrypted using a symmetric key; the steps for encrypting data are outlined earlier in this chapter.

```
dwEPlain=dwPlain;
dwEHash=dwHash;
bResult=CryptEncrypt(hCrypt, 0, FALSE, 0, NULL, &dwEPlain,
    dwPlain);
bResult=CryptEncrypt(hCrypt, 0, FALSE, 0, NULL, &dwEHash,
```

```
        dwHash);
dwEncrypt=dwEPlain+dwEHash;
BYTE *pEncrypt=new BYTE[dwEncrypt];
memcpy(pEncrypt, pPlain, dwPlain);
memcpy(&(pEncrypt[dwEPlain]), pHash, dwHash);
CryptEncrypt(hCrypt, NULL, FALSE, 0, pEncrypt, &dwEncrypt,
        dwEPlain+dwEHash);
```

8. **Persist the key blob and digest to media accessible to the recipient.** In the sample program, hash related information is persisted to a file.

```
HANDLE hCipher=CreateFile(cipher, GENERIC_WRITE, 0,
        NULL, CREATE_ALWAYS, 0, NULL);
if(hCipher == INVALID_HANDLE_VALUE)
{
        MessageBox(NULL, "Invalid File for Encryption", "Error",
                MB_OK);
        return 0;
}
WriteFile(hCipher, &dwBlob, sizeof(dwBlob), &dwTemp,
        NULL);
WriteFile(hCipher, pBlob, dwBlob, &dwTemp,
        NULL);
WriteFile(hCipher, &dwPlain, sizeof(dwPlain), &dwTemp,
        NULL);
WriteFile(hCipher, &dwHash, sizeof(dwHash), &dwTemp,
        NULL);
WriteFile(hCipher, &dwEncrypt, sizeof(dwEncrypt), &dwTemp,
        NULL);
WriteFile(hCipher, pEncrypt, dwEncrypt, &dwTemp,
        NULL);
```

After applying a hashing algorithm to create a digest, the hash should be verified before using the related data.

Verifying the Hash

These are steps for verifying a digest that was created using a hashing algorithm.

1. Retrieve the key blob, cipher, and other relevant data persisted by the sender.

2. Request a provider that supports the desired hashing algorithm and key length.

3. Decrypt the cipher and extract the plain data and hash.

4. Recreate the hash from the plain data.

5. Compare the original and newly created digest. If identical, the hash is verified.

The sample code verifies an existing hash.

```c
#define _WIN32_WINNT 0x0400
#include <windows.h>
int main(int argc, char *argv[])
{
    LPTSTR cipher=argv[1];
    DWORD dwBlob, dwEncrypt, dwHash, dwPlain;
    DWORD dwTemp=0;
    HANDLE hCipher=CreateFile(cipher, GENERIC_READ, 0,
        NULL, OPEN_EXISTING, 0, NULL);
    if(hCipher == INVALID_HANDLE_VALUE)
    {
        MessageBox(NULL, "Invalid Cipher File", "Error",
            MB_OK);
        return 0;
    }
    ReadFile(hCipher, &dwBlob, sizeof(dwBlob), &dwTemp,
        NULL);
    BYTE* pBlob=new BYTE[dwBlob];
    ReadFile(hCipher, pBlob, dwBlob, &dwTemp,
        NULL);
    ReadFile(hCipher, &dwPlain, sizeof(dwPlain), &dwTemp,
        NULL);
    ReadFile(hCipher, &dwHash, sizeof(dwHash), &dwTemp,
        NULL);
    ReadFile(hCipher, &dwEncrypt, sizeof(dwEncrypt), &dwTemp,
        NULL);
    BYTE* pEncrypt=new BYTE[dwEncrypt];
    ReadFile(hCipher, pEncrypt, dwEncrypt, &dwTemp,
        NULL);
    CloseHandle(hCipher);
    HCRYPTPROV hProv=NULL;
    HCRYPTKEY hCrypt=NULL, hExchange=NULL;
    DWORD dwP_H=dwEncrypt;
    CryptAcquireContext(&hProv, NULL, MS_ENHANCED_PROV,
        PROV_RSA_FULL, 0);
    CryptGetUserKey(hProv, AT_KEYEXCHANGE, &hExchange);
    CryptImportKey(hProv, pBlob, dwBlob, hExchange, 0, &hCrypt);
    CryptDecrypt(hCrypt, 0, TRUE, 0, NULL, &dwP_H);
    BYTE *pP_H=new BYTE[dwP_H];
    memcpy(pP_H, pEncrypt, dwP_H);
    CryptDecrypt(hCrypt, 0, TRUE, 0, pP_H, &dwP_H);
    BYTE *pPlain=new BYTE[dwPlain];
    BYTE *pHash=new BYTE[dwHash];
    memcpy(pPlain, pP_H, dwPlain);
    memcpy(pHash, &(pP_H[dwPlain]), dwHash);
    HCRYPTHASH hCompare=NULL;
    DWORD dwCompare=0;
    CryptCreateHash(hProv, CALG_MD5, 0, 0, &hCompare);
```

```
CryptHashData(hCompare, (const unsigned char*) pPlain,
    dwPlain, 0);
CryptGetHashParam(hCompare, HP_HASHVAL, NULL, &dwCompare, 0);
BYTE *pCompare=new BYTE[dwCompare];
CryptGetHashParam(hCompare, HP_HASHVAL, pCompare, &dwCompare, 0);
if(memcmp(pCompare, pHash, dwCompare)==0)
    MessageBox(NULL, "Hashes equal", "Success", MB_OK);
else
    MessageBox(NULL, "Tampering Detected", "Failure", MB_OK);
CryptReleaseContext(hProv, 0);
delete pP_H;
delete pPlain;
delete pHash;
delete pCompare;
delete pEncrypt;
return 0;
}
```

This is a detailed review of the program. For brevity, the explanation from previous sample code is omitted here.

1. Retrieve the key blob, cipher, and other relevant data persisted by the sender.

```
HANDLE hCipher=CreateFile(cipher, GENERIC_READ, 0,
    NULL, OPEN_EXISTING, 0, NULL);
if(hCipher == INVALID_HANDLE_VALUE)
{
    MessageBox(NULL, "Invalid Cipher File", "Error",
        MB_OK);
    return 0;
}
ReadFile(hCipher, &dwBlob, sizeof(dwBlob), &dwTemp,
    NULL);
BYTE* pBlob=new BYTE[dwBlob];
ReadFile(hCipher, pBlob, dwBlob, &dwTemp,
    NULL);
ReadFile(hCipher, &dwPlain, sizeof(dwPlain), &dwTemp,
    NULL);
ReadFile(hCipher, &dwHash, sizeof(dwHash), &dwTemp,
    NULL);
ReadFile(hCipher, &dwEncrypt, sizeof(dwEncrypt), &dwTemp,
    NULL);
BYTE* pEncrypt=new BYTE[dwEncrypt];
ReadFile(hCipher, pEncrypt, dwEncrypt, &dwTemp,
    NULL);
```

2. Request a provider that supports the desired hashing algorithm and key length.

```
CryptAcquireContext(&hProv, NULL, MS_ENHANCED_PROV, PROV_RSA_FULL,
    0);
```

3. Decrypt the cipher and extract the plain data and hash.

```
CryptGetUserKey(hProv, AT_KEYEXCHANGE, &hExchange);
CryptImportKey(hProv, pBlob, dwBlob, hExchange, 0, &hCrypt);
CryptDecrypt(hCrypt, 0, TRUE, 0, NULL, &dwP_H);
BYTE *pP_H=new BYTE[dwP_H];
memcpy(pP_H, pEncrypt, dwP_H);
CryptDecrypt(hCrypt, 0, TRUE, 0, pP_H, &dwP_H);
BYTE *pPlain=new BYTE[dwPlain];
BYTE *pHash=new BYTE[dwHash];
memcpy(pPlain, pP_H, dwPlain);
memcpy(pHash, &(pP_H[dwPlain]), dwHash);
```

4. Recreate the hash from the plain data.

```
HCRYPTHASH hCompare=NULL;
DWORD dwCompare=0;
CryptCreateHash(hProv, CALG_MD5, 0, 0, &hCompare);
CryptHashData(hCompare, (const unsigned char*) pPlain,
        dwPlain, 0);
CryptGetHashParam(hCompare, HP_HASHVAL, NULL, &dwCompare, 0);
BYTE *pCompare=new BYTE[dwCompare];
CryptGetHashParam(hCompare, HP_HASHVAL, pCompare, &dwCompare, 0);
```

5. Compare the original and newly created digest. If they are identical, the hash is verified.

```
if(memcmp(pCompare, pHash, dwCompare)==0)
        MessageBox(NULL, "Hashes equal", "Success", MB_OK);
else
        MessageBox(NULL, "Tampering Detected", "Failure", MB_OK);
```

Steps for encrypting and hashing plaintext have been presented. Digital signatures are the remaining pillar of cryptography that has not yet been discussed.

Digital Signatures

Digital signatures authenticate the sender and validate the integrity of the data. These are the steps to creating a digital signature. The steps are nearly identical to those used to create a digest with a hashing algorithm.

1. Get the signature data.

2. Request a provider that supports the desired cryptographic algorithm and key length.

3. Create an asymmetric key pair.

4. Make a key blob to encapsulate the public key of the private/public key pair.

5. Specify the hashing algorithm, create the hash object, and hash the signature data.

6. Retrieve the resulting digest.

7. Sign the digest.

8. Persist the signature and related data.

```c
#define _WIN32_WINNT 0x0400
#include <windows.h>
int main(int argc, char *argv[])
{
    LPTSTR plain=argv[1];
    LPTSTR sign=argv[2];
    HANDLE hPlain=CreateFile(plain, GENERIC_READ, FILE_SHARE_READ,
        NULL, OPEN_EXISTING, 0, NULL);
    if(hPlain == INVALID_HANDLE_VALUE)
    {
        MessageBox(NULL, "Invalid Plain Text File", "Error",
            MB_OK);
        return 0;
    }
    DWORD dwPlain=GetFileSize(hPlain, NULL);
    BYTE *pPlain=new BYTE[dwPlain];
    BOOL bResult=ReadFile(hPlain, pPlain, dwPlain, &dwPlain, NULL);
    CloseHandle(hPlain);
    HCRYPTKEY hCrypt=NULL, hKey=NULL;
    DWORD dwPos=0, dwBlob=0;
    HCRYPTHASH hHash;
    HCRYPTPROV hProv=NULL;
    CryptAcquireContext(&hProv, NULL, MS_ENHANCED_PROV,
        PROV_RSA_FULL, 0);
    CryptGetUserKey(hProv, AT_SIGNATURE, &hKey);
    CryptExportKey(hKey, NULL, PUBLICKEYBLOB, 0, NULL, &dwBlob);
    BYTE *pBlob=new BYTE[dwBlob];
    CryptExportKey(hKey, NULL, PUBLICKEYBLOB, 0, pBlob, &dwBlob);
    DWORD dwSign=0;
    CryptCreateHash(hProv, CALG_MD5, 0, 0, &hHash);
    CryptHashData(hHash, pPlain, dwPlain, 0);
    CryptSignHash(hHash, AT_SIGNATURE, NULL, 0, NULL, &dwSign);
    BYTE *pSign=new BYTE[dwSign];
    CryptSignHash(hHash, AT_SIGNATURE, NULL, 0, pSign, &dwSign);
    HANDLE hSign=CreateFile(sign, GENERIC_WRITE, 0,
        NULL, CREATE_ALWAYS, 0, NULL);
    if(hSign == INVALID_HANDLE_VALUE)
    {
        MessageBox(NULL, "Invalid File to Write Signed Hash",
            "Error", MB_OK);
        return 0;
    }
    DWORD dwTemp=0;
    WriteFile(hSign, &dwBlob, sizeof(dwBlob), &dwTemp,
        NULL);
```

```
WriteFile(hSign, pBlob, dwBlob, &dwTemp,
    NULL);
WriteFile(hSign, &dwSign, sizeof(dwSign), &dwTemp,
    NULL);
WriteFile(hSign, pSign, dwSign, &dwTemp,
    NULL);
delete pPlain;
delete pBlob;
delete pSign;
CloseHandle(hPlain);
CloseHandle(hSign);
CryptReleaseContext(hProv, 0);
}
```

This is a detailed review of the program. The explanation of steps already provided are omitted for brevity.

1. **Get the signature data.** In the sample code, the signature data used for creating the signature is read from a file.

```
HANDLE hPlain=CreateFile(plain, GENERIC_READ, FILE_SHARE_READ,
    NULL, OPEN_EXISTING, 0, NULL);
if(hPlain == INVALID_HANDLE_VALUE)
{
    MessageBox(NULL, "Invalid Plain Text File", "Error",
        MB_OK);
    return 0;
}
DWORD dwPlain=GetFileSize(hPlain, NULL);
BYTE *pPlain=new BYTE[dwPlain];
BOOL bResult=ReadFile(hPlain, pPlain, dwPlain, &dwPlain, NULL);
```

2. **Request a provider that supports the desired cryptographic algorithm and key length.**

```
CryptAcquireContext(&hProv, NULL, MS_ENHANCED_PROV,
    PROV_RSA_FULL, 0);
```

3. **Create an asymmetric key pair.** CryptGetUserKey is invoked to create an asymmetric key. The constant AT_SIGNATURE requests a signature key pair.

```
CryptGetUserKey(hProv, AT_SIGNATURE, &hKey);
```

4. **Make a key blob to encapsulate the public key of the private/public key pair.** CryptExportKey is called to create a key blob that encapsulates the asymmetric key. PUBLICKEYBLOB exports the public key of the private/ key pair.

```
CryptExportKey(hKey, NULL, PUBLICKEYBLOB, 0, NULL, &dwBlob);
BYTE *pBlob=new BYTE[dwBlob];
CryptExportKey(hKey, NULL, PUBLICKEYBLOB, 0, pBlob, &dwBlob);
```

5. **Specify the hashing algorithm, create the hash object, and hash the signature data.**

```
CryptCreateHash(hProv, CALG_MD5, 0, 0, &hHash);
```

6. **Retrieve the resulting digest.**

```
CryptHashData(hHash, pPlain, dwPlain, 0);
```

7. **Sign the digest.** CryptSignHash will sign the hash using the signature key. The first parameter is a handle to the hash object. The second parameter stipulates the type of key. The third parameter is not used and must be NULL. The fourth parameter is an assortment of flags. The final two parameters contain the results—the location where the signed data is written and the size of the buffer. Both are out parameters.

```
CryptSignHash(hHash, AT_SIGNATURE, NULL, 0, NULL, &dwSign);
BYTE *pSign=new BYTE[dwSign];
CryptSignHash(hHash, AT_SIGNATURE, NULL, 0, pSign, &dwSign);
```

8. **Persist the signature and related data.**

Confirming a Digital Signature

Using the digital signature, the recipient can authenticate the identity of the sender. Here are the steps for confirming a digital signature.

1. Retrieve digital signature.

2. Request a provider that supports the desired cryptographic algorithm and key length.

3. Use a hashing algorithm to create a digest from the plaintext.

4. Verify the signature using the newly created digest and the digital signature of the sender.

Here is some sample code.

```
#define _WIN32_WINNT 0x0400
#include <windows.h>
int main(int argc, char *argv[])
{
    LPSTR plain=argv[1];
    LPSTR sign=argv[2];
    DWORD dwTemp=0, dwBlob=0, dwSign=0;
    HANDLE hSign=CreateFile(sign, GENERIC_READ, FILE_SHARE_READ,
        NULL, OPEN_EXISTING, FILE_ATTRIBUTE_NORMAL, NULL);
    ReadFile(hSign, &dwBlob, sizeof(DWORD), &dwTemp,
        NULL);
    BYTE *pBlob=new BYTE[dwBlob];
    ReadFile(hSign, pBlob, dwBlob, &dwTemp, NULL) ;
    ReadFile(hSign, &dwSign, sizeof(dwSign), &dwTemp,
```

```
        NULL);
    BYTE* pSign=new BYTE[dwSign];
    ReadFile(hSign, pSign, dwSign, &dwTemp, NULL) ;
    DWORD dwPlain=0;
    HANDLE hPlain=CreateFile(plain, GENERIC_READ, FILE_SHARE_READ,
        NULL, OPEN_EXISTING, FILE_ATTRIBUTE_NORMAL, NULL);
    dwPlain=GetFileSize(hPlain, NULL);
    BYTE* pPlain=new BYTE[dwPlain];
    ReadFile(hPlain, pPlain, dwPlain, &dwTemp,
        NULL) ;
    HCRYPTPROV hProv;
    HCRYPTKEY hKey;
    HCRYPTHASH hHash;
    CryptAcquireContext(&hProv, NULL, MS_ENHANCED_PROV,
        PROV_RSA_FULL, 0);
    CryptImportKey(hProv, pBlob, dwBlob, 0, 0, &hKey);
    CryptCreateHash(hProv, CALG_MD5, 0, 0, &hHash);
    CryptHashData(hHash, pPlain, dwPlain, 0);
    if(CryptVerifySignature(hHash, pSign, dwSign,
        hKey, "donis", 0))
        MessageBox(NULL, "Signature Verified",
        "Security Notice", MB_OK);
    delete pBlob;
    delete pPlain;
    delete pSign;
    CloseHandle(hSign);
    CloseHandle(hPlain);
    CryptReleaseContext(hProv, 0);
}
```

This is a detailed review of the program. For brevity, previously explained steps are omitted.

1. Retrieve the input used to create the digital signature.

```
HANDLE hPlain=CreateFile(plain, GENERIC_READ, FILE_SHARE_READ,
    NULL, OPEN_EXISTING, 0, NULL);
if(hPlain == INVALID_HANDLE_VALUE)
{
    MessageBox(NULL, "Invalid Plain Text File", "Error",
        MB_OK);
    return 0;
}
DWORD dwPlain=GetFileSize(hPlain, NULL);
BYTE *pPlain=new BYTE[dwPlain];
BOOL bResult=ReadFile(hPlain, pPlain, dwPlain, &dwPlain, NULL);
```

2. Request a provider that supports the desired cryptographic algorithm and key length.

```
CryptAcquireContext(&hProv, NULL, MS_ENHANCED_PROV,
    PROV_RSA_FULL, 0);
```

3. Use a hashing algorithm to create a digest from the plain text.

```
CryptImportKey(hProv, pBlob, dwBlob, 0, 0, &hKey);
CryptCreateHash(hProv, CALG_MD5, 0, 0, &hHash);
CryptHashData(hHash, pPlain, dwPlain, 0);
```

4. Verify the signature using the newly created digest and the digital signature of the sender. CyptVerifySignature confirms the digital signature of the sender. The first parameter is a handle to the hash object. The second parameter is a pointer to the signature. The third parameter is the size of the signature. The fourth parameter is the handle to the public key. The fifth parameter is no longer used and should be NULL. The final parameter is an assortment of flags. If the signature is verified, thus confirming the identity of the sender, CryptVerifySignature returns true.

```
if(CryptVerifySignature(hHash, pSign, dwSign,
        hKey, "donis", 0))
    MessageBox(NULL, "Signature Verified",
    "Security Notice", MB_OK);
```

So far, the foundation in Win32 has been laid using the CryptoAPI. Fortunately, .NET abstracts much of this detail, making it easier to incorporate cryptography into your managed application. Since .NET leverages the Web, cryptography will play an ever-increasing role in application development.

.NET and Cryptography

As evidenced by previous code, the CryptoAPI can be detailed and complicated. The System.Security.Cryptography namespace is an array of managed classes that abstract much of the complexity of including cryptography in application development. System.Security.Cryptography is more than an abstraction of the CryptoAPI. Managed classes that are wrappers for Crypto-API routines have the suffix Provider, such as SHA1CryptoServiceProvider. Managed classes that provide a pure .NET cryptographic implementation end with a Managed suffix, such as SHA256Managed.

The Cryptography namespace is primarily a hierarchy of managed classes, with the upper tiers representing generic and abstract details, while the bottom tier provides the implementation details. Root algorithms are abstract managed classes for asymmetric, symmetric, and hashing routines, which are in the top tier. These classes define common methods used by categories of cryptographic routines. AsymmetricAlgorithm, SymmetricAlgorithm, and the HashAlgorithm class are examples of root algorithms. The next tier of cryptographic classes are the named algorithms, which are derived from root algorithms. Named algorithms represent specific cryptographic routines. For example, DES, RC2, Rijndael, and TripleDES are named algorithms derived from SymmetricAlgorithm. Implementation algorithms are the bottom tier of the Cryptography hierarchy. DESCryptoProvider is an example of a cryptographic implementation class and is derived from System.Cryptography.DES. Figure 7.5 depicts the hierarchy of cryptographic classes in the System .Security.Cryptography namespace.

In .NET, a specific implementation algorithm can be selected, or a default implementation can be requested from a named algorithm class. To select a specific implementation, create an instance of the implementation algorithm class. Alternately, call the Create method on the named algorithm class, and an instance of the default implementation algorithm will be returned.

Default implementation algorithms can be overridden using the machine .config configuration file. Selecting the default implementation algorithm is preferred to creating an instance of a specific implementation algorithm. Creating a specific instance is not extensible and limits an application's ability to integrate future cryptographic routines as they become available or simply to switch algorithms based on changes in preference.

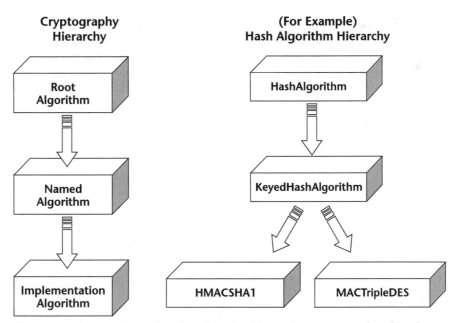

Figure 7.5 For algorithms, there is a three-level hierarchy: root, named, and implementation.

Cryptography is not static. Stronger and more efficient algorithms are published regularly. For this reason, the Create method is the preferred means of obtaining an instance of a cryptographic algorithm. Using the configuration file, an administrator or developer has a code-free method of updating the chosen algorithm.

Cryptography is about transformation. The transformation of plaintext to a hash digest is one such operation. In .NET, CryptoStream is a conduit of cryptographic transformation. CryptoStream is probably the most important class in the cryptography namespace and associates a specific algorithm implementation class with either an input or output data stream. The transformation is between the CryptoStream and a second stream.

CryptoStream

Whether a program is reading from or writing bytes to a CryptoStream, a mutation occurs A second stream is provided to facilitate the transformation. If the mode is CryptoStreamMode.Read, the second stream is the source of the data. If the mode is CryptoStreamMode.Write, it is the target. The stream must be derived from System.IO.Stream. File, memory, and binary streams are examples of valid data streams and can be used with CryptoStream. The secondary stream is stated as the first parameter of the CryptoStream constructor. The mode is listed in the last parameter of the same constructor.

Transform objects are objects that implement ICryptoTransform interface and determine the operation performed on the CryptoStream. The transform object is the second parameter of the CryptoStream constructor. Implementation algorithm classes offer methods that return transform objects, such as the CreateEncryptor and CreateDecryptor methods. CreateEncryptor returns an instance of a transform object that encrypts data.

This is the signature of the CryptoStream constructor:

```
public CryptoStream(Stream stream, ICryptoTransform transform,
    CryptoStreamMode mode)
```

The stream mode does not imply the operation. Write mode does not suggest encryption, and read mode does not hint at decryption. To demonstrate this, two code examples follow. The first encrypts data in Read mode. The second example encrypts data, but uses Write mode.

The first example encrypts plaintext, which is read from a memory stream. The memory stream is initialized with the plaintext. When the CryptoStream object is read, the data is encrypted and a cipher is transferred to a byte buffer.

```
// Example 1
byte [] data=new byte [] {1, 2, 3, 4};
MemoryStream memData=new MemoryStream(data);
RC2CryptoServiceProvider algorithm =
     new RC2CryptoServiceProvider();
CryptoStream stream= new CryptoStream(memData,
     algorithm.CreateEncryptor(algorithm.Key, algorithm.IV),
     CryptoStreamMode.Read);
byte [] cipher=new byte[8];
stream.Read(cipher, 0, (int)8);
memData.Close();
stream.Close();
```

The second example encrypts data written from a byte buffer into a Crypto-Stream object. The data is encrypted during the write. The CryptoStream is wrapped in a binary writer to facilitate writing the plaintext into the stream. After the write, the secondary stream holds the cipher.

```
// Example 2
byte [] numbers=new Byte[] { 1, 2, 3, 4};
MemoryStream inmemory=new MemoryStream();        RC2CryptoServiceProvider
algorithm =
     new RC2CryptoServiceProvider();
CryptoStream estream= new CryptoStream(inmemory,
algorithm.CreateEncryptor(algorithm.Key, algorithm.IV),
     CryptoStreamMode.Write);
BinaryWriter bw=new BinaryWriter(estream);
bw.Write(numbers, 0, numbers.Length);
bw.Close();
```

Configuring .NET Cryptography

As mentioned previously, calling the Create method on a named algorithm class returns the default implementation of that type. Updating or revising the default requires editing the machine.config configuration file. The updated default can be an algorithm from the System.Security.Cryptography namespace or a proprietary algorithm that you developed or purchased from a third-party vendor. Pluggable algorithms make cryptography in .NET highly extensible.

SECURITY ALERT

Cryptography is not static. Using obsolete algorithms increases the likelihood of a successful security attack. Rogue hackers spend their time scheming and plotting new attacks that eventually render existing algorithms ineffectual or trivial. Remaining vigilant and embracing the newest cryptographic algorithms is imperative for building a perimeter that withstands the important test of time.

Machine.config is an XML-based configuration file located in the \%system% \Microsoft.Net\Framework\version#\config subdirectory. .NET configuration files are opened with any text editor or XML parser. Notepad or Visual Studio .NET works well.

NOTE

Machine.config is leveraged by various components of the .NET Framework. A careless insertion or deletion can have dramatic, adverse effects. Most importantly, back up the machine.config file before editing. In addition, do not change anything in the machine.config file without a clear understanding of the impact or repercussions.

Cryptography configuration is found between the <cryptographySettings> paired tags. These tags must be nested within the <configuration><mscorlib> paired tags.

An original machine.config file does not contain any cryptography settings. The initial default algorithms are implied and not explicitly recorded in the configuration file. Changing the default implementation algorithm of a named algorithm requires the following tags.

<cryptographySetting>.   Brackets all cryptographic settings in the machine .config file. It must appear within the <mscorlib> tags.

<cryptoNameMapping>.   Contains two important entries. <cryptoClasses> maps an implementation algorithm to a name available only in the configuration file. <nameEntry> changes the default implementation algorithm of a named algorithm.

<cryptoClasses>.   Holds one or more <cryptoClass> tags.

<cryptoClass>.   Associates a name with an implementation algorithm. This name is only relevant within the machine.config file. These are the attributes of the tag: <cryptoClass configname="classname, assemblyname culture='culture', PublicToken =abcdefgh, Version=1.2.3.4"/>. If the culture is neutral, the culture attribute can be omitted.

<nameEntry>.   Maps a new default implementation algorithm. These are the attributes of the tag: <nameEntry name="named algorithm" class="implementation algorithm"/>. The name attribute is the named algorithm. The friendly name or the managed class is used for this attribute. The friendly name of each algorithm can be found in MSDN documentation. The class attribute uses the name provided in the <cryptoClass> tag.

If ever an example is useful, it is now. The default implementation algorithm of the HashAlgorithm named algorithm is SHA1CryptoServiceProvider. The following code displays "System.Security.Cryptography.SHA1CryptoService-Provider" to a console window.

```
HashAlgorithm algorithm=HashAlgorithm.Create();
Console.WriteLine(algorithm.ToString());.
```

The following fragment from an updated machine.config file changes the default implementation class for HashAlgorithm.

```
<mscorlib>
    <cryptographySettings>
        <cryptoNameMapping>
            <cryptoClasses>
                <cryptoClass
        MD5="System.Security.Cryptography.MD5CryptoServiceProvider,
        MSCorLib, PublicKeyToken=b77a5c561934e089,
        Version=1.0.3300.0"/>
            </cryptoClasses>
            <nameEntry
                name="System.Security.Cryptography.HashAlgorithm"
                class="MD5"/>
        </cryptoNameMapping>
    </cryptographySettings>
</mscorlib>
```

The configuration file names MD5CryptoServiceProvider as the new default for HashAlgorithm. Rerun the preceding code; "System.Security.Cryptography.MD5CryptoServiceProvider" appears in the window.

Cryptographic Parameters

Key containers were discussed earlier in this chapter. CspParameter represents a key container in .NET and a repository of key pairs for asymmetric and digital key algorithms. A CspParameters object, when assigned to a cryptographic provider, provides a location for retrieved keys. CspParameter objects are passed as parameters in the constructor of the implementation class for the algorithm and are only supported by .NET asymmetric providers, such as the RC2CryptoServiceProvider. Randomized container names are generated for asymmetric providers that are not otherwise assigned a CspParameters object.

These are the important members of the CspParameter class:

KeyContainerName.   Name of the container. If the container does not exist, a new container is created and keys are automatically generated.

KeyNumber.   This is an integer value: 1 for AT_KEYEXCHANGE and 2 for AT_SIGNATURE. Each provider sets the most appropriate default. For example, with DSACryptoServiceProvider the default is 2 or AT_SIGNATURE, since AT_KEYEXCHANGE is used for exchanging session keys (for encryption) and DSA does not support encryption.

ProviderName. The string name of the provider. Microsoft Strong Cryptographic Provider and Microsoft Base DSS Cryptographic Provider are examples of provider names.

ProviderType. This is an integer value stipulating the provider type, such as PROV_RSA_FULL. For a full list of provider names and types, review the documentation on CryptAcquireContext of the CryptoAPI.

Flags. This field is an enumerated value: CspProviderFlags.UserMachineKeyStore and CspProviderFlags.UseDefaultKeyContainer. The key container can be machine specific or per user, depending on this flag. UseDefaultKeyContainer is the same as passing a null for the pzContainer parameter to CryptAcquireContext. The container name will be the name of the currently logged on user of the thread.

NOTE
━━━━ Some of the mentioned fields of the PcsParameter class work differently with the RNGCryptoServiceProvider. This provider is dedicated to generating random values for cryptography.

Persistent keys survive the destruction of the related cryptographic provider object and can therefore be reused by other providers. By default, containers created from an explicit key name contain persistent keys. Containers created from randomly generated names are transient and destroyed when the provider object is cleaned up by the garbage collector. The persistence status can be set or altered in the PersistKeyInCsp field of the Cryptographic Provider object. If true, the container is persistent.

Enough information has been provided to begin discussing encryption, decryption, hashing, and creating digital signatures in .NET cryptography. Similarly to the CryptoAPI section earlier in this chapter, the general steps for each of these actions is provided with sample code.

Encryption with .NET

Encrypt and Decrypt Text is an application that accepts plaintext as input, which can then be encrypted and the resulting cipher saved to a physical file. Alternately, the application can decode an encrypted file and display the resulting plaintext in the Plain text box. The application is shown in Figure 7.6.

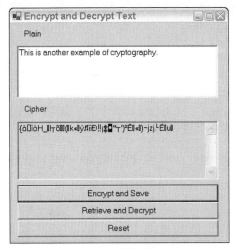

Figure 7.6 A view of the Encrypt and Decrypt Text application.

These are the steps for encrypting plaintext in .NET.

1. Acquire the plaintext.

2. Define the algorithm.

3. Create a CryptoStream class that wraps a data stream.

4. Depending on the CryptoStream mode, read or write from the Crypto-Stream to apply a cryptographic transformation.

5. Persist the key and initialization vector to later decrypt the cipher.

```
private void btnEncrypt_Click(object sender, System.EventArgs e)
{
    FileStream encrypt;
    SaveFileDialog save = new SaveFileDialog();
    if(save.ShowDialog() == DialogResult.OK)
    {
        if((encrypt = (FileStream)save.OpenFile()) == null)
        {
            MessageBox.Show("File I/O error");
            return;
        }
    }
    else
        return;
    MemoryStream memory=new MemoryStream();
    BinaryWriter memorywriter=new BinaryWriter(memory);
```

```
        memorywriter.Write(txtPlain.Text);
        memory.Position=0;


        TripleDES algorithm=TripleDES.Create();
        CryptoStream stream= new CryptoStream(memory,
            algorithm.CreateEncryptor(algorithm.Key, algorithm.IV),
            CryptoStreamMode.Read);
        byte [] cipher=new byte[memory.Capacity ];
        stream.Read(cipher, 0, (int) memory.Capacity);
        char [] temp=new char[memory.Capacity];
        for(int i=0; i<memory.Capacity; temp[i]=(char)(cipher[i++]));
        txtCipher.Text=new String(temp);
        BinaryWriter filewriter=new BinaryWriter(encrypt);
        filewriter.Write(algorithm.Key.Length);
        filewriter.Write(algorithm.Key, 0, algorithm.Key.Length);
        filewriter.Write(algorithm.IV.Length);
        filewriter.Write(algorithm.IV, 0, algorithm.IV.Length);
        filewriter.Write(cipher.Length);
        filewriter.Write(cipher, 0, (int) cipher.Length);
        filewriter.Write(memory.Capacity);
        memory.Close();
        memorywriter.Close();
        encrypt.Close();
        stream.Close();
        filewriter.Close();
    }
```

The following steps apply to the preceding code.

1. **Acquire the plaintext.** The user enters plaintext into a text box on the form.

    ```
    MemoryStream memory=new MemoryStream();
    BinaryWriter memorywriter=new BinaryWriter(memory);
    memorywriter.Write(txtPlain.Text);
    memory.Position=0;
    ```

2. **Define the algorithm.** This application uses TripleDES. Create is called, and the default implementation algorithm is returned.

    ```
    TripleDES algorithm=TripleDES.Create();
    ```

3. **Create a CryptoStream class that wraps a data stream.** The CryptoStream uses a memory stream, which contains the plaintext. CreateEncryptor returns an ICryptoTransform object that encrypts plaintext. The mode is set to CryptoStreamMode.Read. When read from the stream, the plaintext is encrypted.

    ```
    CryptoStream stream= new CryptoStream(memory,
        algorithm.CreateEncryptor(algorithm.Key, algorithm.IV),
        CryptoStreamMode.Read);
    ```

4. **Depending on the CryptoStream mode, read or write from the CryptoStream to apply a cryptographic transformation.** Read the stream into a byte array while encrypting the data.

```
byte [] cipher=new byte[memory.Capacity ];
stream.Read(cipher, 0, (int) memory.Capacity);
```

5. **Persist the key and initialization vector to later decrypt the cipher.** This application writes the key and initialization vector to a file.

```
BinaryWriter filewriter=new BinaryWriter(encrypt);
filewriter.Write(algorithm.Key.Length);
filewriter.Write(algorithm.Key, 0, algorithm.Key.Length);
filewriter.Write(algorithm.IV.Length);
filewriter.Write(algorithm.IV, 0, algorithm.IV.Length);
filewriter.Write(cipher.Length);
filewriter.Write(cipher, 0, (int) cipher.Length);
filewriter.Write(memory.Capacity);
```

Decryption with .NET

Here are steps for decrypting plaintext in .NET. These steps are almost identical to those for encrypting plaintext:

1. Acquire the cipher text.

2. Define the algorithm.

3. Create a CryptoStream class that wraps a data stream.

4. Depending on the CryptoStream mode, read to or write from the CryptoStream to apply a cryptographic transformation.

This is additional sample code from the Encrypt and Decrypt Text application that demonstrates decryption.

```
private void btnDecrypt_Click(object sender, System.EventArgs e)
{
    FileStream encrypt;
    OpenFileDialog open = new OpenFileDialog();
    if(open.ShowDialog() == DialogResult.OK)
    {
        if((encrypt = (FileStream)open.OpenFile()) == null)
        {
            MessageBox.Show("File I/O error");
            return;
        }
    }
    else
        return;
```

```
TripleDESCryptoServiceProvider algorithm =
    new TripleDESCryptoServiceProvider();
BinaryReader filereader=new BinaryReader(encrypt);
int nKeyLen=filereader.ReadInt32();
byte [] key=new byte[nKeyLen];
filereader.Read(key, 0, nKeyLen);
int nIVLen=filereader.ReadInt32();
byte [] iv=new byte[nIVLen];
filereader.Read(iv, 0, nIVLen);
int nCipherLen=filereader.ReadInt32();
byte [] encryptdata=new byte[nCipherLen];
filereader.Read(encryptdata, 0, nCipherLen);
int nMemLen= filereader.ReadInt32();
byte [] byteBuffer=new byte[nMemLen];
MemoryStream memory=new MemoryStream();
CryptoStream stream= new CryptoStream(memory,
    algorithm.CreateDecryptor(key, iv),
    CryptoStreamMode.Write);
stream.Write(encryptdata, 0, nCipherLen);
memory.Position=0;
BinaryReader memoryreader=new BinaryReader(memory);
txtPlain.Text=memoryreader.ReadString();
char [] temp=new char[nMemLen];
for(int i=0; i<nMemLen; temp[i]=(char)(encryptdata[i++]));
txtCipher.Text=new String(temp);
txtPlain.Enabled=false;
}
```

The following comments dissect this code based on the steps for decrypting a cipher. For succinctness, explanations provided previously are not repeated.

1. **Acquire cipher text.** The sample application reads the symmetric key, initialization vector, and encrypted text (cipher) from a file.

```
BinaryReader filereader=new BinaryReader(encrypt);
int nKeyLen=filereader.ReadInt32();
byte [] key=new byte[nKeyLen];
filereader.Read(key, 0, nKeyLen);
int nIVLen=filereader.ReadInt32();
byte [] iv=new byte[nIVLen];
filereader.Read(iv, 0, nIVLen);
int nCipherLen=filereader.ReadInt32();
byte [] encryptdata=new byte[nCipherLen];
filereader.Read(encryptdata, 0, nCipherLen);
int nMemLen= filereader.ReadInt32();
byte [] byteBuffer=new byte[nMemLen];
```

2. **Define the algorithm.**

3. **Create a CryptoStream class that wraps a data stream.** In the Crypto-Stream constructor, CreateDecryptor returns an ICryptoTransform object

that decrypts plaintext. The mode is set to CryptoStreamMode.Write. When written to the stream, the cipher is converted to plaintext.

```
CryptoStream stream= new CryptoStream(memory,
    algorithm.CreateDecryptor(key, iv),
    CryptoStreamMode.Write);
```

4. **Depending on the CryptoStream mode, read or write from the CryptoStream to apply a cryptographic transformation**. The sample application writes the cipher into a byte array while transforming cipher data into plaintext.

```
stream.Write(encryptdata, 0, nCipherLen);
```

Hashing with .NET

Hash Text is an application that first computes and then saves the digest of a file. Figure 7.7 is the user interface of the application.

These are steps for hashing data in .NET. Compared to the steps presented earlier when describing hashing with the CryptoAPI, these steps are refreshingly simple.

1. Retrieve data.

2. Define the algorithm.

3. Compute the hash using a hashing algorithm.

4. Obtain the digest from the hash property of the hash implementation class.

5. Encrypt and then persist the hash.

Here is the relatively sparse code from the HashText application. The application hashes a file and saves the results to another file.

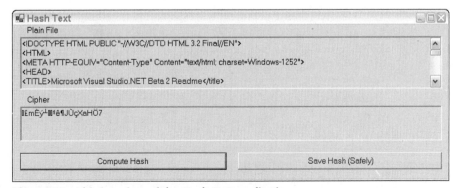

Figure 7.7 This is a view of the Hash Text application.

NOTE
The save code is available on the Web site dedicated to this book.

```
private void btnCompute_Click(object sender, System.EventArgs e)
{
    FileStream file=null;
    OpenFileDialog openfile = new OpenFileDialog();
    openfile.InitialDirectory = @"c:\" ;
    if(openfile.ShowDialog() == DialogResult.OK)
    {
        if((file = (FileStream)openfile.OpenFile())!= null)
        {
        }
            else
        return;
    }
    int filelen=(int) file.Length;
    bytePlain=new byte[filelen];
    if(filelen>32767)
    {
        MessageBox.Show("File to Large");
        return;
    }
    if(filelen == 0)
    {
        MessageBox.Show("File empty");
        return;
    }
    BinaryReader filereader=new BinaryReader(file);
    filereader.Read(bytePlain, 0, filelen);
    file.Position=0;
    char [] plaincharacters=filereader.ReadChars(filelen);
    txtPlain.Text=new string(plaincharacters, 0, filelen);
    SHA1 sha=SHA1.Create();
    sha.ComputeHash(bytePlain, 0, filelen);
    hash=sha.Hash;
    char [] temp=new char[hash.Length];
    for(int i=0; i<hash.Length; temp[i]=(char)(hash[i++]));
    txtDigest.Text=new String(temp);
    filereader.Close();
    file.Close();
}
```

These are the steps for hashing in .NET as applied to the sample code. Repetitive explanations have been excluded.

1. **Retrieve data.**

2. **Define the algorithm.** The sample code selects SHA1, an algorithm that supports hashing.

```
SHA1CryptoServiceProvider sha=new SHA1CryptoServiceProvider();
```

3. **Compute the hash using a hashing algorithm.** ComputeHash, a method of SHA1CryptoServiceProvider, is called to compute the hash from plaintext. The first parameter is a byte array containing the plaintext. The second parameter is an offset in the byte. The hashing algorithm starts at the offset. The final parameter is the number of bytes to hash.

```
sha.ComputeHash(bytePlain, 0, filelen);
```

NOTE

If the offset is zero and the entire byte array is utilized, most methods in .NET are overloaded to accept the byte array as the sole parameter.

4. **Obtain the digest from the hash property of the hash implementation class.** The hash property returns a byte array containing the digest.

```
hash=sha.Hash;
```

5. **Encrypt and then persist the hash.**

Of course, after creating a hash, the next task is to verify the digest and confirm the integrity of the affiliated data.

Verifying a Hash in .NET

Verify Hash is an application that tests a digest and confirms the integrity of data before displaying the contents. From this application, Figure 7.8 shows a successful confirmation of a hash.

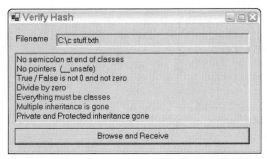

Figure 7.8 A view of the Verify Hash application.

These are the steps to verify a hash; they are similar to the steps for creating the original hash.

1. Retrieve plain data and the original hash.

2. Define the algorithm.

3. Compute the hash using a hashing algorithm.

4. Obtain the digest from the hash property of the hash implementation class.

5. Verify the hash.

Here is the verification code from the Hash Verify application:

```
private void btnBrowse_Click(object sender, System.EventArgs e)
{
    FileStream hashfile=null;
    OpenFileDialog openfile = new OpenFileDialog();
    openfile.InitialDirectory = @"c:\" ;
    if(openfile.ShowDialog() == DialogResult.OK)
    {
        if((hashfile = (FileStream)openfile.OpenFile())== null)
            return;
    }
    txtFilename.Text=openfile.FileName;
    BinaryReader filereader=new BinaryReader(hashfile);
    string key=filereader.ReadString();
    RSACryptoServiceProvider rsa=new RSACryptoServiceProvider();
    rsa.FromXmlString(key);
    MemoryStream plain=new MemoryStream();
    BinaryWriter plainwriter=new BinaryWriter(plain);
    byte [] buffer=new byte[128];
    while(filereader.Read(buffer, 0, 128)!= 0)
    {
        byte [] temp=rsa.Decrypt(buffer, false);
        plainwriter.Write(temp, 0, temp.Length);
    }
    plain.Position=0;
    BinaryReader plainreader=new BinaryReader(plain);
    int lenText=plainreader.ReadInt32();
    byte [] byteText=new byte[lenText];
    plainreader.Read(byteText, 0, lenText);
    int lenHash=plainreader.ReadInt32();
    byte [] byteHash=new byte[lenHash];
    plainreader.Read(byteHash, 0, lenHash);
    MemoryStream textstream=new MemoryStream(byteText);
    BinaryReader textreader=new BinaryReader(textstream);
    char [] plaincharacters=textreader.ReadChars((int)
```

```
        textstream.Length);
txtPlain.Text=new string(plaincharacters, 0, (int)
        textstream.Length);
SHA1CryptoServiceProvider sha=new SHA1CryptoServiceProvider();
sha.ComputeHash(byteText, 0, lenText);
byte [] hash;
hash=sha.Hash;
if(!byte.Equals(hash, byteHash))
{
        MessageBox.Show("Hash matches");
}
        else
            MessageBox.Show("Hash failed");
}
```

Next, the steps are applied to the sample code. For brevity, explanations presented in earlier code snippets are omitted. Except for comparing two hashes, there is almost nothing new in this code. The first five steps are similar to those in previous examples.

1. Retrieve plain data and the original hash.

2. Define the algorithm.

3. Compute the hash using a hashing algorithm.

4. Obtain the digest from the hash property of the hash implementation class.

5. Verify the hash.

```
byte [] hash;
 hash=sha.Hash;
 if(!byte.Equals(hash, byteHash))
 {
        MessageBox.Show("Hash matches");
 }
 else
        MessageBox.Show("Hash failed");
```

The knowledge of creating hashes is sometimes useful when producing a digital signature. Therefore, digital signatures are the next topic.

Digital Signatures in .NET

Sign Data is an application that creates a digital signature, which is saved with the contents of the specified file. The process of creating a digital signature in .NET is trivial. More steps are required to read the data than in the creation of a digital signature. Sign Data is shown in Figure 7.9.

Figure 7.9 The Sign Data application.

These are the steps to create a digital signature.

1. Gather signature data.
2. Define the algorithm.
3. Export the public key of a signature key pair.
4. Call SignData on the implementation algorithm to create the digital signature.
5. Save signature, public key, and other related data.
6. This is sample code from the Sign Data application.

```
private void btnSignSave_Click(object sender, System.EventArgs e)
{
    DSACryptoServiceProvider dsa=new DSACryptoServiceProvider();

    MemoryStream textstream=new MemoryStream();
    BinaryWriter textwriter=new BinaryWriter(textstream);
    textwriter.Write(txtData.Text);
    byte [] signaturedata=textstream.GetBuffer();
    byte [] signature=dsa.SignData(signaturedata);
    string key=dsa.ToXmlString(true);
    FileStream outfile=new FileStream(file.Name+"s",
        FileMode.Create);
    BinaryWriter filewriter=new BinaryWriter(outfile);
    filewriter.Write(key);
    filewriter.Write(signature.Length);
    filewriter.Write(signature, 0, signature.Length);
```

```
filewriter.Write(bytePlain.Length);
filewriter.Write(bytePlain, 0, bytePlain.Length);
MessageBox.Show("Signature saved with file");
textstream.Close();
outfile.Close();
textwriter.Close();
filewriter.Close();
}
```

Next, the steps are applied to the sample code. Redundant explanations are omitted.

1. **Gather signature data.** In the Sign Data application, signature data is read from the form.

2. **Define the algorithm.** The application chooses DSACryptoService-Provider, which supports the creation of digital signatures.

   ```
   DSACryptoServiceProvider dsa=new DSACryptoServiceProvider();
   ```

3. **Export the public key of a signature key pair.** ToXMLString is called on the provider to export the public key into a string. The single parameter is a Boolean. If it is true, the private data of the algorithm is also extracted.

   ```
   string key=dsa.ToXmlString(true);
   ```

4. **Call SignData on the implementation algorithm to create the digital signature.** To create a signature, the SignData method is called on the DSA implementation algorithm. Employing the SHA1 hashing algorithm, SignData creates a hash of the signature data and signs the results. The sole parameter is the signature data, which is a byte array. The resulting digital signature is returned as a byte array.

   ```
   byte [] signature=dsa.SignData(textstream.GetBuffer());
   ```

5. **Save signature, public key, and other related data.**

The final piece to the cryptography puzzle is confirming the signature.

Confirming a Digital Signature in .NET

Confirming a signature in .NET is a simple process. Confirm Signature is an application that confirms a signature from the previous application. If the signature is confirmed, then the file is displayed. The application is shown in Figure 7.10.

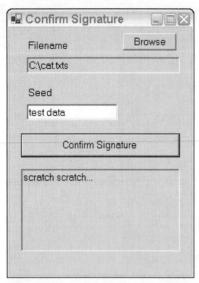

Figure 7.10 The Confirm Signature application.

These are the steps for verifying a signature in .NET:

1. Retrieve the signature, public key, and related information.

2. Define the cryptographic provider and import the key.

3. Call the VerifyData method of the provider to confirm the validity of the digital signature.

This is verification code of the Confirm Signature application:

```
private void btnConfirm_Click(object sender, System.EventArgs e)
{
    BinaryReader filereader=new BinaryReader(file);
    string key=filereader.ReadString();
    int lenSign=filereader.ReadInt32();
    byte [] signature=new byte[lenSign];
    filereader.Read(signature, 0, lenSign);
    DSACryptoServiceProvider dsa=new DSACryptoServiceProvider();
    dsa.FromXmlString(key);
    MemoryStream ms=new MemoryStream();
    BinaryWriter bw=new BinaryWriter(ms);
    bw.Write(txtSeed.Text);
    ms.Position=0;

    if(dsa.VerifyData(ms.GetBuffer(), signature))
        MessageBox.Show("Verified");
    else
    {
        MessageBox.Show("Not verified");
```

```
            txtContent.Text="Not authorized to view";
            return;
        }
        int lenPlain=filereader.ReadInt32();
        char [] plain=new char[lenPlain];
        plain=filereader.ReadChars(lenPlain);
        txtContent.Text=new string(plain);
    }
```

Let us compare the steps to the code in the application.

1. **Retrieve the signature, public key, and related information.** The signature and key are read from a file.

   ```
   BinaryReader filereader=new BinaryReader(file);
   string key=filereader.ReadString();
   int lenSign=filereader.ReadInt32();
   byte [] signature=new byte[lenSign];
   filereader.Read(signature, 0, lenSign);
   ```

2. **Define the cryptographic provider and import the key.** The sample application creates an instance of the DSACryptoServiceProvider. The provider imports the public key using FromXMLString.

   ```
   DSACryptoServiceProvider dsa=new DSACryptoServiceProvider();
   dsa.FromXmlString(key);
   ```

3. **Call the VerifyData method of the provider to confirm the validity of the digital signature.** The first argument of VerifyData is a byte array containing the signature data. The second argument is the signature, also a byte array. VerifyData returns true if the signature is authenticated.

   ```
   if(dsa.VerifyData( ms.GetBuffer(), signature))
       MessageBox.Show("Verified");
   else
   {
       MessageBox.Show("Not verified");
       txtContent.Text="Not authorized to view";
   return;
   }
   ```

What's Next

The next chapter is about customizing the Runtime Security Policy and code access security. The Runtime Security Policy and code access security were reviewed in separate chapters earlier in the book. Many classes were introduced, including permissions, permission sets, code groups, and evidence classes. These classes offered standard objects that addressed general security concerns.

Expanding beyond the usual assortment of objects offers many exciting possibilities. There are many scenarios where customizing security objects could be useful. You can create a new permission that protects a proprietary resource, arrange permission in unique combinations in new permission sets, design code groups offering previously unforeseen categories of code, and test the origin or identity of assemblies using custom evidence.

Despite rumors to the contrary, Microsoft is not omnipotent. Microsoft made .NET security extensible, helping administrators and developers expand the universe of .NET to include a myriad of unique objects. The only limit to .NET security is imagination. Importantly, extensibility means fine-tuning .NET security to solve specific problems with specific solutions.

The challenge of creating custom security objects is achieving the look and feel of a standard object. Your security objects should be well behaved. This requires implementing a host of methods and properties as described in the next chapter. Poorly designed or improperly implemented custom security objects can weaken the overall security of an application. For that reason, custom security objects should be tested and retested.

For those with no interest in custom security objects, the next chapter is nonetheless valuable. In learning about custom objects, you gain important insights into how standard objects are constructed and behave. Anyway, the next chapter is simply fun. We finally get the opportunity to be creative.

CHAPTER

8

Customizing .NET Security

A comprehensive assortment of security objects is available in .NET. Despite this, there are many scenarios where a custom security object might be helpful. First, Microsoft cannot predict the security requirements of every application. Therefore, the predefined security objects represent core requirements of security for most applications. Second, as the universe of sensitive resources widens, the family of objects protecting those resources should also be expandable and thus further the need for custom objects. Third, predefined security objects are static. However, custom security objects can be dynamic, adding another important dimension to protecting a managed application. There are no practical limits to the benefits of custom security objects—only one's imagination.

In .NET, literally everything is customizable, even most security objects, including cryptographic objects, ASP.NET security modules, and more. This chapter focuses on components of the Runtime Security policy, such as code groups, permissions, and Evidence objects. These objects were introduced in the chapter dedicated to the Runtime Security Policy, which is Chapter 3, and are the most visible of all security objects.

The common strategies and techniques for deploying custom security objects are fully demonstrable with the security objects of the Runtime Security Policy. For example, the implementation of the ToXml and FromXml methods for a membership condition permission object is indicative of those methods in any other security object.

Customization of a security object is a detailed proposition. If a picture is worth a thousand words, how valuable is good sample code? The necessity of sample code increases with the complexity of the topic and the difficulty of the code itself. This chapter has plenty of both and an abundance of sample code to help. The primary topics of this chapter are segmented into four topics. First, an overview of a custom object is presented, such as creating a custom code group. Second, the steps for creating the specific custom object are detailed. Third, a scenario is painted where the custom object is deployed. Fourth, sample code from the scenario is presented and explained.

Even those not planning to create a custom object will find this chapter beneficial. An understanding of building custom objects conveys considerable insight—knowledge that is helpful even when writing .NET security with conventional security objects.

Custom evidence, as the most granular of security objects, is a good place to start. At load time, assembly evidence is presented to the common language runtime to categorize assemblies into code groups and grant the appropriate permissions. Evidence, including custom evidence, is published through membership conditions. A review of custom membership conditions follows the details of custom evidence. Membership conditions set membership conditions (naturally) of code groups. For that reason, exploration of custom code groups follows custom membership conditions. Code groups frame assemblies by trust levels. More-trusted assemblies are granted more permissions than less-trusted assemblies. Assigning correct permissions to assemblies is the ultimate goal of the Runtime Security Policy, and custom permissions are the final topic of this chapter.

Custom Evidence

Evidence presented to the common language runtime when an assembly is loaded determines which code groups assemblies are assigned to. Evidence is an array of objects that define the origin or identity of an assembly. Host evidence pertains to the origin of an assembly. Windows Explorer, ASP.NET, and the Windows shell are three de facto hosts in .NET. A URL or application directory object is an example of host evidence. The second type of evidence is assembly evidence and this confers the identity of the assembly. Identity evidence read from the manifest of the assembly includes evidence items such as a strong name and hash.

Host evidence is more trusted then assembly evidence. Untrustworthy assemblies tampering with assembly evidence in an attempt to grab elevated permissions is a security concern. Signing assembly evidence and other techniques are available to make assembly evidence safer. In addition, evaluating assembly evidence along with some host evidence makes the entire proposition safer.

Creating Custom Evidence

Evidence can be anything. There is no specific managed class or interface for evidence. Literally, any managed class is potential evidence. The only requirement is that evidence be serializable.

These are the steps to create custom evidence:

1. Create a strongly named and shared DLL assembly.

2. In the DLL, construct a managed class that supports serialization. In most circumstances, this simply requires adding the SerializableAttribute to the class.

3. Host evidence can optionally inherit the IIdentityPermissionFactory interface. IIdentityPermissionFactory.CreateIdentityPermission creates an identity permission for the evidence object.

4. INormalizeForIsolatedStorage is a second optional interface for evidence classes. Evidence that inherits this interface is used with custom Isolated-Storage classes. For more information, refer to MSDN.

5. To deploy the custom evidence in the Runtime Security Policy, create a membership condition that uses the evidence.

Custom Evidence Scenario

Time is often an important factor in deciding when and whether an application should execute. Time evidence can be used to deny permissions to resource-intensive applications during normal hours, when resources are scarce. Time evidence could also be useful in preventing sequenced applications from executing out of order. Time of execution could also be an important criterion in determining the trust level assigned to an assembly.

Custom Evidence Sample Code

TimeEvidence is custom evidence consisting of a timestamp. Here is the sample code:

```
using System;
namespace TimeEvidence
{
    [Serializable]
    public class Time
    {
        public Time(uint hour, uint minute)
        {
            if((hour>24) || (minute > 60))
                throw new Exception(
                    "Parameters out of bounds.");
            _hour=hour;
            _minute=minute;
        }
        private uint _hour;
        private uint _minute;
        public uint hour
        {
            get
            {
                return _hour;
            }
        }
        public uint minute
        {
            get
            {
                return _minute;
            }
        }
    }
}
```

Other than the serializable attribute, TimeEvidence is a routine managed class and simply a wrapper for time (hour and minute).

Adding Evidence to an Assembly

When an assembly is loaded, the host can contribute evidence known as host evidence. A host is anything that spawns an assembly, such as a parent domain that creates child domains. Theoretically, the host is expected to know the origin of the child assembly and is trusted by the common language runtime to provide that information. Chapter 2, ".NET Security Core Concepts," offers sample code demonstrating a host submitting evidence on behalf of another assembly.

As an alternative to host evidence, evidence can be stored directly in an assembly. This includes custom evidence. Evidence to be included in an assembly must first be persisted to a binary file. Embed binary evidence in an assembly using the assembly generation tool (al.exe) with the evidence option.

These are the steps to persist evidence in a binary format:

1. Define an instance of an initialized evidence object.
2. Create a BinaryFormatter object—found in the System.Runtime.Serialization.Formatters.Binary namespace.
3. Call BinaryFormatter.Serialize to serialize the evidence to a file.
4. From the command line, use the assembly generation tool to merge evidence into the assembly.

Create Evidence is an application that writes time evidence to a binary file. See Figure 8.1.

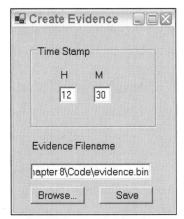

Figure 8.1   A time object, with a timestamp of 12:30, is persisted to evidence.bin file.

In the Create Evidence application, time evidence is saved in the Save button handler. This is the code from that function:

```
private void btnSave_Click(object sender, System.EventArgs e)
{
    try
    {
        TimeEvidence.Time tevidence=new TimeEvidence.Time(
            uint.Parse(txtHour.Text),
            uint.Parse(txtMinute.Text));
        Evidence evid=new Evidence();
        evid.AddAssembly(tevidence);
        BinaryFormatter bf=new BinaryFormatter();
        FileStream fs=new FileStream(txtFilename.Text,
            FileMode.Create, FileAccess.Write);
        bf.Serialize(fs, (object) evid);
        fs.Close();
        MessageBox.Show(
            "Evidence saved to"+txtFilename.Text);
    }
    catch(Exception except)
    {
        MessageBox.Show(except.Message);
    }
}
```

In the sample code, time evidence is created with information gathered in the form. Next a BinaryFormatter is created to convert the evidence to binary, and a file is opened to output the information. BinaryFormatter.Serialize is then called to serialize the evidence to a file.

The sample is a basic assembly where time evidence will be embedded. It is a trivial assembly that only outputs a message to the console. This is source code from the assembly.

```
using System;
class Starter
{
    public static void Main()
    {
        Console.WriteLine("Executing...");
    }
}
```

The following statements, entered at the .NET command prompt, compile Sample.cs into a module and then combine the results with the binary evidence object to formulate an assembly. The final assembly is named Sample.exe and contains evidence of time.

```
csc /t:module sample.cs
al sample.netmodule /target:exe /out:sample.exe
    /evidence:evidence.bin /main:Starter.Main
```

SECURITY ALERT

▬▬▬ **Embedded, or assembly, evidence must be protected from tampering. Use crypto- graphic encryption and hashing algorithms to protect evidence from tampering and confirmation of origin. An example would be to digitally sign the evidence with a private key and verify the authenticity of the signature with the public key.**

Custom Membership Condition

Membership conditions set the membership criteria of a code group. Evidence submitted to the membership condition is checked to approve or deny membership in the applicable code group. Typically, membership is based on a single element of evidence, such as a Web site, URL, or strong name. However, custom membership conditions receive all evidence pertaining to the assembly and can optionally evaluate membership based on several fac- tors. For example, both time and user identity could be submitted as separate evidence to allow the granting of permission to an assembly based on execu- tion time and owner.

The IMembershipCondition.Check method is the heart of a membership con- dition object. It confirms or denies membership. ToXml and FromXml are also important methods. After creating a membership condition, it must be exported to an XML file and then imported into a code group. That is the purpose of the ToXml and FromXml methods.

Creating a Custom Membership Condition

Membership condition objects are the implementation of the IMembership- Condition, ISecurityEncodable, and ISecurityPolicyEncodable interfaces. The implementation IMembershipCondition provides the logic for assessing the membership condition of a code group. ISecurityEncodable and ISecurity- PolicyEncodable offer methods to persist and construct a membership condi- tion from an XML file.

These are the steps for creating a custom membership condition:

1. Create a strongly named and shared DLL assembly.

2. In the DLL, build a managed class for a membership condition that inherits the IMembershipCondition, ISecurityEncodable, and ISecurity- PolicyEncodable interfaces.

3. Membership condition objects must offer a default constructor for creating the object without state information.

4. Implement the IMembershipCondition.Check method. Check accepts assembly evidence as a function parameter. Check evaluates that evidence and returns true if membership is granted. False is returned if membership is denied.

5. Implement the IMembership.Copy method. This method returns a copy of the current membership condition object.

6. ISecurityPolicyEncodable.ToXml returns a SecurityElement object, which contains the state of the membership condition object. SecurityElement is a lightweight XML document.

7. ISecurityPolicyEncodable.FromXml reads a SecurityElement object to update the state of the current membership permission object. Both ToXml and FromXml can be dependent on the policy level.

8. ISecurityEncodable.ToXml is equivalent to ISecurityPolicyEncodable.ToXml minus the policy level. For that reason, ISecurityEncodable.ToXml delegates to ISecurityPolicyEncodable.ToXml, passing a null policy level.

9. Like ISecurityEncodable.ToXml, ISecurityEncodable.FromXml is equivalent to ISecurityPolicyEncodable.FromXml minus the policy level.

10. Export the membership condition to an XML file.

11. Import the membership condition into a code group.

Custom Evidence Scenario

Time was created as evidence in an earlier section. However, the evidence was never integrated into the security policy of .NET—which requires a membership condition. In this section, a membership condition is created that uses time as evidence.

The custom membership condition will locate assemblies scheduled to run after hours but that are attempting to execute during normal hours. These assemblies will be denied permission to execute. Normal hours are considered 8:00 A.M. to 5:00 P.M. The custom membership condition created for this scenario is a perfect example of a dynamic security object. To be effective, the membership condition cannot use static time. Instead, this membership condition uses the current time, which is updated each time the membership condition is evaluated.

Custom Membership Condition Sample Code

The TimeMembershipCondition class implements a custom membership condition. This is code from the class, interspersed with comments. In the default constructor, the date is initialized with the current time:

```
public TimeMembershipCondition()
{
     hour=(uint)DateTime.Now.Hour;
     minute=(uint)DateTime.Now.Minute;
}
uint hour;
uint minute;
```

Most of the heavy lifting for a membership condition is in the Check method. First, all evidence submitted about the assembly is enumerated. Evidence.GetEnumerator returns an enumerator to all evidence. Alternately, Evidence.GetAssemblyEnumerator returns an enumerator to only assembly evidence. Finally, Evidence.GetHostEnumerator returns an enumerator for host evidence.

Several tests are performed in the Check method of this application. If time evidence is located, the timestamp cached in the assembly is extracted. If the timestamp is after 5:00 P.M. but before 8:00 A.M, the assembly is considered an after-hours application. Membership is granted to after-hours applications running during normal hours. The intention is to deny Execute permissions to assemblies that are members of this group and thereby prevent after hours applications from running during normal hours.

```
public bool Check(Evidence evidence)
{
     if(evidence == null)
          return false;
     IEnumerator enumerator=evidence.GetEnumerator();
     while(enumerator.MoveNext())
     {
          if(enumerator.Current is Time)
          {
               Time tm=(Time)enumerator.Current;
               if((tm.hour<8)||(tm.hour>17))
               {
                    if((hour>=8)&&(hour<17))
                         return true;
                    else
                         return false;
               }
          }
     }
     return false;
}
public IMembershipCondition Copy()
{
     return new TimeMembershipCondition();
}
public override string ToString()
```

```
{
    return "Current time:"+hour+":"+minute;
}
```

The ToXml method returns a SecurityElement object. SecurityElement is an abstraction of an XML document and is less complicated than a full-fledged XML document object. ToXml persists the state of the membership condition object to an XML document, beginning with an IMembershipCondition root element. Follow the root element with the class attribute, which contains the namespace and class name of the membership condition object. Call Security-Element.AddAttribute to add the classattribute as a name/value pair to the XML document. Optionally, add an attribute containing the version of the membership condition object. Finally, add attributes that record the unique state of the membership condition object.

The sole argument of ToXml is a PolicyLevel object. PolicyLevel refers to the policy level, such as Enterprise, Machine, User, or Application Domain. When the state of the membership condition varies on policy level, reference the PolicyLevel parameter. Most membership permission objects do not use the policy level argument. Therefore, the sample code ignores the level parameter.

```
public SecurityElement ToXml(PolicyLevel level)
{
    string currentclass=this.GetType().AssemblyQualifiedName;
    SecurityElement se=new
        SecurityElement("IMembershipCondition");
    se.AddAttribute("class", currentclass);
    se.AddAttribute("Version", "1.0.0.0");
    se.AddAttribute("hour", hour.ToString());
    se.AddAttribute("minute", minute.ToString());
    return se;
}
```

FromXml sets the state of a membership condition from a SecurityElement object. As a precaution, a series of tests are performed on the SecurityElement object. First, the identity of the root tag is confirmed, which should be IMembershipCondition. Second, the class type of the current membership condition is compared to the saved type. The types must be identical or an error is reported. If the tests are passed, extract the state information from the SecurityElement object and update the membership condition object.

```
public void FromXml(SecurityElement se, PolicyLevel level)
{
    if(se==null)
        throw new ArgumentNullException("se is null.");
    if(!se.Tag.Equals("IMembershipCondition"))
        throw new ArgumentException(
```

```
                    "Parse Error: invalid se.root tag");
        string classname=se.Attribute("class");
        if(classname == null)
            throw new ArgumentException(
                "Parse Error: invalid se.class attribute");
        string classtype=Type.GetType(classname).ToString();
        if(classtype == null)
            throw new ArgumentException(
                "Parse Error: invalid se.class type");
        string currentclass=this.GetType().ToString();
        if(currentclass != classtype)
            throw new ArgumentException(
                "Parse Error: invalid se.class");
        hour=uint.Parse(se.Attribute("hour"));
        minute=uint.Parse(se.Attribute("minute"));
        }

    public SecurityElement ToXml()
    {
        return ToXml(null);
    }

    public void FromXml(SecurityElement e)
    {
        FromXml(e, null);
    }
```

Using a Custom Membership Condition

Deploying a custom membership condition requires exporting the condition to an XML file and then importing it into a code group.

Test Membership is an application that tests, sets the state, and exports a TimeMembershipCondition object. Data from the form is used to create an instance of time evidence. See Figure 8.2. The time evidence is then used to test the membership condition object.

Figure 8.2 Test Membership both tests and exports the membership condition object.

The relevant code is in the handler for the Test button. An instance of a membership condition and evidence object is created. Evidence.AddAssembly adds Time evidence to the evidence object. The evidence is tested with the IMembershipCondition.Check method and the appropriate message is displayed. At the end, ToXml converts the membership permission object to a SecurityElement object, which is then converted to a string. The Save button saves this string to a file.

```
string xmlcondition;
private void btnTest_Click(object sender, System.EventArgs e)
{
     TimeMembershipCondition mcondition=
          new TimeMembershipCondition();
     Evidence evid=new Evidence();
     evid.AddAssembly(new Time(uint.Parse(txtHour.Text),
          uint.Parse(txtMinute.Text)));
     MessageBox.Show(mcondition.Check(evid)?
          "Passed test":"Failed test");
     xmlcondition=mcondition.ToXml().ToString();
}
```

The next challenge is to import the membership condition into a code group. This will make the membership condition and related evidence part of the security policy. These are the steps to import a membership condition:

1. Open the .NET Framework Configuration tool from the Administrative tools folder in the Control Panel.

2. Expand the applicable policy level in the Runtime Security Policy.

3. Open the Code Group folder and choose New from the context-sensitive menu of the All_Code code group. A wizard appears.

4. From the Identify the New Code Group window, name the new code group and then move to the next pane.

5. The next window is the Choose a Condition Type window, where a custom membership condition is imported. Select custom as the condition type. Click the Import button to import the exported XML file. See Figure 8.3. The membership condition is now attached to the new code group.

6. Move to the final pane, which is the Assign a Permission Set to the Other Group window. Assign the Nothing permission set to prevent after-hour assemblies from executing during normal hours.

7. To test the new policy, execute an assembly that offers time as evidence. Steps in the previous section document how to embed time evidence in an assembly.

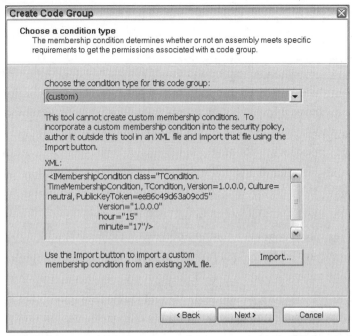

Figure 8.3 The panel for importing a custom membership condition.

Sample and Sample2 are two executables containing time evidence. The time evidence of the Sample assembly is 8:20 P.M. The time saved in Sample2 assembly is 3:20 P.M.. The current time on the computer is 2:40 P.M. Figure 8.4 shows the results of running the two assemblies. As an after-hour assembly, Sample raises an error, since it is not granted permission to run during normal hours. As a normal hours application, Sample2 executes without problems.

Figure 8.4 Output from running Sample and Sample2 assemblies.

Custom Code Groups

Code groups are the essential components of the Runtime Security Policy. The Runtime Security Policy is a hierarchal tree of code groups. Assemblies can belong to one or more code groups and derive permissions from each of these relationships. Membership in a code group is evaluated when an assembly is loaded and is based on meeting membership conditions, which was the focus of the previous section.

Code groups are organized in policy levels: Enterprise, Machine, User, and Application Domain. UnionCodeGroup and FirstMatchCodeGroup are the basic class templates for constructing code groups. UnionCodeGroup objects combine the permissions of a parent node and any child code group where the assembly is a member. FirstMatchCodeGroup objects grant to an assembly the permissions of the first child code group for which membership is permitted. This is called the merge logic.

Differences between standard code and custom code groups are considerable. Standard code groups, such as MY_COMPUTER_ZONE and MICROSOFT _STRONG_NAME, are assigned a membership condition and a permission set. Custom code groups evaluate the membership condition and assign a permission set at run time. This makes custom code groups more flexible than a predefined code group, such as the ability to support dynamic behavior. Custom code groups can implement custom merge logic, or select union or first match assimilation of child permissions.

Creating a Custom Code Group

Custom code groups inherit the CodeGroup managed class. Other code group classes (FileCodeGroup, FirstMatchCodeGroup, NetCodeGroup, and Union-CodeGroup) are sealed and cannot be inherited. CodeGroup.Resolve is the pivotal method of a custom code group. Evidence of an assembly is submitted to Resolve, where the evidence is evaluated to determine membership and, if applicable, any permissions to be granted. Child objects are typically provided an opportunity to comment on the evidence. Their comments are then added to the policy (merge logic). The Resolve method returns a PolicyStatement object. PolicyStatement is a wrapper for a permission set and code group attributes, such as Exclusive and LevelFinal. Exclusive and LevelFinal were described in Chapter 3, "Runtime Security Policy."

These are the steps to implement a custom code group:

1. Create a strongly named and shared DLL assembly.

2. In the DLL, build a managed class for the custom code group. It will inherit the CodeGroup class.

3. Code group must contain a default constructor for creating the object without state information.

4. Implement the CodeGroup.Resolve method. Evidence is passed in as the sole parameter. Enumerate the evidence to determine membership and assign the appropriate permissions. Evidence.GetEnumerator returns an enumerator for iterating each piece of evidence. Next, hand the evidence to each child. The method CodeGroup.Children.GetEnumerator returns an enumerator to all child objects. The parent group enumerates and calls the Resolve method on each child object. Finally, the code group merges its policy with the children. The aggregate policy statement (merge logic) is then returned.

5. Implement the CodeGroup.ResolveMatchingCodeGroups method. Evidence is once again the sole parameter. ResolveMatchingCodeGroups returns an array of code groups—the current code group and any children that would grant membership based on the provided evidence.

6. CodeGroup.CreateXml method is similar to ToXml and accepts Security-Element and PolicyLevel as parameters. Unlike ToXml, this method saves the custom data of the code group object, but not the class type, version, or related information. The implementation of ToXml in the base class saves the common data. If the state of the custom code group is dependent on policy level, reference the PolicyLevel parameter of the method. CodeGroup.ToXml invokes CreateXml in the child object.

7. CodeGroup.ParseXml method is the logical reversal of CreateXml. Parse-Xml also accepts SecurityElement and PolicyLevel objects as parameters. However, the SecurityElement is used to restore the state of the code group object. Only restore proprietary data—common data is handled in the CodeGroup.FromXml method in the base class. CodeGroup.FromXml calls ParseXml in the child.

8. CodeGroup.MergeLogic is a read-only property returning a string that describes the merge logic implemented in the code group.

9. CodeGroup.PermissionSetName is a read-only property, returning a string that describes the permissions offered in the code group.

10. CodeGroup.AttributeString is a read-only property, returning a string that describes the attributes of the code group.

11. Implement the CodeGroup.Copy method, which returns an instance of the object.

Custom Code Group Scenario

An interesting by-product of security policy is that the logic of each customer code group is called whenever *any* assembly is loaded. Anytime and anywhere an assembly is loaded or executed, CodeGroup.Resolve method is called. Of course, the stated purpose is to evaluate membership and granted permission to every assembly. However, developers can be more creative in the Resolve method and implement any behavior.

The sample custom code group provided in this chapter is untraditional and exists to log evidence submitted on behalf on any assembly. A timestamp is recorded with each evidence submission. The evidence submitted to the Resolve method is written to a log file and can be viewed in the Evidence Log tool.

Custom Code Group Sample Code

Log is a managed class derived from CodeGroup. The class logs all evidence submitted by the common language runtime to a predefined filename in the application directory.

This is the required default constructor for the Code Group. The Log managed class has no state information to initialize:

```
public Log() : base(new AllMembershipCondition(),
    (PolicyStatement) null)
{

}
```

Resolve is the heart of any code group. In the following example, a text file is opened for logging. The current time and the number of items of evidence submitted for evaluation is written to the text file. The evidence is then enumerated and the type of each item of evidence is written to the log file. Next, each child is enumerated and asked to resolve the evidence in its context. Since the Log code group is purely for logging, it contains no attributes or permissions. However, the permissions and attributes of the child groups are relevant and returned as the PolicyStatement.

```
string szLog="";
public override PolicyStatement Resolve(Evidence evidence)
{
    if(evidence == null)
        throw new ArgumentNullException("evidence");
    string directory=Environment.GetFolderPath
        (Environment.SpecialFolder.LocalApplicationData);
    string logfilename=directory+@"\evidlog.txt";
    StreamWriter sw=new StreamWriter(logfilename, true);
```

```
szLog=DateTime.Now.ToString()+
    " Items evaluated "+evidence.Count.ToString();
sw.WriteLine(szLog);
IEnumerator enumerator=evidence.GetEnumerator();
while(enumerator.MoveNext())
{
    sw.WriteLine(
        enumerator.Current.GetType().ToString());
}
sw.Close();
PolicyStatementAttribute psattrib=
    PolicyStatementAttribute.Nothing;
PermissionSet pset=new
    PermissionSet(PermissionState.None);
IEnumerator childenumerator=Children.GetEnumerator();
while(childenumerator.MoveNext())
{
    PolicyStatement policy=
        ((CodeGroup)
        enumerator.Current).Resolve(evidence);
    pset.Union(policy.PermissionSet);
    psattrib=psattrib|policy.Attributes;
}
return new PolicyStatement(pset, psattrib);
}
```

ResolveMatchingCodeGroups takes the submitted evidence and confirms membership in this code group or any children. The Log code group is inclusive of all assemblies. The Copy() statement always includes the Log code group in the membership list. The evidence is then offered to the children to evaluate their membership policy.

```
public override CodeGroup ResolveMatchingCodeGroups(Evidence evidence)
{
    if(evidence==null)
        throw new ArgumentNullException("evidence");
    CodeGroup cg=Copy();
    cg.Children=new ArrayList();
    foreach(object child in cg.Children)
    {
        CodeGroup match=(
            (CodeGroup)child).ResolveMatchingCodeGroups(evidence);
        if(match!=null)
            cg.AddChild(match);
    }
    return cg;
}
```

The state of the Log code group is the log string. This is persisted to an XML file in CreateXml and ParseXml.

```
protected override void CreateXml(SecurityElement element,
    PolicyLevel level)
{
    element.AddAttribute("logtext", szLog);
}
```

The remaining methods of the Log code group are self-explanatory.

```
protected override void ParseXml(SecurityElement element,
PolicyLevel level)
{
    szLog=element.Attribute("logtext");
}
public override CodeGroup Copy()
{
    return new Log();
}
public override string MergeLogic
{
    get
    {
        return "Union";
    }
}
public override string PermissionSetName
{
    get
    {
        return "Does not apply permissions.";
    }
}
public override string AttributeString
{
    get
    {
        return
            "Does not use Exclusive or LevelFinal attributes";
    }
}
```

Using a Custom Code Group

Import an XML representation of a custom code group to activate in security policy. The custom code group can be inserted at any policy level and any-where in the hierarchy. Call CodeGroup.ToXml to convert a code group into a

XML document. The following code converts a code group to XML, which is then rendered as a string.

```
string xml=log.ToXml().ToString();
```

Open the .NET Framework Configuration tool to import the custom code group. Select the parent group in which the custom code group is to be inserted as a child. From the context-sensitive menu, pick the New menu item. As shown in Figure 8.5, choose the option Import a Code Group from an XML File. Click the Browse button to select the XML file for the custom code group.

Once installed into the security policy, the Log code group immediately begins tracking evidence as it is submitted to the security policy for evaluation. The results are writing to an evidlog.txt file, which can be viewed in any text editor. In addition, Evidence Log, shown in Figure 8.6, is a viewer for the log file. This tool, including the sample code, is available for download at the Web site dedicated to this book.

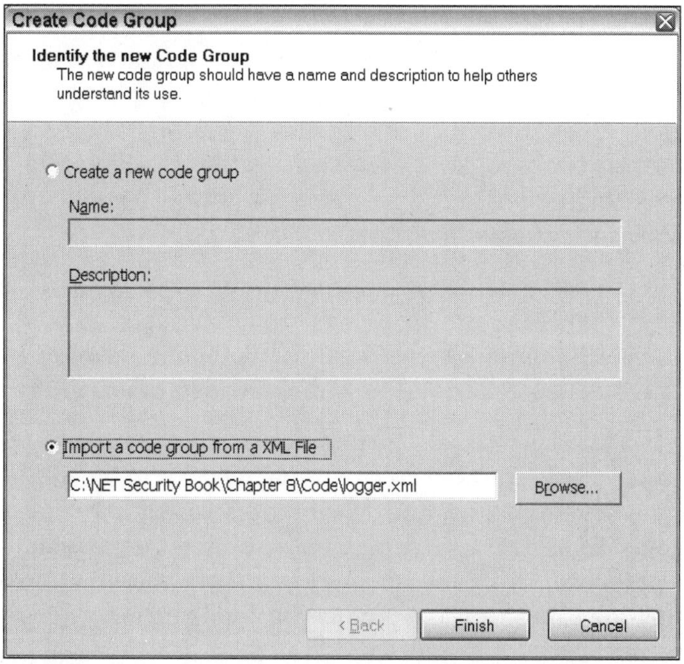

Figure 8.5 Import the XML file for a custom code group to insert into the security policy.

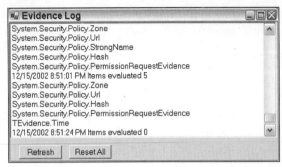

Figure 8.6 Evidence Log list evidence presented to the Runtime Security Policy.

Custom Permissions

Attributing the correct permissions to assemblies based on origin and identity is the ultimate goal of the Runtime Security Policy. The cumulative purpose of evidence, membership conditions, and code groups is to award the correct level of trust to an assembly. The level of permissions granted to an assembly measures trust. Fully trusted assemblies are granted all permissions, while lesser or partially trusted assemblies are assigned lesser privileges. Permissions protect sensitive resource objects, such as files, sockets, and the user interface. Unsafe operations are also protected by permissions, including unmanaged code and the assert permission.

Permissions are not assigned directly to code groups, but are organized into permissions sets. Permission sets are logical grouping of permissions, usually based on trust level. For example, the LocalIntranet_Zone permission set contains suitable permissions for an assembly downloaded from an intranet.

There are myriad reasons to create custom permissions. First, an application may introduce sensitive objects that were unplanned for in the .NET security policy. Second, a vendor may want to distribute a secure library that abstracts unmanaged code. Third, you may want to use a custom permission to extend an existing permission. Finally, the standard permissions are static. Creating a dynamic permission using a custom permission adds capability and flexibility not available otherwise.

When creating a custom permission, three types of permission objects can be considered: Boolean, Flags-based, and Level-based. A Boolean permission is enabled or disabled. If it is enabled, access is granted to the permission. A BankAccountPermission object could grant or deny access to a specific bank account. Flags-based permission is an enumeration of states in which each state can be granted or denied. A DriverPermission object would have a car, motorcycle, bus, airplane, and spaceship flag. Each state could be separately or collectively (unrestricted) allowed or denied. The Level-based permission is also an enumeration of states, except the flags are cumulative. The SecrecyPermission object could offer Top-Secret, Medium, and Unclassified flags. Someone granted the Top-Secret permission would implicitly obtain the permission accorded the Medium and Unclassified flags. The type of permission should be decided before creating the custom permission.

Creating a Custom Permission

Custom Permission must inherit the CodeAccessPermission managed class and implement the IUnrestrictedPermission interface. Build a custom permission class by overriding certain methods of the CodeAccessPermission class and implement other methods of the IUnrestrictedPermission interface.

Permissions can be implemented as a permission or permission attribute class. Permission objects are used imperatively or inline with code. Permission attribute objects adorn methods, classes, or assemblies as attributes. Thus, permission attribute objects must be declared at compile time and are less flexible. Deferring the decision to run time, using a permission object, allows more flexibility in decision making.

These are the steps for implementing a permission object for declarative security.

1. Create a strongly named and shared DLL assembly.

2. In the DLL, create a managed class that inherits the CodeAccessPermission class and IUnrestrictedPermission interface.

3. Implement a single argument constructor, where the sole argument is a PermissionState variable. PermissionState is an enumerated variable and can be assigned the PermissionState.None and PermissionState.Unrestricted values. None grants no access to the sensitive resource. Unrestricted grants full access. Update the state of the permission object to reflect the choice specified.

4. Implement the CodeAccessPermission.Union method. Union offers an IPermission object parameter that is combined with the current permission to create a superset.

5. The CodeAccessPermission.Intersect method is similar to the Union method, except that the intersection of the two permission objects is returned.

6. Implement the CodeAccessPermission.IsSubsetOf method, which also accepts a permission object as a parameter. If the incoming permission is a logical or physical subset of the current permission, return true. Otherwise, return false. BankSavingsAccount and BankCheckingAccount permissions might be considered the subset of a BankingPermission object.

7. The CodeAccessPermission.Copy method returns an instance of the current permission object.

8. A CodeAccessPermission.ToXml and CodeAccessPermission.FromXml method must be created for the custom permission class. The purpose and implementation are identical to the same functions mentioned in earlier custom objects. Both methods use a SecurityElement object as a lightweight XML document to save and retrieve a permission object. The sole deviation from previous code is naming the root element IPermission. This is followed by the class name, version number, and state information of the object, written as name/value pairs into the XML document.

9. The final method to implement is IUnrestrictedPermission.IsUnrestricted. IsUnrestricted returns true if full access to the sensitive resource is granted.

10. Once the XML version of the permission object is imported into the security policy, it is available for use.

Implementing a declarative version or attribute version of a permission requires many fewer steps then imperative security. Here are the steps:

1. Create a serializable managed class for the permission attribute. The class inherits the CodeAccessPermissionAttribute class.

2. The developer decides where the custom permission attribute can be used. Some permission attributes are reserved for classes, while other attributes can decorate anything. The AttributeUsage attribute describes where the permission attribute can be applied. For this reason, all permission attributes should be prefixed with the AttributeUsage attribute.

3. Provide a single argument constructor. The sole parameter is a SecurityAction parameter. SecurityAction is an enumerated value that describes the action desired. Actions include SecurityAction.Demand, SecurityAction.Assert, SecurityAction.Deny, SecurityAction.InheritanceDemand, and many more.

4. Implement the CodeAccessPermissionAttribute.CreatePermission method. CreatePermission returns an instance of the underlying permission object cloned from the state of the permission attribute.

Custom Permission Scenario

I am presently implementing a managed library for the Win32 security APIs. The library will be available to developers wanting to integrate Win32 security concepts, such as security descriptors, SACL, DACL, ACEs, access tokens, and so on, in their .NET applications.

Win32 security APIs are extremely dangerous. First, Win32 security APIs are native or unmanaged code, and not trusted for good reason. Second, the native security APIs are quite powerful and should not be granted blindly to all assemblies. For these reasons, the Win32 Security Library will be deployed with a variety of custom permissions protecting different resources and tasks. An access token is the most commonly used construct in Win32 security and is a primary candidate for protection.

The token permission is implemented both as a permission and permission object attribute. Therefore, it can be used imperatively and declaratively. In the token managed class, the token permission will be demanded to enforce the security policy. This protects security-neutral assemblies from inappropriate use of the token object by lesser-trusted callers.

Custom Permission Sample Code

TokenPermission is designed to protect an access token. This permission is a Boolean permission. True grants access to the token permission, while false denies usage. The state of the permission object is kept in the _granted variable. The TokenPermissionAttribute managed class follows the TokenPermission and is the attribute class of the token permission. The final class provided in this scenario is the token class. The token class is a wrapper for an access token. The TokenPermission, TokenPermissionAttribute, and Token class are contained in the same library.

This is the token permission sample code interspersed comments. TokenPermission offers two constructors. The first constructor maps PermissionState.Unrestricted to full access and PermissionState.None to no access.

```
public class TokenPermission: CodeAccessPermission,
    IUnrestrictedPermission
{
    public TokenPermission(PermissionState state)
    {
        if(state==PermissionState.Unrestricted)
            _granted=true;
        else
            _granted=false;
    }
```

```
    public TokenPermission(bool grant)
    {
         _granted=grant;
    }
     public TokenPermission()

{

             granted=false;
        }
```

IPermission.Union merges the incoming permission, OtherPermission, with the current permission. Several tests are performed in this method. First, the types of both permissions are compared. If the permissions are not similar objects, an exception is thrown. If the permission objects are similar and either is granted access to the token object (true), the combined state is Permission-State.Unrestricted. Otherwise, the combined state is PermissionState.None.

```
    public override IPermission Union(IPermission
        otherPermission)
    {
        if(GetType()==otherPermission.GetType())
        {
            if((granted==true) ||
                    ((TokenPermission)
                    otherPermission).granted==true)
                return new
                    TokenPermission(
                    PermissionState.Unrestricted);
            else
                return new
                    TokenPermission(
                    PermissionState.None);
        }
        else
            throw new ArgumentException(
                "Must be TokenPermission permission");
    }
```

Intersect is similar to the Union method. The difference is in the comparison of the two permission objects. If the permission objects are similar and either denies access to the token object (false), the combined state is Permission-State.None. Otherwise, the combined state is PermissionState.Unrestricted.

```
    public override IPermission Intersect(IPermission
        otherPermission)
    {
        if(otherPermission==null)
            return Copy();
        if(GetType()==otherPermission.GetType())
        {
```

```
        if((granted==false) ||
                ((TokenPermission)
                otherPermission).granted==false)
            return new
                TokenPermission(
                PermissionState.None);
        else
            return new
                TokenPermission(
                PermissionState.Unrestricted);
        }
    else
        throw new ArgumentException(
            "Must be TokenPermission permission");
}
```

IsSubsetOf compares two permission objects. If the incoming permission is a
subset of the current permission, true is returned. In the security policy,
nothing is a subset of the token permission. For this reason, in the sample code,
true is returned only when the incoming and current permissions are of the
same type.

```
public override bool IsSubsetOf(IPermission otherPermission)
{
    if(otherPermission==null)
        return !granted;
    else if(GetType()==otherPermission.GetType())
        return true;
    else
        return false;
}
```

The Copy, ToXml, and FromXml methods are similar to the identical methods
in earlier sample code:

```
public override IPermission Copy()
{
    if(granted)
        return new TokenPermission(
            PermissionState.Unrestricted);
    else
        return new TokenPermission(
            PermissionState.None);
}
public override SecurityElement ToXml()
{
    string currentclass=
        this.GetType().AssemblyQualifiedName;
    SecurityElement se=new
        SecurityElement("IPermission");
```

```
            se.AddAttribute("class", currentclass);
            se.AddAttribute("Version", "1.0.0.0");
            se.AddAttribute("Granted", granted.ToString());
            return se;
        }
        public override void FromXml(SecurityElement se)
        {
            if(se==null)
                throw new ArgumentNullException("se is null.");
            if(!se.Tag.Equals("IPermission"))
                throw new ArgumentException(
                    "Parse Error: invalid interface");
            string classname=se.Attribute("class");
            if(classname == null)
                throw new ArgumentException(
                    "Parse Error: invalid se.class attribute");
            string classtype=Type.GetType(classname).ToString();
            if(classtype == null)
                throw new ArgumentException(
                    "Parse Error: invalid se.class type");
            string currentclass=this.GetType().ToString();
            if(currentclass != classtype)
                throw new ArgumentException(
                    "Parse Error: invalid se.class");
            if(se.Attribute("Granted")=="true")
                _granted=true;
            else
                _granted=false;
        }
```

The IsUnrestricted method returns true if the Boolean state (_granted) is true. Otherwise, false is returned.

```
        public bool IsUnrestricted()
        {
            return _granted;
        }
        private bool _granted=false;
        public bool granted
        {
            get
            {
                return _granted;
            }
        }
    }
```

The TokenPermissionAttribute managed class follows next. The class is preceded with the AttributeUsage attribute to list where the TokenPermissionAttribute attribute can be used.

```
[AttributeUsage(AttributeTargets.Method |
AttributeTargets.Constructor |
AttributeTargets.Class | AttributeTargets.Struct |
AttributeTargets.Assembly, AllowMultiple = true,
Inherited=false)]
[Serializable]
sealed public class TokenPermissionAttribute:
CodeAccessSecurityAttribute
{
    public TokenPermissionAttribute(SecurityAction action)
        : base(action)
    {

    }
```

The one argument constructor implements the requested security action by invoking the same constructor in the base class. CodeAccessSecurityAttribute contains an appropriate implementation. For that reason, the constructor simply delegates to the base class.

CreatePermission returns an instance of a TokenPermission:

```
public override IPermission CreatePermission()
{
    return new TokenPermission(_granted);
}
private bool _granted=false;
public bool granted
{
    get
    {
        return _granted;
    }
}
}
```

Using a Custom Permission

Import an XML representation of a permission object into a permission set to include in the security policy. The following code creates a file containing the XML representation of the token permission. The permission can now be imported and deployed in the security policy.

```
TokenPermission perm=new TokenPermission(false);
string xmlPermission=perm.ToXml().ToString();
StreamWriter sw=new StreamWriter(filename);
sw.Write(xmlPermission);
sw.Close();
```

Custom permissions are imported into a permission set. Assign the permission set to a new or existing code group to add the custom permission to the security policy. Here are the steps to import a custom permission:

1. Open the Microsoft .NET Framework Configuration tool.

2. Select the Permission Set folder in the policy level where the custom permission will be used.

3. From the context-sensitive menu of the Permission Set folder, choose the New menu item. The Create Permission Set wizard appears.

4. Enter the name of the permission set in the first screen and then move to the next screen.

5. From the Assign Individual Permission to Permission Set window, click the Import button to import the XML file of a custom permission. See Figure 8.7.

6. As demonstrated in the Token class, the permission is ready it integrate into a managed application as part of the security policy infrastructure.

NOTE You will need to add the assembly containing the permission to the list of Policy Assemblies for the level.

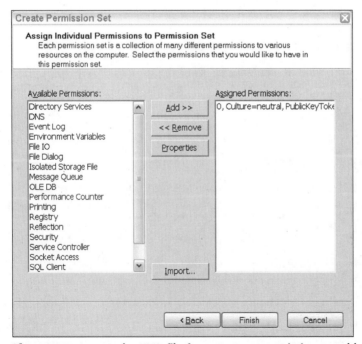

Figure 8.7 Import the XML file for a custom permission to add the permission to the security policy.

We are now prepared to create a Token class that leverages the token permission. The Token class abstracts two native calls: LogonUser and CloseHandle. DllImport is used to import a reference to both functions.,LogonUser has two parameters, where the credentials of the user are inputted, and returns a handle to an authenticated token. CloseHandle invalidates a handle and lowers the outstanding references on the related object. Authentication is performed in the Token.SetToken method.

Importantly, at the beginning of this method a TokenPermission is created and demanded to protect access to an access token. This narrows the protection specifically to the token, which is the sensitive resource, and not unmanaged code in general. Token.SetToken is callable directly as a public method or indirectly from the two-argument constructer, where credentials are also submitted.

This is the code from the Token class:

```
[SuppressUnmanagedCodeSecurityAttribute()]
public class Token
{
    public Token()
    {
    }
    public Token(string _username, string _password)
    {
        SetToken(_username, _password);
    }
    ~Token()
    {
        CloseHandle(_hToken);
    }
    [DllImport("Advapi32.dll")]
    public static extern bool LogonUser(
        string Username,
        string Domain,
        string Password,
        System.Int32 dwLogonType,
        System.Int32 dwLogonProvider,
        ref IntPtr phToken);
    [DllImport("Kernel32.dll")]
    public static extern bool CloseHandle(
        IntPtr hObject);
    public void SetToken(string _username, string _password)
    {
        TokenPermission permission=new TokenPermission(true);
        permission.Demand();

        if((_username==null) || (_password==null))
            throw new ArgumentNullException(
                "Invalid username or password");
```

```
        if(_hToken != IntPtr.Zero)
                return;
        username=_username;
        password=_password;
        bool resp=LogonUser(username, "", password,
                LOGON32_LOGON_NETWORK,
                LOGON32_PROVIDER_DEFAULT,
                ref _hToken);
        if(resp==false)
                throw new Exception("Authentication failed");
    CodeAccessSecurity.RevertAssert();
}
private string username=null;
private string password=null;
private const int LOGON32_LOGON_NETWORK=3;
private const int LOGON32_PROVIDER_DEFAULT=0;
private const int TOKEN_TYPE=8;
private IntPtr _hToken=IntPtr.Zero;
public IntPtr hToken
{
    get
    {
        return _hToken;
    }
}
```

The token object is ready to be deployed. Here is code that uses the token and token permission attribute. If constructed correctly, the TokenPermission can be used as easily as a standard permission. All the hard work and code used to create the custom permission should be transparent.

```
class Class1
{
    [STAThread]
    [TokenPermission(SecurityAction.Deny)]
    static void Main(string[] args)
    {
        Token thetoken=new Token("ovid", "1260");
        IntPtr hToken=thetoken.hToken;
    }
}
```

Using the TokenPermissionAttribute, the preceding code denies the Token permission to the Main method. When the Token, with credentials, is created inside the Main method, an implicit demand for the TokenPermission occurs from the SetToken method and an exception is triggered. Remember, Main is denied this permission. The sample code effectively tests both the TokenPermission and TokenPermissionAttribute classes. Figure 8.8 shows the exception incurred when the application is run.

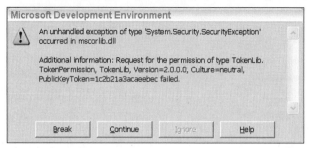

Figure 8.8 This error message confirms that the TokenPermission and attribute are working correctly.

What's Next

The final two chapters of the book are an overview of the System.Security and System.Security.Permissions namespaces. The System.Security namespace is the base namespace of .NET security and includes important classes, such as the PermissionSet, SecurityManager, SecurityException, and other classes. The System.Security.Permissions namespace is the interface for creating and managing permissions. This namespace consists mainly of the predefined permissions used in the Runtime Security Policy. These are the two most important security namespaces in .NET security.

The continued motto in this book is that more sample code is better. The next two chapters offer an abundance of code snippets to clarify important concepts and demonstrate implementation details.

System.Security Namespace

S ystem.Security is the base namespace of .NET security. This namespace has the core class interfaces and base classes to key components of .NET security. In addition, System.Security aggregates other key namespaces of .NET security—see Figure 9.1. The only exception is System.Web.Security, which is a separate namespace. Chapter 6, "ASP.NET Security," describes components of the System.Web.Security namespace.

Classes in the System.Security Namespace

An explanation of each class in the System.Security namespace follows. For brevity, some methods and properties are omitted from the descriptions.

CodeAccessPermission

CodeAccessPermission is the base class for most permissions objects, such as FileIOPermission and SocketPermission. The notable exception is the PrincipalPermission object, which is not inherited from this class. CodeAccessPermission is an abstract class and cannot be instantiated independently. Methods of CodeAccessPermission include:

CodeAccessPermission.Assert.   Assert exempts callers from demands of specific permissions. This short-circuits the stack walk and access to related resources is granted.

```
public void Assert().
```

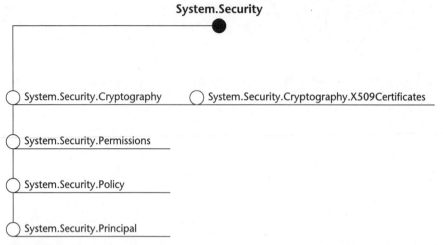

Figure 9.1 The System.Security namespace and nested namespaces.

CodeAccessPermission.Copy. This method duplicates the current permission object.

```
public abstract IPermission Copy().
```

CodeAccessPermission.Demand. This method forces an immediate stack walk seeking the specified permissions. Callers not granted the sought permissions throw a SecurityException.

```
public void Demand()
```

CodeAccessPermission.Deny. This method blocks access to secured resources by denying specified permissions to called (upstream) functions.

```
public void Deny()
```

CodeAccessPermission.FromXml. This method initializes a permission object using XML that is retrieved from a security element object.

```
public abstract void FromXml(SecurityElement elem)
```

CodeAccessPermission.Intersect. This method intersects the current permission object with another. The resulting permission object holds the permissions common to both.

```
public abstract IPermission Intersect(IPermission target)
```

CodeAccessPermission.IsSubsetOf. This method tests the current permission as a subset of another permission object.

```
public abstract bool IsSubsetOf(IPermission target)
```

CodeAccessPermission.PermitOnly. PermitOnly lists those permissions that are allowed in called (upstream) functions. Called functions have access to resources granted by the designated permissions.

```
public void PermitOnly()
```

CodeAccessPermission.RevertAll. This method removes any Assert, Deny, or PermitOnly that is pending on the stack. Only one Assert, Deny, or PermitOnly command can be pending. Issuing a second identical command raises an exception. The pending command must be reverted first.

```
public static void RevertAll()
```

CodeAccessPermission.RevertAssert. This method reverts a pending Assert only.

```
public static void RevertAssert()
```

CodeAccessPermission.RevertDeny. This method reverts a pending Deny only.

```
public static void RevertDeny()
```

CodeAccessPermission.RevertPermitOnly. This method reverts a pending PermitOnly only.

```
public static void RevertPermitOnly()
```

CodeAccessPermission.ToXml. This method converts a permission object into XML, which is cached in a SecurityElement object.

```
public abstract SecurityElement ToXml()
```

CodeAccessPermission.Union. This method combines the permissions of the current object with another. The returned permission contains the permissions of both principals. Demands on the returned permission are treated as an *or* condition. For example, Principal Permission A and B are combined with the Union method. The result is Principal Permission C. Demands on Principal Permission C succeed if the current principal is A or B.

```
public virtual IPermission Union(IPermission other)
```

NamedPermissionSet

A permission set groups one or more permissions. Named permissions sets are predefined in the Runtime Security Policy and are instances of the NamedPermissionSet class. NamedPermissionSet is sealed and cannot be inherited by another class. Methods of the Named PermissionSet include:

NamedPermissionSet.AddPermission. This method adds a permission to the permission set. Combines that permission and with any other permission of the same type that already exists in the permission set.

```
public virtual IPermission AddPermission(IPermission perm)
```

NamedPermissionSet.Assert.   Assert exempts callers from demands of specific permissions found in a permission set. This short-circuits the stack walk and access to related resources is granted.

```
public virtual void Assert()
```

NamedPermissionSet.ContainsNonCodeAccessPermissions.   If the permission set contains a permission that is not derived from CodeAccessPermission, this methods returns false.

```
public bool ContainsNonCodeAccessPermissions()
```

NamedPermissionSet.Copy.   This methodDuplicates the current named permission set object.

```
public override PermissionSet Copy();
public NamedPermissionSet Copy(string);
```

NamedPermissionSet.CopyTo.   This method copies the permission objects of a permission set into an array, beginning at index.

```
public virtual void CopyTo(Array array, int index)
```

NamedPermissionSet.Demand.   This method forces an immediate stack walk of each permission in the permission set. Callers not granted any of the contained permissions raise a SecurityException.

```
public virtual void Demand()
```

NamedPermissionSet.Deny.   This method blocks access to secured resources by denying specified permissions from a permission set to called (upstream) functions.

```
public virtual void Deny()
```

NamedPermissionSet.FromXml.   This method initializes a permission set using XML that is retrieved from a security element object.

```
public abstract void FromXml(SecurityElement elem)
```

NamedPermissionSet.GetEnumerator.   This method returns an enumerator to the permissions in the permission set.

```
public virtual IEnumerator GetEnumerator();
```

NamedPermissionSet.GetPermission.   This method returns a permission object of the specified type, if it exists in the permission set.

```
public virtual IPermission GetPermission(Type permClass)
```

NamedPermissionSet.Intersect.   This method intersects the current permission set object and another. The resulting permission object set holds the common permissions of both.

```
public virtual PermissionSet Intersect(PermissionSet other)
```

NamedPermissionSet.IsEmpty.   IsEmpty returns false if permission set contains one or more permissions.

```
public virtual bool IsEmpty()
```

NamedPermissionSet.IsSubsetOf.   For this method, a subset is defined as the target permission set containing every permission of the current permission set. If the current permission set is a subset of the target, this method returns true.

```
public virtual bool IsSubsetOf(PermissionSet target)
```

NamedPermissionSet.IsUnrestricted.   If a permission set is unrestricted, this method returns true.

```
Public virtual bool IsUnrestricted()
```

NamedPermissionSet.PermitOnly.   PermitOnly permits only those permissions of the permission set to be granted to called functions. Called (upstream) functions only have access to resources granted by the designated permissions.

```
public virtual void PermitOnly()
```

NamedPermissionSet.RemovePermission.   This method removes a permission object of a specific type from a permission set.

```
public virtual IPermission RemovePermission(Type permClass)
```

NamedPermissionSet.SetPermission.   While AddPermission combines the attributes of matching permissions, SetPermission replaces the matching permission in the permission set.

```
public virtual IPermission SetPermission(IPermission perm)
```

NamedPermissionSet.ToXml.   This method converts a permission set into XML, which is then cached in a SecurityElement object.

```
public override SecurityElement ToXml()
```

NamedPermissionSet.Union.   This method combines the permissions of the current permission set object with another. The returned permission set contains the permissions of both.

```
public virtual PermissionSet Union(PermissionSet other)
```

NamedPermissionSet.Count.   This method provides the number of permissions in the permission set.

```
public virtual int Count {get;}
```

NamedPermissionSet.Description.   This method gets and sets the description of a permission set.

```
public string Description {get; set;}
```

NamedPermissionSet.Name.   This method gets and sets the name of a permission set.

```
public string Name {get; set;}
```

PermissionSet

A permission set groups one or more permissions. PermissionSet is the base class of the NamedPermissionSet. Methods of the PermissionSet include:

PermissionSet.AddPermission.   This method adds a permission to the permission set. It combines that permission and with any other permission of the same type that already exists in the permission set.

```
public virtual IPermission AddPermission(IPermission perm)
```

PermissionSet.Assert.   Assert exempts callers from the demands of specific permissions found in a permission set. This short-circuits the stack walk, and access to related resources is granted.

```
public virtual void Assert()
```

PermissionSet.ContainsNonCodeAccessPermissions.   If a permission set contains a permission that is not derived from CodeAccessPermission, this methods returns false.

```
public bool ContainsNonCodeAccessPermissions()
```

PermissionSet.Copy.   This method duplicates the current named permission set object.

```
public override PermissionSet Copy();
public PermissionSet Copy(string);
```

PermissionSet.CopyTo.   This method copies the permission objects of a permission set into an array, beginning at index.

```
public virtual void CopyTo(Array array, int index)
```

PermissionSet.Demand.   This method forces an immediate stack walk of each permission in the permission set. Callers not granted any of the contained permissions raise a SecurityException.

```
public virtual void Demand()
```

PermissionSet.Deny.   This method blocks access to secured resources by denying specified permissions from a permission set to called (upstream) functions.

```
public virtual void Deny()
```

PermissionSet.FromXml.   This method initializes a permission set using XML that is retrieved from a security element object.

```
public virtual void FromXml(SecurityElement se)
```

PermissionSet.GetEnumerator.   This method returns an enumerator to the permissions in the permission set.

```
public virtual IEnumerator GetEnumerator()
```

PermissionSet.GetPermission.   This method returns a permission object of the specified type if it exists in the permission set.

```
public virtual IPermission GetPermission(Type permClass)
```

PermissionSet.Intersect.   This method intersects the current permission set object and another. The resulting permission object set holds the common permissions of both.

```
public virtual PermissionSet Intersect(PermissionSet other)
```

PermissionSet.IsEmpty.   IsEmpty returns false if permission set contains one or more permissions.

```
public virtual bool IsEmpty()
```

PermissionSet.IsSubsetOf.   For this method, a subset is defined as the target permission set containing all the permissions of the current permission set. If the current permission set is a subset of the target, this method returns true.

```
public virtual bool IsSubsetOf(PermissionSet target)
```

PermissionSet.IsUnrestricted.   If a permission set is unrestricted, this method returns true.

```
public virtual bool IsUnrestricted()
```

PermissionSet.PermitOnly.   PermitOnly permits only those permissions of the permission set to be granted to called functions. Called (upstream) functions only have access to resources granted by the designated permissions.

```
public virtual void PermitOnly()
```

PermissionSet.RemovePermission.   This method removes a permission object of a specific type from a permission set.

```
public virtual IPermission RemovePermission(Type permClass)
```

PermissionSet.SetPermission.   While AddPermission combines the attributes of matching permissions, SetPermission replaces the matching permission in the permission set.

```
public virtual IPermission SetPermission(IPermission perm)
```

PermissionSet.ToXml.   This method converts a permission set into XML, which is then cached in a SecurityElement object.

```
public virtual SecurityElement ToXml()
```

PermissionSet.Union.   This method combines the permissions of the current permission object with another. The returned permission contains the permissions of both.

```
public virtual PermissionSet Union(PermissionSet other)
```

PermissionSet.Count. This method provides the number of permissions in the permission set.

```
public virtual int Count {get;}
```

SecurityElement

The SecurityElement is a specialty XML document object model for .NET Security. It does not have the functionality of the generic XML document object model. The XML of a .NET security object can be cached and manipulated as part of a SecurityElement object. Methods of the SecurityElement include:

SecurityElement.AddAttribute. This method adds a name/value attribute to the current element.

```
public void AddAttribute(string name, string value)
```

SecurityElement.AddChild. This method adds a child tag to the existing element.

```
public void AddChild(SecurityElement child)
```

SecurityElement.Attribute. This method locates an attribute and returns its corresponding value.

```
public string Attribute(string name)
```

SecurityElement.Escape. This method removes invalid XML characters and substitutes a correct escape sequence.

```
public static string Escape(string str)
```

SecurityElement.IsValidAttributeName. This method tests a proposed attribute name. If it is valid, true is returned and the name can be added to the security element.

```
public static bool IsValidAttributeName(string name)
```

SecurityElement.IsValidAttributeValue. This method tests a proposed value. If it is valid, true is returned and the value can be added to the security element.

```
public static bool IsValidAttributeValue(string name)
```

SecurityElement.IsValidTag. This method tests the proposed value of a tag. If valid, true is returned and the value can be added to the security element.

```
public static bool IsValidTag(string tag)
```

SecurityElement.IsValidText. This method tests the appropriateness of text as a value between paired tags. If the result is valid, true is returned and the value can be added to the security element.

```
public static bool IsValidText(string text)
```

NOTE Use the methods IsValidAttributeName, IsValidAttributeValue, IsValidTag, and IsValid-Text to test an item before adding it to a security element.

SecurityElement.SearchForChildByTag. This method searches for and returns the first child element that is a tag of the specified value.

```
public SecurityElement SearchForChildByTag(string tag)
```

SecurityElement.SearchForTextOfTag. This method searches for and returns the inner text of the first child element that is a tag of the specified value.

```
public string SearchForTextOfTag(string tag)
```

SecurityElement.Attributes. This method gets or sets the name/value pair of attributes within the current element. Attributes are offered as a hash table.

```
public Hashtable Attributes {get; set;}
```

SecurityElement.Children. This method gets or sets the child elements as an ArrayList. The children are returned as an array of security elements.

```
public ArrayList Children {get; set;}
```

SecurityElement.Tag. This method gets or sets the tag of the current element.

```
public string Tag {get; set;}
```

SecurityElement.Text. This method gets or sets the inner text of the current element.

```
public string Text {get; set;}
```

Sample Code

The following code enumerates each policy level, searching for the Machine policy level. PolicyHierarchy first returns the policy level enumerator. IEnumerator.MoveNext then enumerates each policy level. PolicyLevel.Label returns the name of the policy level, which is used to confirm the exact policy level. When the Machine policy level is confirmed, the LocalIntranet named permission set is requested and converted to XML. Converting the policy level to XML returns a SecurityElement object. The SecurityElement.Children property is then used to return an ArrayList of security elements for child tags. Last, the child elements are iterated and each name is written to the console window.

```
using System;
using System.Security;
using System.Collections;
using System.Security.Policy;
public class Starter
{
```

```
    public static void Main()
    {
        IEnumerator policies=SecurityManager.PolicyHierarchy();
        while(policies.MoveNext())
        {
            PolicyLevel policy=(PolicyLevel) policies.Current;
            string policyname=policy.Label;
            Console.WriteLine(
                "\nAt policy level "+policyname+".\n");
            if(policyname=="Machine")
            {
                Console.WriteLine("Processing...");
                NamedPermissionSet permset=
                    policy.GetNamedPermissionSet(
                    "LocalIntranet");
                Console.WriteLine(
                    "PermissionSet Name: "
                    +permset.Name+"\n");
                SecurityElement se=permset.ToXml();
                ArrayList children=se.Children;
                foreach(SecurityElement child in children)
                {
                    string classname=
                        child.Attribute("class");
                    Console.WriteLine(classname);
                }
            }
        }
    }
}
```

SecurityException

SecurityException is the generic exception thrown when you use code access security. Conversely, a PolicyException is thrown in role-based security. System.SecurityException inherits from System.SystemException, which is derived from System.Exception. System.Exception is the base class of all exception objects in .NET. The methods of SecurityException include:

SecurityException.GetBaseException. This is the root exception in a chain of exceptions. If this is an unaccompanied or root exception, the Inner-Exception property is null and this method returns the current exception.

```
public virtual Exception GetBaseException()
```

SecurityException.HelpLink. This method gets or sets the URL or URN that references the help file for the current exception.

```
public virtual string HelpLink {get; set;}
```

SecurityException.InnerException. In a chain of exceptions, this is the exception that threw the current exception. Walk through successive InnerExceptions to traverse a chain of exceptions, starting at the current exception and ending at the root (base) exception.

```
public Exception InnerException {get;}
```

SecurityException.Message. This method returns the description of an exception.

```
public virtual string Message {get;}
```

SecurityException.PermissionState. This method encodes a XML tag that describes the related permission object.

```
public string PermissionState {get;}
```

SecurityException.PermissionType. This method retrieves the type of permission object that raised the exception.

```
public Type PermissionType {get;}
```

SecurityException.Source. This method gets the name of the core assembly where the exception was raised. When a standard permission, such as FileIOPermission, raises an exception, the source is mscorlib.

```
public virtual string Source {get; set;}
```

SecurityException.StackTrace. This method gets a snapshot of the stack frame when the exception occurred.

```
public virtual string StackTrace {get;}
```

SecurityException.TargetSite. This method gets the method that caused the exception.

```
public MethodBase TargetSite {get;}
```

Sample Code

This program voluntarily denies the FileIOPermission of Test.txt for the Main entry routine. When the code subsequently attempts to access that file, a SecurityException is thrown. In the catch block, the properties of the SecurityException object are used to display various data pertaining to the exception.

```
using System;
using System.Security;
using System.Security.Permissions;
using System.Reflection;
using System.IO;
class Starter
{
```

```
[FileIOPermission(SecurityAction.Deny, All = @"c:\test.txt")]
public static void Main()
{
    try
    {
        StreamWriter sw=new StreamWriter(@"c:\test.txt");
        sw.WriteLine("test");
    }
    catch(SecurityException se)
    {
        Console.WriteLine("Exception message is: {0}\n",
            se.Message);
        Console.WriteLine("Permission state is: {0}\n",
            se.PermissionState);
        Console.WriteLine("Exception source is: {0}\n",
            se.Source);
        MethodBase mb=se.TargetSite;
        Console.WriteLine("Exception thrown by: {0}\n",
            mb.Name);
    }
}
}
```

SecurityManager

The security system of .NET grants permission to assemblies based on code groups, checks callers for required permissions, and performs other security-related tasks. The SecurityManager managed class is an interface to the security system. .NET classes use this class to communicate with the security system. SecurityManager is a static class, containing only static methods. Methods of the SecurityManager include:

SecurityManager.IsGranted. This method tests caller for permission. If caller is granted permission, this method returns true.

```
public static bool IsGranted(IPermission perm)
```

SecurityManager.LoadPolicyLevelFromFile. This method reads the runtime security policy of a specific level from a file. This is an XML-encoded file.

```
public static PolicyLevel LoadPolicyLevelFromFile(string path,

    PolicyLevelType type)
```

SecurityManager.LoadPolicyLevelFromString. This method reads the runtime security policy of a specific level from a string. The string is in an XML format.

```
public static PolicyLevel LoadPolicyLevelFromString(string str,

    PolicyLevelType type)
```

SecurityManager.PolicyHierarchy.   This method returns an enumerator to the policy levels. When iterated, the enumerator returns successive PolicyLevel managed objects.

```
public static IEnumerator PolicyHierarchy()
```

SecurityManager.ResolvePolicy.   This method returns a set of permissions that is granted based on the provided evidence.

```
public static PermissionSet ResolvePolicy(Evidence,
    PermissionSet, PermissionSet, PermissionSet, PermissionSet)
public static PermissionSet ResolvePolicy(Evidence)
```

SecurityManager.ResolvePolicyGroups.   This method returns an enumerator of code groups that match the stipulated evidence.

```
public static IEnumerator ResolvePolicyGroups(Evidence evidence)
```

SecurityManager.SavePolicy.   This method saves previous policy changes from policy objects, such as PolicyLevel objects. Otherwise, modifications are lost when the current application closes.

```
public static void SavePolicy()
```

SecurityManager.SavePolicyLevel.   A policy level can be loaded from a file using the LoadPolicyLevelFromFile method. SavePolicyLevel saves a policy level to the originating file. Otherwise, modifications are lost when the current application closes.

```
public static void SavePolicyLevel(PolicyLevel level)
```

SecurityManager.CheckExecutionRights.   If this property is true, which it is normal, the security system checks for the Execute permission and allows only assemblies with this permission to execute. Setting the property to false authorizes the security system to skip this verification and improves performance. Programs without the Execute permissions will not be allowed to run.

```
public static bool CheckExecutionRights {get; set;}
```

SecurityManager.SecurityEnabled.   If this is false, security checks are disabled and all demands succeed. Typically, this parameter is true for normal operations, and demands are strictly enforced.

```
public static bool SecurityEnabled {get; set;}
```

SECURITY ALERT
Disabling the security system is inadvisable and lowers the security curtain to expose the entire .NET Framework, including any running .NET application. However, administrators may choose this option for performance reasons. If it is disabled, other systems should be in place to protect sensitive resources.

Sample Code

The following code changes and then saves the security policy. The CheckExecutionRights property is set to false, which allows assemblies not granted the Execution permission to load and execute. SavePolicy then persists the policy change.

```
using System;
using System.Security;
public class Starter
{
    public static void Main()
    {
        SecurityManager.CheckExecutionRights=false;
        SecurityManager.SavePolicy();
    }
}
```

SuppressUnmanagedCodeSecurityAttribute

This attribute is used in declarative code access security to exempt code from the unmanaged code permission check. This attribute allows a method to freely call unmanaged code.

VerificationException

This exception is thrown when code is not verified as being code safe. VerificationException inherits from System.SystemException, which is derived from System.Exception. Methods of VerificationException include:

VerificationException.GetBaseException. This is the root exception in a chain of exceptions. If this is an unaccompanied or root exception, the InnerException property is null and this method returns the current exception.

```
public virtual Exception GetBaseException()
```

VerificationException.HelpLink. This method gets or sets the URL or URN that references the help file for the current exception.

```
public virtual string HelpLink {get; set;}
```

VerificationException.InnerException. In a chain of exceptions, this is the exception that threw the current exception. Walk through successive InnerExceptions to traverse a chain of exceptions, starting at the current exception and ending at the root (base) exception.

```
public Exception InnerException {get;}
```

VerificationException.Message. This method returns a description of the security exception.

```
public virtual string Message {get;}
```

VerificationException.Source.   This method gets the name of the core assembly where the exception is raised. When a standard permission, such as FileIOPermission, raises an exception, the source is mscorlib.

```
public virtual string Source {get; set;}
```

VerificationException.StackTrace.   This method gets a snapshot of the stack frame when the exception occurred.

```
public virtual string StackTrace {get;}
```

VerificationException.TargetSite.   This method gets the method that caused the exception.

```
public MethodBase TargetSite {get;}
```

XmlSyntaxException

This exception is thrown when the XML Parser encounters a syntactical error. System.XmlSyntaxException inherits from System.SystemException, which is derived from System.Exception.

XmlSyntaxException.GetBaseException.   This is the root exception in a chain of exceptions. If this is an unaccompanied or root exception, the InnerException property is null and this method returns the current exception.

```
public virtual Exception GetBaseException()
```

XmlSyntaxException.HelpLink.   This method gets or sets the URL or URN that references the help file for the current exception.

```
public virtual string HelpLink {get; set;}
```

XmlSyntaxException.InnerException.   In a chain of exceptions, this one threw the current exception. Walk through successive InnerExceptions to traverse a chain of exceptions, starting at the current exception and ending at the root (base) exception.

```
public Exception InnerException {get;}
```

XmlSyntaxException.Message.   This method returns a description of the exception.

```
public virtual string Message {get;}
```

XmlSyntaxException.Source.   This method gets the name of the core assembly where the exception is raised.

```
public virtual string Source {get; set;}
```

XmlSyntaxException.StackTrace.   This method gets a snapshot of the stack frame when the exception occurred.

```
public virtual string StackTrace {get;}
```

XmlSyntaxException.TargetSite.   This method gets the method that caused the exception.

```
public MethodBase TargetSite {get;}
```

What's Next

This chapter reviewed the System.Security namespace and core security classes. The next chapter covers the System.Permission namespace, which is one of the most important namespaces nested in System.Security.

CHAPTER 10

System.Security.Permissions Namespace

S ystem.Security.Permissions is an essential namespace nested in the System.Security namespace. Permissions play an important role in .NET security and grant code access to sensitive resources or tasks.

The System.Security.Permissions namespace contains the standard permissions, both the declarative and imperative objects, for code access security and role-based security. The namespace also includes base classes, such as CodeAccessSecurityAttribute, which define common services implemented by related permission objects.

Classes of System.Security.Permissions

This section summarizes each class in the System.Security.Permissions namespace and offers sample code where helpful. Unless otherwise indicated, it is assumed that all sample code runs from a local drive. For brevity, some methods and properties are excluded. Except for PrincipalPermission, the remaining permission classes derive from CodeAccessPermission. The inherited methods and properties of this class are explained in Chapter 9 and omitted here.

Services specific to the functionality of a particular permission are explained. Most permission objects have related access flags, which are enumerations. Usually, access flags contain bitwise values that can be combined with the bitwise operator.

In the next section, the CodeAccessSecurityAttribute class is fully described, but not repeated for each derived class, such as FileIOPermissionAttribute.

CodeAccessSecurityAttribute

CodeAccessSecurityAttribute is an abstract class that defines the common services of permission attribute objects. It is the base class of every permission attribute object. EnvironmentPermissionAttribute, FileDialogPermissionAttribute, and PrincipalPermissionAttribute are among the permission attribute classes that derive from CodeAccessSecurityAttribute.

METHODS

CodeAccessSecurityAttribute.CreatePermission.   This method creates a permission object that can be serialized to the metadata of an assembly.

```
public abstract Ipermission CreatePermission()
```

CodeAccessSecurityAttribute.IsDefaultAttribute.   Classes may have default attributes. IsDefaultAttribute tests the current permission. If it is a default attribute, the method returns true.

```
public virtual bool IsDefaultAttribute()
```

PROPERTIES

CodeAccessSecurityAttribute.Action.   This property gets or sets the prescribed action of a permission attribute object. The action is a SecurityAction enumeration. The range of values is Assert, Demand, Deny, Inheritance-Demand, LinkDemand, PermitOnly, RequestMinimal, RequestOptional, and RequestRefuse.

```
public SecurityAction Action (get; set;)
```

CodeAccessSecurityAttribute.Unrestricted.   This method gets or sets the access mode of the permission attribute object. Unrestricted is a Boolean attribute. If it is true, full access is granted to the sensitive resource guarded by the permission object. If false, limited access is provided.

```
public bool Unrestricted (get; set;)
```

EnvironmentPermission

An EnvironmentPermission object grants access to system and user environment variables. EnvironmentPermission inherits common permission services from the CodeAccessPermission class.

METHODS

EnvironmentPermission constructor.   The EnvironmentPermission class has two constructors. The first constructor takes a single argument, which is the permission state. The permission state is either Unrestricted or None. The second constructor has two arguments: access permission and a semicolon-delimited list of environment variables. EnvironmentPermissionAccess is an enumeration with the values AllAccess, NoAccess, Read, and Write.

```
public EnvironmentPermission(PermissionState state)
public EnvironmentPermission(EnvironmentPermissionAccess flag,
    )
```

EnvironmentPermission.AddPathList.   This method adds environment variables to the list of variables already guarded by the permission object. The parameters are the same as the two for the argument constructor.

```
public void AddPathList(EnvironmentPermissionAccess flag, string
    pathList)
```

EnvironmentPermission.GetPathList.   This method retrieves the list of environment variables from the permission object. Only environment variables that match the access flag are included in the list.

```
public string GetPathList(EnvironmentPermissionAccess flag)
```

EnvironmentPermission.SetPathList.   SetPathList reinitializes the permission object. The access permissions and environment variables of the method replace the current state of the object.

```
public void SetPathList(EnvironmentPermissionAccess flag,
    String pathList)
```

Sample Code

The following program copies the environment variables into an array. The names of the environment variables are then displayed to the console for the user. Next, an instance of an EnvironmentPermission object is created for the USERNAME and OS environment variables, with permission set to AllAccess. Main then denies this permission using the Deny method. GetUser is called from Main and throws an exception when an attempt is made to get the User-Name. Since it denied all access to the username, the stack walk fails at Main.

```
using System;
using System.Collections;
using System.Security.Permissions;
```

```
public class Starter
{
    public static void Main()
    {
        IDictionary environ=
            Environment.GetEnvironmentVariables();
        ICollection keys=environ.Keys;
        System.Object [] values=new System.Object[environ.Count];
        keys.CopyTo(values, 0);
        foreach(string s in values)
            Console.WriteLine(s);
        string environvars="USERNAME;OS";
        EnvironmentPermission ep=new EnvironmentPermission(
            EnvironmentPermissionAccess.AllAccess,
            environvars);
        ep.Deny();
        GetUser();
    }
    public static void GetUser()
    {
        string user=Environment.UserName;
    }
}
```

EnvironmentPermissionAttribute

EnvironmentPermissionAttribute is a custom attribute and the declarative version of the EnvironmentPermission object. This class inherits from the CodeAccessPermissionAttribute class, which was described earlier in this chapter. To avoid repetitiveness, the methods and attributes of the CodeAccessPermissionAttribute are not repeated here.

FileDialogPermission

Files and directories are often accessible through dialog boxes. The best example is the Open File dialog box. As sensitive resources, files and directories access should always be protected, even from dialog boxes. A FileDialogPermission grants dialog boxes permission to files and directories. FileDialogPermission inherits common permission services from the CodeAccessPermission class.

METHODS

FileDialogPermission constructor. The FileDialogPermission class has two constructors. The first constructor takes a single argument, which is the permission state. The permission state is either Unrestricted or None. The second constructor is also a single-argument constructor, which describes the type of access that is granted. FileDialogPermissionAccess is an enumeration with the values None, Open, OpenSave, and Save.

```
public FileDialogPermission(PermissionState state)
public FileDialogPermission(FileDialogPermissionAccess access)
```

PROPERTIES

FileDialogPermission.Access.   This property gets or sets access permission to files and directories.

```
public FileDialogPermissionAccess Access {get; set;}
```

FileDialogPermissionAttribute

FileDialogPermissionAttribute is a custom attribute and the declarative version of the FileDialogPermission object. This class inherits from the CodeAccessPermissionAttribute class, which is described earlier in this chapter. The methods and attributes of the CodeAccessPermissionAttribute are not repeated here.

FileIOPermission

As mentioned previously, files and directories are sensitive resources. Considerable havoc can be wreaked by malicious code with unfettered access to the file system. The FileIOPermission grants permission to files and directories. FileDialogPermission inherits common permission services from the Code-AccessPermission class.

METHODS

FileIOPermission constructor.   The FileIOPermission class offers three constructors. The first constructor takes a single argument, which is the permission state. The permission state is either Unrestricted or None. The second constructor is a two-argument constructor: file access permission and a path identifying a file or directory. The third constructor also has two arguments, which are the file access permission and an array of paths. FileIOPermissionAccess is an enumeration with the values AllAccess, Append, NoAccess, PathDiscovery, Read, and Write.

```
public FileIOPermission(PermissionState state)
public FileIOPermission(FileIOPermissionAccess access,
    string path)
public FileIOPermission(FileIOPermissionAccess, access, string[]
    pathList)
```

FileIOPermission.AddPathList.   AddPathList adds additional paths and the associated permissions to the current FileIOPermission object. This method is overridden twice. One version takes permission flags and a single path, while the second version accepts an array of paths.

```
public void AddPathList(FileIOPermissionAccess, string)
public void AddPathList(FileIOPermissionAccess, string[])
```

FileIOPermission.GetPathList.   This method returns a string array of items in the FileIOPermission object. Only paths with the stated permission, the sole argument, are returned.

```
public string[] GetPathList(FileIOPermissionAccess access)
```

FileIOPermission.SetPathList.   SetPathList resets the state of the FileIOPermission object. There is a single and multipath version of this method.

```
public void SetPathList(FileIOPermissionAccess access, string
    path)
public void SetPathList(FileIOPermissionAccess access, string[]
    pathList)
```

PROPERTIES

FileIOPermission.AllFiles.   This property gets or sets the file permission associated with the paths of the permission object.

```
public FileIOPermissionAccess AllFiles {get; set;}
```

FileIOPermission.AllLocalFiles.   This property is similar to the AllFiles attribute, but limited to paths that refer to local files and directories, not a network drive or share.

```
public FileIOPermissionAccess AllLocalFiles {get; set;}
```

FileIOPermissionAttribute

FileIOPermissionAttribute is a custom attribute and the declarative version of the FileIOPermission object. This class inherits from the CodeAccessPermissionAttribute class, which was described earlier in this chapter. The methods and attributes of the CodeAccessPermissionAttribute are not repeated here.

Sample Code

The following code employs both declarative and imperative FileIOPermission objects. First, a FileIOPermissionAttribute object denies the methods of the Starter class access to the files in the c:\sample directory. In Main, a filename is read from the console. Then the WriteToFile method is called and passed the filename. Inside this method, a FileIOPermission object is created and initialized with the filename and the Write permission. Before writing to the file, Demand is called to confirm that callers are granted the necessary permissions. If the file is located in the c:\sample directory, a SecurityException will be thrown and caught.

```
// Full paths must be entered (drive:\path\filename)
using System;
using System.IO;
using System.Security;
using System.Security.Permissions;
[FileIOPermission(SecurityAction.Deny, All=@"c:\sample")]
public class Starter
{
    public static void Main()
    {
        Console.WriteLine("Enter path or file name:");
        string filename=Console.ReadLine();
        FileIO.WriteToFile(filename);
    }
}
public class FileIO
{
    public static void WriteToFile(string filename)
    {
        FileIOPermission fp=new FileIOPermission(
            FileIOPermissionAccess.Write,
            filename);
        try
        {
            fp.Demand();
            Console.WriteLine("Application can write to file");
            StreamWriter sw=new StreamWriter(filename, true);
            sw.WriteLine(DateTime.Now.ToString());
            sw.Close();
        }
        catch(SecurityException)
        {
            Console.WriteLine(
                "Application Cannot write to file");
        }
    }
}
```

IsolatedStorageFilePermission

IsolatedStorageFilePermission grants permission to the virtual file system, which provides isolated storage to Intranet and Internet applications and protects the file system of the local computer. IsolatedStorageFilePermission inherits common permission services from the CodeAccessPermission class.

METHODS

IsolatedStorageFilePermission constructor.   The IsolatedStorageFilePermission class has a single constructor with one argument, which is the permission state. The permission state is either Unrestricted or None.

```
public IsolatedStorageFilePermission(PermissionState state)
```

PROPERTIES

IsolatedStorageFilePermission.UsageAllowed.   This property gets or sets the type of isolated storage represented by this object. IsolatedStorageContainment is an enumeration with the values AdministerIsolatedStorageByUser, AssemblyIsolationByRoamingUser, AssemblyIsolationByUser, DomainIsolationByRoamingUser, DomainIsolationByUser, UnrestrictedIsolatedStorage, and None.

```
public IsolatedStorageContainment UsageAllowed {get; set;}
```

IsolatedStorageFilePermission.UserQuota.   This method gets or sets the quota size for a particular user.

```
public long UserQuota {get; set;}
```

IsolatedStorageFilePermissionAttribute

IsolatedStorageFilePermissionAttribute is a custom attribute and the declarative version of the IsolatedStorageFilePermission object. This class inherits from the CodeAccessPermissionAttribute class, which was described earlier in this chapter. The methods and attributes of the CodeAccessPermissionAttribute are not repeated here.

PermissionSetAttribute

PermissionSetAttribute tests code for the permissions of a permission set. This class is a custom attribute and is applied using declarative security. This class inherits from the CodeAccessPermissionAttribute class, which was described earlier in this chapter. The methods and attributes of the CodeAccessPermissionAttribute are not repeated here.

METHODS

PermissionSetAttribute constructor.   The PermissionSetAttribute class exposes a single constructor. The constructor has a single argument, which is the permission state. The permission state is either Unrestricted or None.

```
public PermissionSetAttribute(SecurityAction action)
```

PROPERTIES

PermissionSetAttribute.File.   This property gets or sets the file containing an XML representation of the internal permission set.

```
public string File {get; set;}
```

PermissionSetAttribute.Name.   This property gets or sets the name of the internal permission. Names are restricted to the named permission sets found in the default runtime security policy.

```
public string Name {get; set;}
```

PermissionSetAttribute.UnicodeEncoded.   This property gets or sets the related XML file as Unicode or ASCII encoded.

```
public bool UnicodeEncoded {get; set;}
```

PermissionSetAttribute.XML.   This property gets or sets the XML of the internal permission set.

```
public string XML {get; set;}
```

Sample Code

In the following code, the PermissionSetAttribute is applied to the Starter class. The attribute denies the permissions of the Internet permission set to methods of the Starter class. When MessageBox.Show is called in the Main method, a SecurityException is thrown. The Internet permission set includes the User Interface permission, which is denied because of the PermissionSetAttribute.

```
using System;
using System.Windows.Forms;
using System.Security.Permissions;
[PermissionSet(SecurityAction.Deny, Name="Internet")]
public class Starter
{
    public static void Main()
    {
        MessageBox.Show("Hello, World!");
    }
}
```

PrincipalPermission

PrincipalPermission objects are used in role-based security, where the primary objects are typically Identity and Principal. For developers knowledgeable about code-access security, PrincipalPermissions objects offer familiar characteristics, such as the Demand method to test for a particular role or identity. PrincipalPermission has methods and attributes similar to those of standard permission objects used in code access security. Although this is a permission object, there are notable differences between a PrincipalPermission object and a standard permission. A complete discussion of the PrincipalPermission class is found in Chapter 5, "Role-Based Security."

METHODS

PrincipalPermission constructor.   The PrincipalPermission class offers three constructors. The first constructor takes a single argument, which is the permission state. The permission state is either Unrestricted or None. The second constructor has two parameters. The parameters are the identity and role of the user. The third constructor has three parameters: the identity, role, and authentication status of the user.

```
public PrincipalPermission(PermissionState state)
public PrincipalPermission(string name, string role)
public PrincipalPermission(string name, string role,
    bool isAuthenticated)
```

PrincipalPermission.Demand.   Demand tests the current code for the role and identity of the principal object. Unlike a standard permission object, Demand does not enforce a stack walk. Therefore, callers are not checked. To check callers, use impersonation or some other technique.

```
public void Demand()
```

PrincipalPermission.IsSubsetOf.   This method compares two permissions. If the current permission is a subset of the target permission, true is returned.

```
public bool IsSubsetOf(IPermission target)
```

PrincipalPermission.ToXml.   This method converts a permission object into XML, which is cached in a SecurityElement object.

```
public SecurityElement ToXml()
```

PrincipalPermission.Union.   Union combines the permissions of the current principal with another. The resulting permission includes the permissions of both permission objects.

```
public IPermission Union(IPermission other)
```

PrincipalPermissionAttribute

PrincipalPermissionAttribute is a custom attribute and the declarative version of the PrincipalPermission object. This class inherits from the CodeAccessPermissionAttribute class, which is described earlier in this chapter. The methods and attributes of CodeAccessPermissionAttribute are not repeated here.

PublisherIdentityPermission

A PublisherIdentityPermission object is a permission for a specific software vendor. The identity of the publisher is established with an X.509 Certificate. PublisherIdentityPermission inherits common permission services from the CodeAccessPermission class.

METHODS

PublisherIdentityPermission constructor. The PublisherIdentityPermission class has two constructors. The first constructor has a single argument, which is the permission state. The permission state is either Unrestricted or None. The second constructor also takes a single argument, which is a certificate for the software publisher.

```
public PublisherIdentityPermission(PermissionState state)
public PublisherIdentityPermission(X509Certificate certificate)
```

PROPERTIES

PublisherIdentityPermission.Certificate. This property gets or sets the identity of the software publisher using an X.509 certificate.

```
public X509Certificate Certificate {get; set;}
```

Sample Code

In this sample, a library and an executable are created. The library is signed with a software publisher's signature. These are the steps for signing the library:

```
makecert -sk sample sample.cer
cert2spc sample.cer sample.spc
signcode -spc sample.spc -k sample dog.dll
```

Since there is no timestamp, a warning is reported on the last step. For simplicity, creating a timestamp is omitted. This will not prevent the signing of the library.

In Dog.Barking, an X509Certificate object is created and initialized with the sample certificate used to sign the library. Next, an instance of PublisherIdentityPermission is created from the certificate object. A demand is performed on the resulting permission to ensure that all callers are signed with the same software publisher's certificate as the library.

In this example, the objective is to confirm that the library and caller are from the same software vendor. If the demand is successful, then processing continues. Otherwise, a security exception is thrown.

Here is the source file for Dog.cs, which was compiled into Dog.dll:

```
using System;
using System.Security;
using System.Security.Permissions;
using System.Security.Cryptography.X509Certificates;
public class Dog
{
    public void Barking()
    {
        try
        {
            X509Certificate cert=
                X509Certificate.CreateFromCertFile("sample.cer");
            PublisherIdentityPermission pidentity=
                new PublisherIdentityPermission(cert);
            pidentity.Demand();
            Console.WriteLine("Dog barking...");
        }
        catch(SecurityException)
        {
            Console.WriteLine("This dog does not bark");
        }
    }
}
```

Following is the source file for PublisherIdentity.cs, compiled into an executable, which is not signed. When Dog.Bark is called, an exception is raised and "This dog does not bark" is displayed.

```
using System;
using System.Windows.Forms;
using System.Security.Permissions;
public class Starter
{
    public static void Main()
    {
        Dog fido=new Dog();
        fido.Barking();
    }
}
```

PublisherIdentityPermissionAttribute

PublisherIdentityPermissionAttribute is a custom attribute and the declarative version of the PublisherIdentityPermission object. This class inherits from the CodeAccessPermissionAttribute class, which is described earlier in this chapter. The methods and attributes of CodeAccessPermissionAttribute are not repeated here.

ReflectionPermission

ReflectionPermission grants access to metadata of an assembly. At run time, reflection can be used to browse types defined in an assembly, and even create new instances of these types. Reflection is also used to read information contained in the manifest, including attributes. Reflection can expose public, protected, and even private data. Since reflection can expose sensitive data, access should be controlled.

SECURITY ALERT

▬▬▬ Private data should be considered sensitive information. Data hiding is important for abstraction and security. Reflection can be used to sidestep private access. With reflection, a hacker can gain important knowledge about the composition of an assembly, which can be used later to skirt security. Internet and intranet applications should have restricted access to metadata, including no access to private metadata.

METHODS

ReflectionPermission constructor. The ReflectionPermission class has two constructors. The first constructor takes a single argument, which is the permission state. The permission state is either Unrestricted or None. The second constructor also has a single argument a ReflectionPermissionFlag. ReflectionPermissionFlag is an enumeration with the values AllFlags, MemberAccess, NoFlags, ReflectionEmit, and TypeInformation. NoFlags protects private data.

```
public ReflectionPermission(PermissionState state)
public ReflectionPermission(ReflectionPermissionFlag flag)
```

PROPERTIES

ReflectionPermission.Flags. Gets or sets the access permission flags of the ReflectionPermission object.

```
public ReflectionPermissionFlag Flags {get; set;}
```

Sample Code

Banana is a class with private and public members compiled into a separate library. Following banana.cs is the source code for reflection.cs, which is compiled into an executable. In Main of reflection.cs, a ReflectionPermission object is created and permission is set to AllFlags. The AllFlags permission permits access to all members, including private methods. The LateBinding method is then called. LateBinding uses reflection to create an instance of the Banana type and invoke the DisplayInfo method. The private method successfully executes and displays information in the console window. This is not good: DisplayInfo is supposedly hidden! Move the comments in Main to create a ReflectionPermission object using the NoFlags permission. NoFlags prevents access to private members. Rerun the application and an exception is correctly thrown when the private DisplayInfo method is invoked.

```
// Banana.cs
using System;
public class Banana
{
      private DateTime date;
      private string color;
      public Banana()
      {
           date=DateTime.Now;
           color="Yellow";
      }
      private void DisplayInfo()
      {
           Console.WriteLine("Banana timestamp is "+date.ToString());
           Console.WriteLine("Banana color is {0}.", color);
      }
      public void Eat()
      {
           Console.WriteLine("Eating banana...");
           DisplayInfo();
      }
}
```

This is the source code for reflection.cs:

```
using System;
using System.Reflection;
using System.Security.Permissions;
public class Starter
{
      public static void Main()
      {
//        ReflectionPermission r=new
//            ReflectionPermission(ReflectionPermissionFlag.NoFlags);
          ReflectionPermission r=new
              ReflectionPermission(ReflectionPermissionFlag.AllFlags);
          r.PermitOnly();
          LateBinding();
      }
      public static void LateBinding()
      {
```

```
FileIOPermission f=new
    FileIOPermission(PermissionState.Unrestricted);
f.Assert();
Assembly a = Assembly.LoadFrom ("banana.dll");
Type t=a.GetType("Banana");
Object o=Activator.CreateInstance(t);
t.InvokeMember ("DisplayInfo",
    BindingFlags.InvokeMethod|
    BindingFlags.Instance|BindingFlags.NonPublic,
    null, o, new object [] {});
    }
}
```

RegistryPermission

Nightmarish stories involving the Registry are folklore in the Windows community. The Registry contains system, application, and user-profiling information. In addition, the Registry is the data store for COM registration and the security database[1]. Malicious code with access to the Registry can literally debase an entire system. Time bombs can be planted in the Registry that will sprout when users least expect and attack their system. For this and other reasons, limit access to the Registry.

NOTE When debugging code that affects the Registry, back up the registry first! This simple precaution can save hours, and possibly days, of heartache.

METHODS

RegistryPermission constructor. The RegistryPermission class has two constructors. The first constructor takes a single argument, which is the permission state. The permission state is either Unrestricted or None. The second constructor has arguments. RegistryPermissionAccess controls access to the Registry and is an enumeration with the values AllAccess, Create, NoAccess, Read, and Write. PathList is a semicolon-delimited list of Registry variables associated with this permission object.

```
public RegistryPermission(PermissionState state)
public RegistryPermission(RegistryPermissionAccess access,
    string pathList)
```

RegistryPermission.AddPathList. This method adds additional Registry variables to the RegistryPermission object with the stated permission.

```
public void AddPathList(RegistryPermissionAccess access,
    pathList)
```

---

[1]The security protocol determines if the Registry is used as a store for the security database.

RegistryPermission.GetPathList. GetPathList returns the Registry variables of the permission object, delimited by semicolons, that have the stipulated access.

```
public string GetPathList(RegistryPermissionAccess access)
```

RegistryPermission.SetPathList. SetPathList resets the state of the RegistryPermission object using a new list of Registry variables and access permissions.

```
public void SetPathList(RegistryPermissionAccess access,
    string pathList)
```

RegistryPermissionAttribute

RegistryPermissionAttribute is a custom attribute and the declarative version of the RegistryPermission object. This class inherits from the CodeAccessPermissionAttribute class, which is described earlier in this chapter. The methods and attributes of the CodeAccessPermissionAttribute are not repeated here.

ResourcePermissionBase

ResourcePermissionBase is the base class for standard permissions, such as System.Diagnostics.EventLogPermission, System.Diagnostics.PerformanceCounterPermission, System.DirectoryServices.DirectoryServicesPermission, and System.ServiceProcess.ServiceControllerPermission. These derived classes provide access to Win32 system resources. ResourcePermissionBase is an abstract class and cannot be created directly.

METHODS

ResourcePermissionBase constructor. The ResourcePermissionBase class has two constructors. There is a default (parameterless) and a one-argument constructor. The sole argument for the second constructor is the permission state. The permission state is either Unrestricted or None. Derived classes of ResourcePermissionBase must implement these two constructors and a third method that gathers the permission entries for the derived object. ResourcePermissionBaseEntry is the base class of a permission entry. The constructors of this class are protected.

```
protected ResourcePermissionBase()
protected ResourcePermissionBase(PermissionState state)
```

ResourcePermissionBase.AddPermissionAccess. This method adds a permission entry to the ResourcePermissionBase derived object.

```
protected void AddPermissionAccess(ResourcePermissionBaseEntry entry)
```

ResourcePermissionBase.Clear. This method clears the permission entries of the permission object.

```
protected void Clear()
```

ResourcePermissionBase.GetPermissionEntries. This method returns an array of permission entries for the current object.

```
protected ResourcePermissionBaseEntry[] GetPermissionEntries()
```

ResourcePermissionBase.RemovePermissionAccess. This method removes a single permission from the permission object.

```
protected void RemovePermissionAccess(ResourcePermissionBaseEntry
    entry)
```

PROPERTIES

ResourcePermissionBase.PermissionAccessType. This method gets or sets the permissions of the derived object. Type the base type of an enumeration set in the derived class.

```
protected Type PermissionAccessType {get; set;}
```

ResourcePermissionBase.Tagnames. String names of the resources protected by the permission object.

```
protected string[] TagNames {get; set;}
```

ResourcePermissionBaseEntry

A ResourcePermissionBaseEntry object is the smallest manageable unit of code access security. Classes derived from ResourcePermissionBase manage resource units, which are derived from ResourcePermissionBaseEntry.

METHODS

ResourcePermissionBaseEntry constructor. The ResourcePermissionBaseEntry class has two constructors. There is a default and two-argument constructor. The first parameter of the two-argument constructor is permissionAccess, which is an enumeration of access permission. Refer to ResourcePermissionBase.PermissionAccessType. The second parameter permissionAccessPath lists the affected resources, using a string array.

```
public ResourcePermissionBaseEntry()
public ResourcePermissionBaseEntry(int permissionAccess,
    string[] permissionAccessPath)
```

PROPERTIES

ResourcePermissionBaseEntry.PermissionAccess. This property gets the permission level as defined in ResourcePermissionBase.PermissionAccess-Type.

```
public int PermissionAccess {get;}
```

ResourcePermissionBaseEntry.PermissionAccessPath. This property gets the array of resources guarded by the ResourcePermissionBaseEntry object.

```
public string[] PermissionAccessPath {get;}
```

SecurityAttribute

SecurityAttribute is an abstract class and is inherited by the CodeAccessSecurityAttribute class. SecurityAttribute contributes common services used by declarative permission objects.

METHODS

SecurityAttribute constructor. The SecurityAttribute constructor has one parameter, which is the action requested by the attribute. SecurityAction is an enumeration with the values Demand, Deny, InheritanceDemand, LinkDemand, PermitOnly, RequestMinimal, RequestOptional, and RequestRefuse.

```
public SecurityAttribute(SecurityAction action)
```

SecurityAttribute.CreatePermission. This method may be overridden in the derived class. This method creates a permission object that can be serialized to the metadata of an assembly. Since it is an abstract method, the derived class must implement CreatePermission or it will also be abstract.

```
public abstract IPermission CreatePermission()
```

SecurityAttribute.IsDefaultAttribute. Classes can have default attributes. If this instance equates to a default value, the method returns true.

```
public virtual bool IsDefaultAttribute();
```

PROPERTIES

SecurityAttribute.Action. This property gets or sets the action of the permission attribute.

```
public SecurityAction Action {get; set;}
```

SecurityAttribute.Unrestricted. This property gets or sets the status of the permission attribute. This is a Boolean attribute. If access to the attribute is unrestricted, the value is true.

```
public bool Unrestricted {get; set;}
```

SecurityPermission

SecurityPermission is not a single permission, but a basket of permissions. The SecurityPermissionFlag is an enumeration that identifies the specific permission represented by the SecurityPermission object. The permission values of the SecurityPermissionFlag are AllFlags, Assertion, ControlAppDomain, ControlDomainPolicy, ControlEvidence, ControlPolicy, ControlPrincipal, ControlThread, Execution, Infrastructure, RemotingConfiguration, SerializationFormatter, SkipVerification, UnmanagedCode, and NoFlags.

METHODS

SecurityAttribute constructor. The SecurityAttribute class has two constructors. The first constructor takes a single argument, which is the permission state. The permission state is either Unrestricted or None. The SecurityPermissionFlag is the sole argument of the second constructor.

```
public SecurityPermission(PermissionState state)
public SecurityPermission(SecurityPermissionFlag flag)
```

PROPERTIES

SecurityPermission.Flags. This property gets or sets the internal SecurityPermissionFlag of the SecurityPermission object.

```
public SecurityPermissionFlag Flags {get; set;}
```

Sample Code

SecurityPermission.cs is compiled into an executable, while orange.cs is used to create a library. In Main, a SecurityPermission object is created for the Assertion permission, which is then denied. Then, an instance of the Orange class is created, and FuncA is called. In Orange.FuncA, when the Assertion permission is demanded, it fails and a SecurityException is thrown.

```
// SecurityPermission.cs
using System;
using System.Reflection;
using System.Security.Permissions;
public class Starter
{
    public static void Main()
     {
         SecurityPermission p=new
             SecurityPermission(SecurityPermissionFlag.Assertion);
         p.Deny();
         Orange o=new Orange();
         o.FuncA();
     }
```

```
    }
// Orange.cs
using System;
using System.Security.Permissions;
public class Orange
{
    public void FuncA()
    {
        SecurityPermission p=new
            SecurityPermission(SecurityPermissionFlag.Assertion);
        p.Demand();
    }
}
```

SecurityPermissionAttribute

SecurityPermissionAttribute is a custom attribute and the declarative version of the SecurityPermission object. This class inherits from the CodeAccessPermissionAttribute class, which is described earlier in this chapter. The methods and attributes of the CodeAccessPermissionAttribute are not repeated here.

SiteIdentityPermission

SiteIdentityPermission limits access to code from callers of particular Web sites. The site description must be a URL and support the HTTP, HTTPS, or FTP protocol. The site itself is the core portion of the URL, such as www.wiley.com. There is restricted use of wildcards (*). The wildcard is used to replace segments of the URL, as delimited by dots, with an *any* value. For example, www.wiley.* uses the wildcard correctly.

METHODS

SiteIdentityPermission constructor. The SiteIdentityPermission class offers two constructors. The first constructor takes a single argument, which is the permission state. The permission state is either Unrestricted or None. The second constructor also has a single parameter, which is the full URL path of the targeted site.

```
public SiteIdentityPermission(PermissionState state)
public SiteIdentityPermission(string site)
```

PROPERTIES

SiteIdentityPermission.Site. This property gets or sets the site affiliated with this SiteIdentityPermission object.

```
public string Site {get; set;}
```

SiteIdentityPermissionAttribute

SiteIdentityPermissionAttribute is a custom attribute and the declarative version of the SiteIdentityPermission object. This class inherits from the CodeAccessPermissionAttribute class, which is described earlier in this chapter. The methods and attributes of CodeAccessPermissionAttribute are not repeated here.

StrongNameIdentityPermission

This permission objects use strong names as the criteria to grant access to code. The strong name can be found in the metadata of an assembly. StrongName-IdentityPermission objects check the strong name of each caller before granting access to code.

METHODS

StrongNameIdentityPermission constructor.   The StrongNameIdentity-Permission class has two constructors. The first constructor takes a single argument, which is the permission state. The permission state is either Unrestricted or None. The second constructor has three parameters. Strong-NamePublicKeyBlob is a wrapper class for a strong name. The constructor of the wrapper class accepts a byte representation of the strong name. The name parameter is the name of the target assembly.

```
public StrongNameIdentityPermission(PermissionState state)
public StrongNameIdentityPermission( StrongNamePublicKeyBlob blob,
    string name, Version version)
```

PROPERTIES

StrongNameIdentityPermission.Name.   This property gets or sets the simple name of the StrongNameIdentityPermission object.

```
public string Name {get; set;}
```

StrongNameIdentityPermission.PublicKey.   This property gets or sets the identity of the strong name. The wrapper class is StrongNamePublicKeyBlob.

```
public StrongNamePublicKeyBlob PublicKey {get; set;}
```

StrongNameIdentityPermission.Version.   This property gets or sets the version number used with the StrongNameIdentityPermission object.

```
public Version Version {get; set;}
```

StrongNameIdentityPermissionAttribute

StrongNameIdentityPermissionAttribute is a custom attribute and the declarative version of the StrongNameIdentityPermission object. This class inherits from the CodeAccessPermissionAttribute class, which is described earlier in this chapter. The methods and attributes of CodeAccessPermissionAttribute are not repeated here.

UIPermission

UIPermission grants access to the user interface elements, such as the clipboard and certain windows. Malicious code often attacks the user interface. This sort of an attack is often trivialized, but can be much more than a nuisance. When escalated, attacks of this ilk lead to user dissatisfaction or, worse, denial of service. The result is fewer clients and less revenue. Now you have a real problem!

METHODS

UIPermission constructor.   The UIPermission class exposes four constructors. The first constructor takes a single argument, which is the permission state. The permission state is either Unrestricted or None. The second constructor sets access to the clipboard using a UIPermissionClipboard type. UIPermissionClipboard is an enumeration with the values AllClipboard, NoClipboard, and OwnClipboard. The third constructor sets access to particular windows using the UIPermissionWindow type, which is also an enumeration. UIPermissionWindow values are AllWindows, NoWindows, SafeSubWindows, and SafeTopLevelWindows. The fourth constructor sets the access rights of the clipboard and windows simultaneously.

```
public UIPermission(PermissionState state)
public UIPermission(UIPermissionClipboard clipboardFlag)
public UIPermission(UIPermissionWindow windowFlag)
public UIPermission(UIPermissionWindow windowFlag,
    UIPermissionClipboard clipboardFlag)
```

PROPERTIES

UIPermission.Clipboard.   This property gets or sets access to the clipboard.

```
public UIPermissionClipboard Clipboard {get; set;}
```

UIPermission.Window.   This property gets or sets access to windows.

```
public UIPermissionWindow Window {get; set;}
```

UIPermissionAttribute

UIPermissionAttribute is a custom attribute and the declarative version of the UIPermission object. This class inherits from the CodeAccessPermissionAttribute class, which is described earlier in this chapter. The methods and attributes of the CodeAccessPermissionAttribute are not repeated here.

UrlIdentityPermission

UrlIdentityPermission limits access to code from callers of a specific URL. The identity must be a URL and support the HTTP, HTTPS, FTP, and file protocols. The URL includes the entire path from the protocol to the filename. There is restricted use of wildcards (*). The wildcard is used to replace segments of the URL, as delimited by dots, with an *any* value.

METHODS

UrlIdentityPermission constructor. The UIPermission class has two constructors. The first constructor takes a single argument, which is the permission state. The permission state is either Unrestricted or None. The second constructor names the URL.

```
public UrlIdentityPermission(PermissionState state)
public UrlIdentityPermission(string Url)
```

PROPERTIES

UrlIdentityPermission.Url. This property gets or sets the URLs of the permission object.

```
public string Url {get; set;}
```

UrlPermissionAttribute

UrlPermissionAttribute is a custom attribute and the declarative version of the UrlPermission object. This class inherits from the CodeAccessPermissionAttribute class, which is described earlier in this chapter. The methods and attributes of CodeAccessPermissionAttribute are not repeated here.

ZoneIdentityPermission

ZoneIdentityPermission grants access to code based on zone of origin. This allows an application to categorize callers as intranet, Internet, or another type of application, and to grant access depending on origin.

METHODS

ZoneIdentityPermission constructor. The ZonePermission class has two constructors. The first constructor takes a single argument, which is the permission state. The permission state is either Unrestricted or None. The second constructor states the zone, using the SecurityZone type. SecurityType is an enumeration with the values Internet, Intranet, MyComputer, NoZone, Trusted, and Untrusted.

```
public ZoneIdentityPermission(PermissionState state)
public ZoneIdentityPermission(SecurityZone zone)
```

PROPERTIES

ZoneIdentityPermission.SecurityZone. This property gets or sets the zone of the permission object.

```
public SecurityZone SecurityZone {get; set;}
1 The security protocol determines if the Registry is used as a store
for the security database.
```

A

access control entries (ACEs), 53–54
Active Directory, 132
Added Code Access groups,
    Runtime Security Policy, 85
AddRef, 4
ADO, 16
ADO.NET, 3, 11, 16–18
algorithms, cryptography, 209
All_Code group, 73, 85
allowOverride attribute, 176
AllowPartiallyTrustedCallers
    attributes, 81
anonymous access, ASP.NET
    security, 156–157
APIs, Win32 security, 54
Application Domain level policy, 77
application domains, .NET security,
    26, 32–36
Application policy level, 60
ASP.NET
  about, 3
  beta versions, 163
  impersonation, 163–164
  user, 161–163
  Web Forms, 12–13
  worker process of, 32
ASP.NET security
  about, 151–153
  anonymous access, 156–157
  ASP.NET impersonation, 163–164

ASP.NET user, 161–163
authentication, 165–172
authentication application, 169–171
basic authentication, 156
configuration files, 158–161
cookie security, 168–169
credentials in web.config file,
    167–168
delegation, 157
digest authentication, 156
file authorization, 152, 153, 173–175
forms authentication, 165–169
IIS, 152, 153
IIS security, 154–155
integrated Windows authentica-
    tion, 156
None authentication, 172
passport authentication, 171–172
pipeline, 153–154
tags configuration file, 175–177
URL authorization, 172–173
Windows authentication, 165
assembly, 7
assembly permissions, Runtime
    Security Policy, 88–89
AssemblyAlgIDAtrribute, 39
AssemblyCulture, 37
AssemblyEvidence.ListEvidence, 65
AssemblyInfo.cs file, 37
AssemblyKeyFile, 37
Assembly.LoadFrom, 50

AssemblyVersion, 37
asserts, Code Access Security, 93, 112–116
asymmetric keys, 183–184, 192
ATL (Active Template Library), 4
attributes, code groups, 73
auditing, .NET security, 45–51
authentication
  application, 169–171
  ASP.NET security, 165–172
  role-based security, 127
authentication tag, Visual Studio .NET, 170
AuthenticationType, 132
auxiliary functions, 187

B
basic authentication, ASP.NET security, 156
Basic C# applications, 22–24
beta versions, ASP.NET, 163
bool IsInRole, 135
BooleanSwitch class, 47

C
C#, 2, 21
C language, 1, 6, 11
CallContext, 138–141, 143–146
CallContext.GetData, 141
CallContext.SetData, 141
CApple, 109
Caspol (Code Access Security Policy), 62
casting, Code Access Security, 109
certificate and certificate store, 187
Certificate Trust Lists (CTL), 187
certificate verification functions, 187
cipher, 185
cipher text, 185
CloseHandle, 149
CLS validation, 29

Code Access Security
  about, 91–94
  asserts, 93, 112–116
  casting, 109
  declarative access security, 96–99
  Demand, 104–107
  demand, 93
  deny, 116–117
  evidence, 65–66
  imperative security, 100–101
  inheritance demand, 107–112
  LinkDemand, 104–107
  luring attacks, 92
  managed classes, 94, 110
  overview, 94–96
  performance optimizations, 122
  PermitOnly, 117–118
  ReverseAssert, 118–120
  ReverseDeny, 118–120
  RevertAll, 118–120
  RevertPermitOnly, 118–120
  stack walks, 101–103
  unmanaged code, 120–122
code groups, Runtime Security Policy, 60, 72–76
code verification
  common language runtime, .NET security, 29–31
  tests performed, 30
CodeAccessPermission, 261–263
CodeAccessPermission class, 249
CodeAccessPermission.Assert, 261
CodeAccessPermission.Copy, 262
CodeAccessPermission.Demand, 262
CodeAccessPermission.Deny, 262
CodeAccessPermission.FromXml, 262
CodeAccessPermission.Intersect, 262

CodeAccessPermission.IsSubsetOf, 262

CodeAccessPermission.PermitOnly, 262

CodeAccessPermission.RevertAll, 263

CodeAccessPermission. RevertAssert, 263

CodeAccessPermission.RevertDeny, 263

CodeAccessPermission.Revert- PermitOnly, 263

CodeAccessPermission.ToXml, 263

CodeAccessPermission.Union, 263

CodeAccessSecurityAttribute, 278

CodeGroup class, 75

COM (Component Object Model)
  about, 3, 92
  coding at API level, 4
  component versioning, 4
  libraries, 36
  objects, 25
  objects lifetime, 4
  as Windows standard, 4

Common Language Infrastructure (CLI), 3, 19

common language runtime, .NET security
  about, 25, 27–28
  code verification, 29–31
  metadata verification, 28
  Portable Executable (PE), 28

Common Language Specification (CLS), 6–7

Common Type System (CTS), 7–8

Computer Management tool, 161

configuring .NET cryptography, 211–213

cookie security, 168–169

COrange, 109, 111

CORBA (Common Object Request Broker Architecture), 92

CPear, 109, 111

credentials in web.config file, 167–168

CryptEncrypt, 193

CryptHashData, 199

CryptoAPI, 187–208

CryptoAPI interface, 182

Cryptographic Service Providers (CSP), 187

cryptography
  about, 179–182
  algorithms, 209
  configuring .NET cryptography, 211–213
  confirming digital signatures, 206–208, 225–227
  CryptoAPI, 187–208
  cryptographic parameters, 213–214
  CryptoStream, 210–211
  decryption, 194–196
  decryption with .NET, 217–219
  digital signatures, 203–206, 223–225
  encryption, 190–193, 214–217
  hashing, 196–200, 219–221
  .NET and, 208–227
  random number generation, 189–190
  transformation, 210
  verifying hash, 200–203, 221–223

CryptoStream, 210–211

custom code groups
  creating, 242–243
  sample code, 244–246
  scenario, 244

custom evidence
  about, 230
  creating, 231

custom evidence *(continued)*
  sample code, 232
  scenario, 231, 236
custom membership condition
  about, 235
  sample code, 236–239
custom permissions
  about, 248–249
  creating, 249–250
  sample code, 251–255
  scenario, 251
  using, 255–259

D

data integrity, 180
data privacy, 179
Debug class, 47
declarative access security, Code
  Access Security, 96–99
declarative, role-based security, 138
decoding certificates, 188
decryption, 188, 194–196, 217–219
decryptionKey attribute, 176
DefaultTraceListener, 47
delayed signing, .NET security,
  39–40
delegation, ASP.NET security, 157
Demand, Code Access Security, 93,
  104–107
Demeanor, 52
Deny, Code Access Security, 116–117
DES (Data Encryption Standard
  algorithm), 183
digest, 185
digest authentication, ASP.NET
  security, 156
digital signatures, 185–186, 188,
  203–206, 223–225
D11ImportAttribute class, 54

directory, Global Assembly Cache
  (GAC), 37–38
Discretionary Access Control List
  (DACL), 53
DLL Hell, 4, 36
Dog.Bark call, 31
Dog.Barking, 136
DoSomething method, 144
Dotfuscator, 52
download cache, .NET security,
  26–27, 41–45
Driver application, 34–35
DSA (Digital Signature algorithm),
  184

E

encoding certificates, 188
encryption, 188, 190–193, 214–217
enterprise applications, role-based
  security, 126
Enterprise policy level, 60, 77
EnvironmentPermission, 278–280
EnvironmentPermissionAttribute,
  278–280
error validation checks, 29
Event Log audit information, 51
EventLogTraceListener, 47
evidence, Runtime Security Policy,
  59, 63–66
evidence to assembly, customizing
  .NET security, 232–235
Exclusive attribute, 78
ExecuteAssembly command, 35

F

file authorization, ASP.NET security,
  152, 153, 173–175
FileDialogPermission, 280–281
FileDialogPermissionAttribute, 281
FileIOPermission, 281–282

FileIOPermission attributes, 67, 87
FileIOPermissionAttribute, 282–283
firewalls, 132
Flags, 214
Foo application, 65
ForeignPrincipal class, 143–144
forms authentication, ASP.NET
 security, 165–169
Forth.NET, 7
Framework Class Library (FCL),
 6, 45
FromXml, 253
FullTrust, 44, 59
fully trusted assemblies, Runtime
 Security Policy, 81–82

G
Garbage Collector, 4, 8, 20–22
Gates, Bill, 2
generations, Garbage Collector
 and, 21
generic identity, role-based security,
 132
GenericIdentity constructors,
 role-based security, 133
GetAnonymous, 134
GetCurrent, 134
GetFileSecurity, 55
Global Assembly Cache (GAC), 29,
 37–38

H
hash
 about, 185
 verifying, 200–203, 221–223
hashing, 39, 188, 196–200, 219–221
Hello assembly, 34
Hello World application, 22–24
HTML, 12–13
HTTP, 2, 3
HttpHandler, 160–161

I
IConnectionPoint, 4
identity, role-based security, 132
identity theft, 125
IDispatch, 4
IIS security, ASP.NET security, 152,
 153, 154–155
ILogicalThreadAffinative, 143
Imperative, role-based security,
 137–138
imperative security, Code Access
 Security, 100–101
Impersonate, 134
impersonate attribute, 176
impersonation, role-based security,
 127, 146–149
inheritance demand, Code Access
 Security, 107–112
initialization vector, 184–185
instrumentation, .NET security,
 45–51
integrated Windows authentication,
 ASP.NET security, 156
integrating in .NET, Win32 security,
 54–56
Interface Definition
 Language (IDL), 6
Internet permission set, 59
Internet_Zone, 74
interoperability classes, Win32
 security, 54
intersection of permissions, 76
invalid MSIL, 29
IPermission.ToXml, 88
IsAnonymous, 134
IsAuthenticated, 132
IsGuest, 134
Isolated File Storage, 73
IsolatedStorageFilePermission,
 283–284

IsolatedStorageFilePermission-
Attribute, 284
IsSystem, 134
IUnknown, 4

J
Java, similarities to .NET, 1
Java Virtual Machine (JVM), 3

K
Kerberos, 52
key blob, 192
key generation, 188
key length, 186
KeyContainerName, 213
KeyNumber, 213

L
Lam, Hoang Q., 1
level attribute, 177
LevelFinal, 78
LinkDemand, Code Access Security,
104–107
LocalIntranet_Zone, 73
LogicalCallContext managed
class, 143
loginUrl attribute, 175
luring attacks, Code Access
Security, 92

M
Machine policy level, 60, 77
machine.config, 212
Main function, 35
managed class permissions,
Runtime Security Policy, 69
managed classes, Code Access
Security, 110
managed heap, Garbage Collector
and, 21

membership condition, code
groups, 73
message functions, 187
MessageBox.Show, 99
metadata, 6
metadata verification, common
language runtime, 28
MFC (Microsoft Foundation
Classes), 4
Microsoft, 2
Microsoft Enhanced Cryptographic
Provider, 191
Microsoft Foundation Classes, 15
Microsoft Intermediate Language
(MSIL), 6, 26, 29–30
Microsoft Management Console
(MMC), 62
Microsoft .NET. *See* .NET
Microsoft Office, 3
Microsoft SQL, 16
mobile code, .NET security, 26–27
mode attribute, 175
Mscorcg (Microsoft Core Configura-
tion), 62–63, 66
MyComputer zone evidence, 66
My_Computer_Zone, 73

N
Name, 132
name attribute, 175, 177
NamedPermissionSet, 263–265
NamedPermissionSet.Add-
Permission, 263
NamedPermissionSet.Assert, 264
NamedPermissionSet.ContainsNon-
CodeAccessPermissions, 264
NamedPermissionSet.Copy, 264
NamedPermissionSet.CopyTo, 264
NamedPermissionSet.Demand, 264
NamedPermissionSet.Deny, 264

NamedPermissionSet.FromXml, 264
NamedPermissionSet.Get-
    Enumerator, 26
NamedPermissionSet.Get-
    Permission, 264
NamedPermissionSet.Intersect, 264
NamedPermissionSet.IsEmpty, 264
native code, Code Access Security,
    115
.NET
  about, 1
  any platform language, 2–3
  benefit to users, 4
  common language runtime, 3, 19
  common language specification,
    6–7
  components, 3–4
  cryptography, 208–227
  Just-in-Time Compilation, 19–20
  languages, 5–6, 6–7
  memory manager, 4
  open standards, 3
  similarities to Java, 1
  similarities to Win32, 1
  Web-enabled, 3
.NET Framework
  about, 1
  architecture, 5–6
  remoting objects, 18–19
.NET Framework Class Library
    (FCL)
  about, 8–11, 52, 146
  classes, 9
  prefixing, 10
  System root namespace, 10
.NET Framework Configuration
    Tool, 38
.NET Framework Configuration
    Wizard, 42, 44

.NET Framework Essentials (Thai and
    Lam), 1
.NET IL-Obfuscator, 52
.NET Remoting, 18–19
.NET security
  about, 25–27
  application domains, 26, 32–36
  COM objects, 25
  common language runtime, 25,
    27–31
  delayed signing, 39–40
  download cache, 26–27, 41–45
  hashing of shared assembly, 39
  instrumentation and auditing,
    45–51
  mobile code, 26–27
  obfuscators, 51–52
  policy level modifiers, 78
  programming, 1
  rings, 78
  strongly named and shared
    assemblies, 36–40
  unmanaged applications, 25
  verification, 26
  Win32 security, 52–54
9Rays, 52
None authentication, ASP.NET
    security, 172
NoPrincipal, 129
Nothing permission set, 59
NT Lan Manager (NTLM), 52

O

obfuscators, .NET security, 51–52
object-oriented languages, 1–2
OLE DB, 16
OnDoubleClick handler, 89
open standards, .NET, 3
OtherPermission, 252

P

partially trusted assemblies,
Runtime Security Policy, 81–82
passport authentication, ASP.NET
security, 171–172
Passport Service, 171
password attribute, 175, 176, 177
passwordFormat attribute, 175
path attribute, 175, 176
performance optimizations, Code
Access Security, 122
permission sets
code groups, 73
Runtime Security Policy, 59, 67–72
PermissionSet, 266–268
PermissionSetAttribute, 284–285
PermissionState, 251
PermitOnly, Code Access Security,
117–118
PersistentCookie, 167
personal digital assistants (PDAs), 3
PEVerify, 30, 31
pipeline, ASP.NET security, 153–154
policy defaults, role-based security,
129–131
policy level modifiers, .NET security
policy, 78
policy levels, Runtime Security
Policy, 60, 76–78
policyFile attribute, 177
PolicyHierarchy attribute, 75
PolicyLevel class, 75
Portable Executable (PE), 7
PreEmptive Solutions, 52
prefixing, .NET Framework Class
Library (FCL), 10
Principal, role-based security,
135–136
PrincipalPermission, role-based
security, 128, 136–137

PrincipalPermissionAttribute,
136, 286
Professional Developers
Conference, 2
propagating principals, role-based
security, 141–143
Protection attribute, 169, 175
ProviderName, 214
ProviderType, 214
PublisherIdentityPermission,
287–288
PublisherIdentityPermission
Attribute, 288

R

random number generation,
cryptography, 189–190
RC2 (Rivest's Cipher algorithm), 183
RedirectFromLoginPage, 167
ReflectionPermission, 289–291
Registry, 6
RegistryPermission, 291–292
RegistryPermissionAttribute, 292
relative identifier (RID), 53
Release, 4
remoting objects
.NET Framework, 18–19
role-based security, 143–146
RemotingConfiguration.Register-
WellKnownServiceType, 19
RequestMinimum option, 82
RequestOptional option, 82
RequestRefused option, 82–83
ResourcePermissionBase, 292–293
ResourcePermissionBaseEntry,
293–294
Restricted_Zone, 74
ReverseAssert, Code Access
Security, 118–120

ReverseDeny, Code Access Security, 118–120

RevertAll, Code Access Security, 118–120

RevertPermitOnly, Code Access Security, 118–120

Richter, Jeffrey, 22

Rijndael (Rijndael Cryptographic algorithm), 183

role-based security
  about, 125–128
  authentication, 127
  CallContext, 138–141, 143–146
  declarative, 138
  enterprise applications, 126
  generic identity, 132
  GenericIdentity constructors, 133
  identity, 132
  Imperative, 137–138
  impersonation, 127, 146–149
  policy defaults, 129–131
  Principal, 135–136
  PrincipalPermission, 128, 136–137
  propagating principals, 141–143
  remoting, 143–146
  Windows identity, 133–134
  WindowsIdentity constructor, 134–135

roles attribute, 176

RootCodeGroup attribute, 75

RSA (Rivest, Shamir, Adleman), 184

Runtime Security Policy
  about, 44, 57–58
  Added Code Access groups, 85
  Code Access Security and, 91
  code group hierarchy, 74–76
  code groups, 60, 72–76
  evidence, 59, 63–66
  fully trusted vs partially trusted assemblies, 81–82

managed class permissions, 69
permission and permission sets, 59, 67–72
policy levels, 60, 76–78
in practice, 83–84
refining, 79, 82–83
resolving assembly permissions, 88–89
security neutral code, 79–81
security permission flags, 70–71
tools, 62
Win32 security and, 61–62
WriteToFile, 84–87
WriteToFile3 security policy, 88

S

safeness levels, MSIL, 29–30
salt value, 186–187
security identifier (SID), 53
Security Manager, 64
security neutral code, Runtime Security Policy, 79–81
security permission flags, Runtime Security Policy, 70–71
SecurityAction attribute, 82
SecurityAction.Assert, 96
SecurityAction.Demand, 96
SecurityAction.Deny, 96
SecurityAction.Inheritance-Demand, 96
SecurityAction.LinkDemand, 96
SecurityAction.PermitOnly, 96
SecurityAttribute, 294
SecurityAttributes parameter, 53
SecurityElement, 268–270
SecurityException, 270–272
SecurityManager, 272–274
SecurityManager.ResolvePolicy, 88
SecurityPermission, 295–296
SecurityPermissionAttribute, 296

session key, 192
SetPrincipalPolicy, 129
SHA-1 algorithm, 39
shared assemblies, .NET security, 36–40
SIMPLE_BLOB, 192
SingleCall objects, 19
SiteIdentityPermission, 296
SiteIdentityPermissionAttribute, 297
SMTP, 3
SOAP, 3
SocketPermission objects, 67–68
stack walks, Code Access Security, 101–103
StartDomain function, 35
StreamWriter, 94
strongly named assemblies, .NET security, 36–40
StrongNameIdentityPermission, 297
StrongNameIdentityPermission-Attribute, 297–298
SuppressUnmanagedCodeSecurity-Attribute, 122, 274
switches, 47
symmetric key, 182–183
System Access Control List (SACL), 45, 53
System.AppDomain class, 33
System.Data.OleDb, 16
System.Data.SqlClient, 16
System.Diagnostics namespace, 46
System.Int32 object, 7
System.Object, 7–8
System.Runtime.Remoting, 18
System.Security namespace
  about, 261
  CodeAccessPermission, 261–263
  NamedPermissionSet, 263–265
  PermissionSet, 266–268
  SecurityElement, 268–270

SecurityException, 270–272
SecurityManager, 272–274
SuppressUnmanagedCode-SecurityAttribute, 274
VerificationException, 274–275
XmlSyntaxException, 275
System.Security.Cryptography, 182
System.Security.Permissions namespace
  about, 277
  CodeAccessSecurityAttribute, 278
  EnvironmentPermission, 278–280
  EnvironmentPermissionAttribute, 278–280
  FileDialogPermission, 280–281
  FileDialogPermissionAttribute, 281
  FileIOPermission, 281–282
  FileIOPermissionAttribute, 282–283
  IsolatedStorageFilePermission, 283–284
  IsolatedStorageFilePermission-Attribute, 284
  PermissionSetAttribute, 284–285
  PrincipalPermission, 285–286
  PrincipalPermissionAttribute, 286
  PublisherIdentityPermission, 287–288
  PublisherIdentityPermission-Attribute, 288
  ReflectionPermission, 289–291
  RegistryPermission, 291–292
  RegistryPermissionAttribute, 292
  ResourcePermissionBase, 292–293
  ResourcePermissionBaseEntry, 293–294
  SecurityAttribute, 294
  SecurityPermission, 295–296
  SecurityPermissionAttribute, 296
  SiteIdentityPermission, 296

SiteIdentityPermissionAttribute, 297
StrongNameIdentityPermission, 297
StrongNameIdentityPermission-Attribute, 297–298
UIPermission, 298
UIPermissionAttribute, 298
UrlIdentityPermission, 299
UrlPermissionAttribute, 299
ZoneIdentityPermission, 299–300
System.ValueType, 7

T
tag, 159
tags configuration file, ASP.NET security, 175–177
TextWriterTraceListener, 47
Thai, Thun L., 1
timeout attribute, 175
Token, 134
TokenPermission, 251
ToXml, 253
Trace class, 47
TraceBoolean class, 47
TraceSwitch class, 47
transformation, cryptography, 210
TripleDES (Triple Data Encryption Standard algorithm), 183
Trust an Assembly, 44
Trusted_Zone, 74
type-safe MSIL, 29

U
UIPermission, 298
UIPermissionAttribute, 298
UnauthenticatedPrincipal, 129
union, 76
unmanaged applications, .NET security, 25

unmanaged code, Code Access Security, 120–122
URL authorization, ASP.NET security, 172–173
UrlIdentityPermission, 299
UrlPermissionAttribute, 299
User policy level, 60, 77
userName attribute, 176, 177
users attribute, 176

V
valid MSIL, 30
validation attribute, 176
validationKey attribute, 176
value types, 7
verbs attribute, 176
verifiable MSIL, 30
verification, .NET security, 26
VerificationException, 274–275
verifying hash, cryptography, 200–203, 221–223
Visual Basic, 4
Visual Basic .NET, 2
Visual C++, 15–16
Visual Studio, 24, 37
Visual Studio .NET, 14, 18

W
warning validation, 29
Web code, .NET security, 26–27
Web Forms, ASP.NET, 12–13
Win32, 1, 32
Win32 libraries, 36
Win32 security
  about, 24
  access token, 53
  APIs, 54
  integrating in .NET, 54–56
  .NET security, 52–54
  Runtime Security Policy, 61–62

Win32Api type, 149
Windows 2000, 32
Windows authentication, ASP.NET
    security, 165
Windows Forms, 3, 15–16
Windows identity, role-based
    security, 133–134
Windows NT, 32
Windows Registry, 4
Windows XP, 32
WindowsIdentity constructor
  about, 146
  role-based security, 134–135
WindowsIdentity.GetCurrent, 164
WindowsPrincipal, 129
WinLogon process, 61
WiseOwl, 52
worker process of ASP.NET, 32
Wrapper.dll, 98
Write, 48

WriteIf, 48
WriteLine, 48
WriteLineIf, 48
Writer, 41–42
Writer2.exe, 48, 50
WriteToFile, Runtime Security
    Policy, 84–87
WriteToFile3 security policy,
    Runtime Security Policy, 88

X
XAge, 23
XML, 2, 3, 16–17
XML Web services, 3, 13–15
    XmlSyntaxException, 275
XMLWeb services, 18

Z
ZoneIdentityPermission, 299–300
zones, code groups, 73–74